T0330408

Economic Crisis Management

Dedication

To my loving wife Souraya

Other books published by Tran Van Hoa

Causes and Impact of the Asian Financial Crisis (editor with C. Harvie)

China's Trade and Investment After the Asia Crisis (editor)

Contributions to Consumer Demand and Econometrics (editor with R. Bewley)

Economic Development and Prospects in the ASEAN (editor)

National Income and Economic Progress (editor with D.S. Ironmonger and J.O.N. Perkins)

Prospects in Trade, Investment and Business in Vietnam and East Asia (editor)

Sectoral Analysis of Trade, Investment and Business in Vietnam (editor)

The Asia Crisis: The Cures, their Effectiveness, and the Prospects After (editor)

The Asia Recovery (editor)

The Macroeconomic Mix in the Industrialised World (co-author with J.O.N. Perkins)

The Social Impact of the Asia Crisis (Editor)

Vietnam: Market Intelligence and Business Analysis (author – in preparation)

Vietnam's Reforms and Economic Growth (co-author with C. Harvie)

Economic Crisis Management

Policy, Practice, Outcomes and Prospects

Edited by

Tran Van Hoa

University of Wollongong, Australia

Edward Elgar
Cheltenham, UK • Northampton, MA, USA

Published by
Edward Elgar Publishing Limited
Glensanda House
Montpellier Parade
Cheltenham
Glos GL50 1UA
UK

Edward Elgar Publishing, Inc.
136 West Street
Suite 202
Northampton
Massachusetts 01060
USA

A catalogue record for this book
is available from the British Library

ISBN 1 84064 692 6

Printed and bound in Great Britain by Biddles Ltd, *www.biddles.co.uk*

Contents

List of Tables

List of Figures

Notes on the Contributors

Wilai Auepiyachut is Lecturer in Economics, Buraphau University, Thailand.

Charles Harvie is Associate Professor, Department of Economics, Director, Centre for SME Research and Development, and Deputy Director, International Business Research Institute, University of Wollongong.

Hyun-Hoon Lee is Associate Professor, Division of Economics and International Trade, Kangwon National University, Korea, and Managing Director of the *Journal of the Korean Economy.*

Junggun Oh is Chief Economist, Human Resource Development Institute, Bank of Korea.

J.O.N Perkins is Emeritus Professor of Economics, Department of Economics, University of Melbourne.

Jeffrey Sachs is Professor of Economics, Center for International Development and Department of Economics, Harvard University, USA.

Tran Van Hoa is Associate Professor of Economics, and Director, Vietnam Research Program, Faculty of Commerce, University of Wollongong.

Xiaokai Yang is Personal Professor of Economics, Faculty of Business and Economics, Monash University, and Fellow, Center for International Development, Harvard University, USA.

Wing Thye Woo is Professor of Economics, Department of Economics, University of California at Davis, USA.

Acknowledgements

The book is the fifth in a series of books on the Asia crisis that started in July 1997 in Thailand and has spread to other countries in Southeast and East Asia and beyond. It complements the four previous books prepared by the editor on the subject matter (*Causes and Impact of the Asian Financial Crisis*; *The Asia Crisis: The Cures, their Effectiveness, and the Prospects After*; *The Social Impact of the Asia Crisis*; and *The Asia Recovery*).

Nearly four years on, the crisis still persisted in the region even though in its milder form and, importantly, its impact was still being felt deep by the people and government in crisis economies. The implication is that the management policy prescribed for this economic and financial crisis, stridently advocated by international organisations and adopted voluntarily or under pressure by crisis governments and authorities, has failed to bring about recovery and sustainable high development and growth in countries in trouble. The aim of the book therefore is to find or articulate a paradigm from this experience and time-tested economic theory and policy that is capable of delivering better solutions to similar future crises.

The book is a collection of scholarly studies with practical interest on contemporary economic policy and its application to major crisis economies in Asia. It provides concise and relevant statistical data and critical analysis of the process of economic management in these economies, its step-by-step implementation and sector-by-sector outcomes. It also provides recommendations or suggestions on how to prevent or avoid future economic and financial crises or, if that is impossible, to reduce their damaging impact and contagion, economic, financial, political and social. The book's topicality and coverage are of interest not only to national and international economic policy makers, academics, government advisers, business economists, development economists, researchers and consultants, and students of economics and commerce, but also to corporate planners and commerce analysts.

The editor wishes to thank Edward Elgar for his continuously strong and prompt support for the book concept. Discussions with colleagues and students in Australia and overseas on interest and aspects of economic management in general and in Asian crisis economies in particular had been most useful to the inception of the book's subject-matter. The editor also wishes to thank his contributing authors for their great efforts in their research and reportage to meet the strict deadline for the book typescripts.

The support and sacrifice of my family during the preparation of this book are again deeply appreciated.

Tran Van Hoa
University of Wollongong
April 2001

1 Economic Crisis Management: An Overview

Tran Van Hoa

1.1 MAIN OBJECTIVES

Economic management has been the main issue of corporate, government and international governance especially in our contemporary economies. Good corporate management can produce great success for corporations, benefits for shareholders and good opportunities for investors. Good government governance can improve the wellbeing, pride and financial ranking of a nation and, on the short-term basis, the satisfaction of the electorate. Bad management at the international level can generate, for the economies affected by this management, bankruptcy for corporations, collapse of giant industries, damaging recession (that is, slow, stagnant or even negative growth), deterioration of the living standard for the people in a country, social and ethnic unrest, and regional or global instability.

The book deals with the theory and policy of economic management in a contemporary context and focuses especially on its adoption and implementation in the recent economic and financial crises in East Asia. It also deals with the outcomes of the prescriptions for crisis management recommended or imposed by international organisations and adopted by a number of major economies in trouble in the Asian region. Early in 2001, it appeared that the impact of the crisis was still lingering in these crisis economies, and the major rescue packages and reforms had not been able to arrest this damaging effect. An implication was that the management of economic and financial crises had not been successful.

The principal objective of the book is, importantly, to assess the suitability and effectiveness of this crisis management policy adopted by the major economies in trouble during the Asia crisis. It also explores new initiatives or develops more appropriate approaches to better manage similar economic and financial crises in the future.

1.2   THE BOOK'S COVERAGE

In Chapter 2, Tran Van Hoa gives a brief survey of recent economic and financial crises and their impact on the affected countries both in the Asian region and in the US and the European Union. An assessment of available official data and analyses prepared by international organisations and agencies, national statistical offices, universities, research institutes and relevant webpages seems to indicate two important findings. First, the impact of the Asia crisis starting in Thailand in 1997 is of a long-term nature, and the prescriptions adopted by crisis governments and authorities have been inappropriate and ineffective in dealing with the crisis and in trying to jumpstart the recovery. Second, due to the globalised nature of contemporary economic relations, economies in North America and Europe that seemed to have escaped the short-term contagion of the Asia crisis have been caught up in its long-term impact. The chapter calls for new initiatives and policies to deal more effectively with this kind of problems facing the world economy.

Chapter 3, written by J.O.N. Perkins, deals with general issues of economic and financial crises and their remedies or policies. It starts on the premise that the crises in Asian economies, and their repercussions on the world as a whole, prompt reflections on policies to deal with any future crises. It also reminds us to bear in mind, however, that future crises may well focus upon somewhat different types of economies, and will certainly have special features of their own. We may reasonably draw lessons from the experience of the past, but, to avoid failures, we need also to consider how those lessons may need to be adapted if future crises originate in different types of economy. In particular, we need to consider how these remedies may need to be adapted to problems originating in larger economies, even one as large as the USA or Japan (a current world observation as of March 2001).

Some of the features of certain Asian economies in the past – large current account deficits and a high level of external liabilities – are certainly characteristic also of the USA at present. In addition, for any country that receives assistance from the International Monetary Fund, it is important to consider what sort of conditions (conditionality) should be attached to the availability of any special drawings on the Fund that are made available to deal with the crisis. The chapter finally addresses the need to consider what fiscal and monetary policies are appropriate not only to countries experiencing a crisis but also to other countries whose aim is to minimise the repercussions on them.

Chapter 4, written by Jeffrey Sachs, Wing Thye Woo and Xiaokai Yang, provides another perspective, long neglected by economists on transition economies both in the West and the East, on understanding economic and financial crises and also how to best manage them in this context. They propose that constitutional transition may be not only an important part of economic reforms but also a generator of restructuring risks of both internal and external characters. Rivalry and competition between states and between political forces within each country are the driving forces for constitutional transition. They use Russia and China as two examples of economic reforms with and without constitutional transition respectively. Under political monopoly of the ruling party however, economic transition will be hijacked by state opportunism, and the dual track approach to economic transition may generate very high long-term cost of constitutional transition (including economic and financial crises or meltdown and social unrest) that might well outweigh its short-term benefit of buying out the vested interests (and posting economic gains).

In Chapter 5, Wilai Auepiyachut and Charles Harvie first assess the causal factors and damaging impact of the Asia crisis on Thailand, the first Asian country to witness its currency devaluation problems and the ensuing economic and financial turmoil and contagion to the region. They then focus upon the development of a macroeconomic model for the country for crisis studies and solutions. This model has a number of features. It can be utilised to identify the impact upon the macroeconomy arising from financial shocks. It can also be used, through the conduct of a numerical simulation analysis, to compare and contrast the economic outcomes from the implementation of alternative policy options in response to such shocks. The suitability or effectiveness of the policies for economic management prescribed by international organisations for or adopted by Thailand are rigorously discussed within the context of this model and its findings under a number of feasible scenarios.

Chapter 6 discusses management issues of Korea's economic and social collapse since the Asia turmoil in July 1997 in Thailand, and the country's prospects and major obstacles to reform and restructuring in the medium term. Written by Junggun Oh, Hyun-Hoon Lee and Charles Harvie, the chapter first provides a comprehensive review and assessment of Korea's macroeconomic management and remedial process to cope with the unprecedented financial crisis in the Korean economy. It then critically discusses the macroeconomic management stance adopted by the country's monetary authority in an effort to stabilise the currency, and to recover and maintain macroeconomic stability. This is followed by an analysis of the structural reform process pursued by the government in an effort to address more fundamental weaknesses in the economy and its outcomes. The chapter finally identifies external and internal challenges that Korea has to accommodate to achieve a full recovery from the crisis and maintain sustainable growth.

Chapter 7, written by Tran Van Hoa, first surveys pertinent aspects of economic and financial management in Vietnam during and immediately after the emergence of the Asia crisis. It then provides a critical analysis of the country's current agenda for further reforms in state-owned enterprises (SOEs), equitisation process, the banking system, and promotion and development of small and medium-size enterprises (SMEs). The reforms are urgent and imperative because they are necessary for further development, growth and poverty reduction, and they are to be implemented in the regional and international context of Vietnam being an Asia Pacific Economic Cooperation Forum member and a potential member of the World Trade Organization in the near future.

In Chapter 8, Tran Van Hoa focuses on the Philippines and its crises and especially economic crisis management in recent years. The country is seen as unique in the Asian region: 90 per cent of its population are Christian, English is the official language, and its culture has more Western (namely Spanish and American) affinities than any other Asian countries. The chapter first surveys the historical trends and pattern of Philippine international trade and the role played by its major trading partners and leading export–import sectors in shaping its development and growth since its independence from the US in 1946. It then discusses the pertinent aspects and issues of the country's crises and economic crisis management. Critical comments on the Philippines' economic management and its outcomes during and after the Asia crisis in 1997 are finally given. Remarks on ways to formulate an appropriate economic policy with plausible and effective resolutions for a country that has had more than its share of problems after 333 years of Spanish rule and 48 years of the US tutelage are also discussed.

The economic and social problems of Indonesia and its economic management and outcomes since the Asia currency crisis in 1997 and its subsequent contagion to the country are discussed by Charles Harvie in Chapter 9. The major objective of the chapter is to identify progress made by the authorities in tackling the crisis that has overwhelmed the country, focusing upon, in particular, progress made in regard to the country's major economic management policy: banking and corporate sector reform. In doing so, it first identifies recent macroeconomic developments that have occurred in the wake of the crisis. It then identifies the reform and policy framework operative after the crisis. Finally, it outlines the issues that remain to be tackled in the short and long terms if sustainable growth is to be re-established for the country. From his analysis, Harvie predicts that the tasks facing the country are enormous, and only if there is a determined, credible, and transparent government policy response to tackle and overcome these will investor confidence and sustained growth be possible. Added to the tasks are ongoing political instability, regional and ethnic tensions and general social unrest, a dimension to the recovery process not apparent, to anywhere near the same degree, in other crisis afflicted economies in the Asian region.

Chapter 10, written by Tran Van Hoa, focuses on a small and successful economy in Asia, namely Singapore, and its economic management in recent years. After reviewing the country's economic successes which had been based chiefly on international trade and investment from the foundation of the city-state or more appropriately from its independence from Britain in the mid-1960s, the chapter then analyses current issues that may have some significant impact on its future growth paths and international economic relations. Being an exports-oriented economy, Singapore often pursues an economic management style that is regarded as pragmatic or flexible and dependent upon volatile international trade conditions. This style has also been considered highly regulated and not completely compatible with a fully fledged market economy especially in the context of current globalisation and borderless commerce. Singapore's challenges are numerous after 2001 as world demand for its key exports was declining and the spectre of an economic recession or slowdown in the US and Japan was growing unabated early in 2001.

Finally, Chapter 11 gives a synthesis of major aspects and issues that have been discussed in the book, and points out pertinent and fundamental problems facing governments and authorities in managing the current lingering impact of the 1997 Asia crisis and in accelerating the recovery. It also foreshadows the difficulties the world has to deal with in the near and medium-term future as a result of new international developments with subsequent serious economic, financial and social implications. These include the political and social unrest in a number of important Asian economies and their declining demand for non-Asian world products, the slowdown in the economies of the US and Japan, and the collapse of the new economy that many Asian economies have crucially depended on for their high economic growth and development in the past few decades.

2   Economic Management and Recent Financial Crises

Tran Van Hoa

2.1   ECONOMIC AND FINANCIAL CRISES

Economic and financial crises are not new to contemporary economies or even to the economies of the colonial days. The bank-run crisis in Australia in the 1890s is one such early example of financial turmoil with its subsequent great damages and hardship on the people involved then. Recent economic and financial crises with their widespread impact on the region could however be traced back to the early 1980s and 1990s, and Mexico is one such example for Latin America.

The economic and financial crisis that started in July 1997 in Thailand and, subsequently, spread to other once 'miracle economies' in East and South East Asia, then to a lesser extent, Russia, South and North Americas, and the European Union is another example of recent crises with great impact worldwide. This so-called Asia crisis has brought about untold damages to the prestige, growth, development and social improvement plans of the crisis countries. It has now become well known that the high-growth Asian economies of the 1970s, 1980s, and early 1990s, had not only experienced a negative growth and a stunt development in the late 1990s, but they have really become the needy ones desperately asking for urgent outside help.

A summary of the rates of growth of gross domestic product (GDP) in a number of developing member countries of the Asian Development Bank (ADB) during the period 1994–99 is given in Table 2.1. From this table we note the decline in growth rates of all except three countries under study. These three countries are located in the subcontinent and include India, Pakistan and Myanmar. It is also interesting to note that both groups of countries in the table, namely developing free-market (such as Singapore and Taiwan) and developing transition economies (such as China and Vietnam), equally suffered from the impact of the Asia crisis. Some form of economic recovery (in terms of small growth) was observed for crisis economies listed in the table. However this recovery was small and nowhere near the rate of pre-crisis growth. In addition, new developments in the world economy during 2000 and early in 2001

Table 2.1
Rates of Growth of GDP[a] in Selected Major Developing ADB-Member Countries (DMC) in Asia and Subcontinent (1994–99) (%)

DMC	1994	1995	1996	1997	1998	1999
Cambodia[c]	3.9	6.7	5.5	3.7	1.8	5.0
China, People's Republic of	12.7	10.5	9.6	8.8	7.8	7.1
Hong Kong, China	5.4	3.9	4.5	5.0	−5.1	3.0
India[b]	7.8 *	4.2	7.5	5.0	6.8	6.4
Indonesia	7.5	8.2	7.8	4.7	−13.2	0.2
Korea, Republic of	8.3	8.9	6.7	5.0	−6.7	10.7
Lao PDR[d]	8.1	7.0	6.9	6.9	4.0	5.2
Malaysia	9.2	9.8	10.0	7.5	−7.5	5.4
Mongolia	2.3	6.3	2.4	4.0	3.5	3.0
Myanmar	7.5	6.9	6.4	5.7	5.8	5.7
Pakistan[d]	3.9	5.1	5.0	1.2	1.2	2.7
Philippines	4.4	4.7	5.8	5.2	-0.6	3.3
Singapore	11.4	8.0	7.5	8.4	0.4	5.4
Sri Lanka[b]	5.6	5.5	3.8	6.3	4.7	4.3
Taipei,China	7.1	6.4	6.1	6.7	4.6	5.7
Thailand	9.0	8.9	5.9	−1.7	−10.2	4.2
Vietnam	8.8	9.5	9.3	8.2	5.8	4.8

a   Unless otherwise indicated, figures are based on constant market prices.
b   Data for real GDP and sectoral growth rates are all based on constant factor cost.
c   Data for sectoral growth rates are based on constant basic prices.
d   Data for real GDP are based on constant market prices, while sectoral growth rates are based on constant factor cost.
Sources: ADB Member Country sources; ADB datafile 2001.

(such as a stagnant Japanese economy and a slowed down US) would make this recovery short-lived.

On the social aspect, the number of people in Asia alone made poor (not only poorer) by the crisis was estimated by the international organisations and agencies to be 200 million. This poverty-rendering effect was associated with social harmony deterioration, rising ethnic unrest and region-wide political instability.

As of March 2001, the crisis economies in Asia seemed to be still in the midst of their economic turmoil with widespread economic slow-downs, political instability, social unrest and an uncertain immediate future (see below). In addition, the world seemed to have lost its interest in and enthusiasm for financial reforms and wellbeing in the Asian region. This attitude, pervasive in agenda, meetings, fora and publications of international organisations in recent years, was based on the erroneous assumption that the impact, short- and long-term, of the Asia crisis had been benign or irrelevant on other economies, especially in North America and the European Union (see Chapter 10). The chief international organisation responsible for assisting in managing Asian crisis economies had been under fierce attacks for having initiated inappropriate remedial policies and, subsequently, met with failures not only in Asia but also in Turkey, Russia and Mexico. 'IMF (International Monetary Fund) needs bail-out' had been the banner of some influential media in Asia, crying out for urgent reform of the organisation (*The Straits Times* 15 March 2001, and 21 March 2001).

2.2   LONG-TERM IMPACT OF ECONOMIC AND FINANCIAL CRISES IN ASIA AND CRISIS MANAGEMENT

At the time of writing (late in April 2001), the damages of the 1997 Asia crisis were still lingering and troubling a great number of people and societies in the region (even though not so in other regions outside Asia). This long-term impact of economic and financial crises is well documented (see for example, Tran Van Hoa 2001) despite the claims by international organisations and agencies with interest in Asian economies that the crisis was over and the recovery was well in sight or was coming with increasing downside risks (Asian Development Bank 2001). Our assessment of the long-term impact of the Asia crisis and obstacles to a recovery in East Asia can be amplified further below for a number of countries involved in or affected by the meltdown.

In Thailand in February 2001, the new government of Prime Minister Thaksin Shinawatra announced a plan to buy out 1.2 trillion bath of bad loans from the state-owned and private banks. The plan is necessary to jumpstart the economy which is still in the doldrums with falling exports and rising government debt almost four years after the emergence of the Asia crisis. According to Thailand's Prime Minister, the country still needed to pursue a (more effective) crisis management strategy (*Australian Financial Review* 2001). Thailand's growth rate in 2000 was 4.3 per cent, almost a percentage point higher than that forecast earlier. A rate of 4.6 per cent had been predicted earlier for 2001, but this rate was cut down to between three and four per cent in April 2001. Early in March 2001, Prime Minister Thaksin also set up an economic 'dream team' to expand GDP growth in the year, in defiance of projections that Thailand's main engine of growth, namely, exports, will run out of steam due to slowdowns in the US and Japan. Late in April 2001, he went further by announcing his government's intention to adopt new 'inward-looking' economic policies and to reject the attempts of the G7 nations to introduce greater transparency to Asian economies through tougher banking and financial regulations.

Late in 2000, in Indonesia, ethnic and social unrest was so vicious and widespread that plans by the government of President Wahid and international organisations and agencies to introduce democratic reforms and to restore the seriously damaged economy as a result of the crisis may not be carried out as they were originally intended. The problem appeared to get worse rather than better in April 2001 with the prospect of impeachment of the President on corruption and economic plundering charges. The economic situation in Indonesia seemed in a better shape early in 2000 with a posted growth rate of 3.6 per cent for 2000:1 and 4.1 per cent for 2000:2, and, for the whole year, 5.8 per cent (compared to 0.31 per cent in 1999). An update in November 2000 revised this figure to four per cent. Before the emergence of a US slowdown, the ADB predicted a robust growth rate of five per cent for Indonesia in 2001. This figure has to be revised downwards later on to take into account the US economy's health and increasing domestic economic and social problems. Added to Indonesia's woes early in April 2001 was the announcement that Toyota Motor Corporation's Indonesian partner, Astra International, South East Asia's biggest car maker, had suspended its production on 19 March 2001 as a result of a strike at a local car seat maker.

Late in 2000, the giant company of Daewoo in Korea was declared bankrupt and thousands of workers took to the street early in 2001 to protest against what can be described as slow and ineffective reforms by the government. In March 2001, the South Korea Finance Minister, Mr Jin Nyum, predicted that his country's growth could dip to less than four per cent also as a result of domestic restructuring obstacles and the downturn in the US and Japan. The forecast figures for Korea's growth rate were five to six per cent only a week or so before. In 1999 and 2000, Korea's GDP growth rates were higher at 10.7 and 7.5 per cent respectively (Wong 2001). In April 2001 however, various indicators did not augur well for the Korean economy. The first week in April saw the Korean currency, the won, fall in one week by 2.7 per cent to a new low (since October 1998) at KW1368 to a US dollar. This new financial crisis had spurred the country's President, Kim Dae Jung, to summon his economic ministers and advisers to an urgent meeting and to come up with measures to stabilise the worsening trend in the economy.

The Philippines late in 2000 and early in 2001 still suffered from the impact of a slowed down economy and the associated uncertainties on its future direction. It had also to put up with political unrest and corruption charges and arrest at the highest level of the government (culminating in a traumatic transfer of executive power) and increasing religiously motivated armed terrorism (the Mindanao crisis and the status of and relief efforts for displaced persons). In the past two years, the country achieved a small but steady growth rate of 3.3 (1999) and 3.8 per cent (2000). The forecast growth for 2001 was slightly higher at 4.3 per cent. But this forecast was made before the prospect of an economic slowdown in the US and Japan. Judged from the country's historical demographic, social and especially trade make-up, this slow-down will have more profound adverse effects on the Philippine economy and society. In April 2001, the National Statistical Office reported an expected inflation rate of over 6 per cent for the year. This forecast has deflated the Philippine economy further and limited the central bank's ability to use its monetary policy to cut interest rates to spur economic growth in a faltering economy (*Australian Financial Review* 2001).

Malaysia, after its adoption of the controversial currency control policy during the Asia crisis, seemed to have weathered out some of the worst of the crisis impact. On the other hand, its long-term growth and development policy in an increasingly globalised economy appears to be at odds with this non-market initiative by the government that has been deemed to have adverse trade and investment prospects with its investors and trading partners. The ramifications of the long-running and still growing political instability in the country and rising security issues are also causes for concern in relation to Malaysia's economic development and growth. In spite of these concerns, the country posted a good growth rate of six per cent (compared to an earlier estimate of 3.8 per cent) in 2000 and the forecast by the ADB for 2001 is of similar magnitude (or 6.1 per cent). In April 2001, Malaysia's credit-rating outlook was cut by Standard & Poor following concern that its foreign reserves were shrinking, growing political uncertainty, slippage in external position, and the fact that the government had not done enough to reduce its budget deficit. The revised outlook has the effect of making it harder and more costly for Malaysia to raise money through debt sale and funds through international market. It also came at a time when the country planned to spend an extra three billion ringgit to build schools and houses and to boost domestic consumption in a bid to stimulate the economy as global growth slowed (*Australian Financial Review* 2001).

Singapore, whose economy and growth depend principally on international trade, had predicted an expansion of total trade of between seven and nine per cent in 2001, compared to 22.9 per cent in 2000, a sharp decline. Real GDP growth was forecast at nine per cent for 2000 but an update in November 2000 put it more realistically at 67 per cent of this forecast or 5.9 per cent. For 2001, Singapore's GDP growth rate was forecast at five to seven per cent but the ADB (2000) admitted that a figure of about 6.2 per cent was more reasonable. Singapore's non-oil retained imports of intermediate goods, a short-term indicator for manufacturing activities, turned in slower growth rates late in 2000. The greatest risk for Singapore's economy in 2001 was that the US economy may go into a recession. Under this scenario, the global economy will fall sharply and the growth prospects of Singapore's exports could be severely affected (Singapore Trade Development Board 2001).

Japan, the world's second richest economy and the major economic force in Asia and an alleged trigger of the Asian turmoil in 1997 with its devaluation of the yen, had suffered a period of crisis in terms of its dramatic income per head decline a year or so before the Asia crisis (see Chapter 10), and an economy in the doldrums during 1998–2000. It had not done well early in 2001 either. As of March 2001, Japan's various fiscal stimulus packages and reforms in the past decade seemed to have failed to revive the economy. But these packages and reforms had created massive public debts that reached the highest level in the developed world of 666 trillion yen or 130 per cent of its nominal gross domestic product. In addition, the cost of debt servicing had soared from 30 per cent of tax revenue to nearly 70 per cent in just over a decade.

In Japan's crisis of 1998, it was accepted that exports and public-works were all that had kept the economy above water. Without government money, bankruptcies, already at a record level, were likely to surge further (Callick 2001 and Cornell 2001).

In his report in March 2001 to the Parliament of Japan, the Finance Minister, Mr Kiichi Miyazawa, admitted that the country had run out of money to support growth, its fiscal situation was close to collapse, and fundamental financial restructuring was desperately needed. He also admitted that fixing the fiscal mess in Japan would take from ten to twenty years, and an immediate dose of fiscal discipline was unlikely with the economy being so weak and the political situation so volatile and uncertain. Early in 2001, the country saw a worse machinery order, a still slowing economy, slipping household spending and more pessimistic corporate confidence survey data. Unemployment which already was at a record high may be pushed up further. Following the celebration of a new easier money policy from the Bank of Japan that was announced a few weeks earlier, latest commitments to push aggressively ahead with corporate reforms and clean up a decades-old mess in the banking system also began to sour in March 2001.

Japan, which has powerful impact on the rest of the world's economies (developed and developing), has to rethink about and redesign its macroeconomic policy to suit its contemporary economic environment and its fundamental status as an economy dependent on trade (exports and imports). The new approach, which focuses more forcefully on implementing reform even with painful short-term hardships on the country's population, has been announced by Japan's new Prime Minister, Mr Junichiro Koizumi, late in April 2001, and may assist Japan in restructuring and managing the economy better. It should be clear by now that Japan's adopted fiscal (demand management) and monetary (zero interest rates) policy and its outcomes during the 1990s had not been appropriate and effective in managing its economy.

All the new developments in major Asia economies described above were happening in the climate of a deteriorating relationship between China and the US over the 1 April 2001 US spy-plane incidence and the subsequent US arms sale to Taiwan, and, in addition, between China and Japan amidst the signs that Japan planned to remove the constitutional restrictions on its military.

2.3 ECONOMIC AND FINANCIAL CRISES OUTSIDE ASIA

Outside Asia, the whole world was troubled with a slow-down in the growth of high-tech industries and its impact on employment, high crude oil prices from the OPEC (Organization of the Petroleum Exporting Countries), and the rise of conflicts in the Middle East and the Balkans.

Early in 2001, the US Federal Reserve Board successively introduced interest rate cuts in its apparently desperate attempt to arrest the economy's slow-down. This slow-down would certainly bring with it damaging impact on the global scale. In fact, in March 2001, the International Monetary Fund (IMF) predicted that the US Federal Reserve Board was likely to cut its key federal fund rates to 4.5 per cent in the near term as the recent steep dive in US equity prices could dampen consumer spending for up to two years and the US economy was in danger of a hard landing. The statistics reported in April 2001 by the US Commerce Department did not bring good news. It showed instead a slackening demand for industrial equipment, including computers and machine tools, that helped to drive orders to US factories in February to their lowest point in 16 months (since October 1999). Factory orders fell by an unusually large 0.4 per cent (or US$363 billion in seasonally adjusted value) while many analysts had expected only 0.2 per cent (*Australian Financial Review* 2001).

According to a report by the Munich-based Ifo economic research institute, German business confidence sank in February 2001 to an 18-month (from July 1999) low and the nation's leading companies were issuing warnings about the impact of contracting global growth (especially a slowing US demand) on earnings. This had put pressure on the European Central Bank to act swiftly to cut interest rates to counter slowing economic growth on the continent. Late in March 2001, European leaders were however confident that the fallout from the deteriorating economic condition in the US and Japan (see above) would have minimal effect on the European Union (the economic safe haven of the developed world). This is in spite of a slowing of their own economies and divisions on all but one item from an ambitious agenda for microeconomic reform. However, the European economic commissioner, Mr Pedro Solbes, had to admit late in March 2001 that even a limited fallout effect from the US alone would mean that the EU had to revise downwards its forecast three per cent growth rate for 2001.

2.4   THE BOOK'S SYNOPSIS ON CRISIS MANAGEMENT

With a focus on the major Asian crisis countries alone and their problems since the emergence of the economic turmoil in 1997 (or slightly earlier as is the case with Japan), it appears that the governments of these countries have not an appropriate and effective management plan to deal with economic and financial crises. Since the international organisations such as the IMF, the World Bank (WB), and the ADB assisted, directly or indirectly, the non-Japan governments in crisis management, it is therefore reasonable to infer that the cures and remedies proposed or imposed by these international organisations on Asian crisis economies seem to have been inappropriate and ineffective. For Japan which had adopted both neo-Keynesian (with budget deficits) and orthodox monetary (with almost zero interest rates) policies, the discussions above also show that its economic and financial crisis management had not been appropriate or effective.

The present book is a collection of country-by-country studies, written by scholars and experts, of the economic crisis and its issues in economic crisis management in general, and with particular emphasis on a number of major Asian economies in trouble since 1997. It first provides a critical survey of the traditional tools (or methodologies) in economic management that can be used by contemporary governments for their countries' fiscal and monetary policy. These tools can and have been adopted by international organisations with economic management responsibilities worldwide as an essential part of their assistance to crisis economies. It then critically analyses the adoption, implementation, and success or failure of these tools in the countries in crisis. Finally and more importantly, the book provides suggestions and recommendations in economic crisis management for the countries under study with a view to improve the suitability, quality and effectiveness of crisis management either in crisis economies in Asia or, equally, in other regions. The book therefore provides an agenda for better regional economic and financial strategy (WB 2001) to deal with future crises of the kind we have experienced in Latin America or East Asia during the 1990s.

REFERENCES

Asian Development Bank (ADB) (2001), Asian data resources, <www.adb.org>.
Australian Financial Review, 5 and 6 April 2001, <www.afr.com>.
Callick, R. (2001), 'Finally facing the truth – but still the yen falls', *Australian Financial Review*, 9 March.
Cornell, A. (2001), 'Japan's finances "close to collapse"', *Australian Financial Review*, 9 March.
Singapore Trade Development Board (2001), 'Review of Year 2000 Trade Performance and Outlook for Year 2001', <www.tdb.gov.sg/newsroom/press/pr-00301.shtml>. March 2001.
Tran Van Hoa (2001), *The Asia Recovery*, Cheltenham, UK and Northampton, MA: Edward Elgar.
Wong, K.Y. (2001), 'Economic Growth of Selected Asian Countries', <http://faculty.washington.edu/karyiu/>, March 2001.
World Bank (2001), 'Regional Strategy', <wbln0018.worldbank.org/eap/eap.nsf/>, February 2001.

3 Monetary and Fiscal Policy and Crisis Economies

J.O.N. Perkins

The crises in Asian economies, and their repercussions on the world as a whole, prompt reflections on policies dealing with any future crises. It is important to bear in mind, however, that future crises may well focus upon somewhat different types of economies, and will certainly have special features of their own. We may reasonably draw lessons from the experience of the past, but we need also to consider how those lessons may need to be adapted if future crises originate in different types of economy. In particular, we need to consider how these remedies may need to be adapted to problems originating in larger economies, even one as large as the USA. For some of the features of certain Asian economies in the past – large current account deficits and a high level of external liabilities – are certainly characteristic also of the USA at present. Individually, other developed, industrialised countries may also have problems associated with external deficits and indebtedness. In particular, there is a need to consider what policies would be appropriate in the event of one European country belonging to the euro exchange rate system facing some sort of financial crisis. In addition, for any country that receives assistance from the International Monetary Fund, it is important to consider what sort of conditions should be attached to the availability of any special drawings on the Fund that are made available to deal with the crisis.

There is also a need to consider what fiscal and monetary policies are appropriate not only to countries experiencing a crisis but also to other countries whose aim is to minimise the repercussions on them. Indeed, these issues are associated with whatever prescriptions are made in relation to policies for any crisis economies. For the policies recommended for any crisis economy must necessarily take account of the policies being adopted in the rest of the world.

Part of the process of dealing with any crisis obviously involves correcting any deficiencies of policy that have been responsible for the crisis arising. These policies may or may not include deficiencies of monetary and fiscal policies. But they may well involve deficiencies of other sorts, and the assumption made here will be that

14

those deficiencies are being met, though that process will inevitably take time, during which macroeconomic and other special measures will be required to meet any immediate crisis. Attention in this chapter will be focused mainly on the contributions to overcoming the crisis that can be made by monetary and fiscal policies.

Section 3.1 discusses the problems of relatively small, less developed, countries, both those appropriate for the crisis economy and those that can usefully be followed by the rest of the world including the International Monetary Fund. Section 3.2 extends the discussion to the problems that may arise if a larger, more developed economy is the source of the crisis, including the possibility that it may be one within the euro exchange rate system. Section 3.3 discusses some general issues and suggests some conclusions.

3.1   CRISES IN DEVELOPING ECONOMIES

The main lesson that has been widely drawn from the experience of the Asian countries in 1997–99 is that the conditions attached to the assistance provided to alleviate their crisis probably imposed too tight an overall regime of fiscal and monetary policy upon several of them. It seems likely that past experience of crises in Latin American countries where government deficits were a major precipitating factor of crises led to the imposition on some Asian countries of conditions relating to fiscal and monetary policy that were not appropriate. For excessive private sector borrowing – rather than government deficits – was a principal factor in precipitating the crises in several of the Asian counties. There has been some discussion of whether it was the setting of fiscal policy or that of monetary policy that was made too tight in dealing with the crisis. But the main consideration was surely the overall setting – which presumably led to a loss of output and consequent costs in terms of social welfare that would have been otherwise avoided.

Having said this, however, it may be appropriate to ask whether it is the setting of fiscal policy or of monetary policy that is likely to have the greater bearing on the degree of confidence in a country that is felt by external investors, especially if the precipitating factor in the crisis has been the withdrawal of funds by private investors. It is doubtful whether any general answer to this question can be made: for clearly it depends mainly on whether the setting of fiscal policy was initially thought to be too slack, or whether it was monetary policy that was widely believed to be too easy.

There is one general consideration, however, that appears to favour concentrating upon tightening monetary rather than fiscal policy in a country suffering a financial crisis. This is that a tightening of monetary policy is probably the more likely to strengthen the exchange rate, by making the country a more attractive place to which to lend (and a more expensive place in which to borrow) at any given level of activity. It has been argued by the International Monetary Fund (IMF)'s Deputy Managing Director that if the Fund had not imposed high interest rates on the crisis countries they would have had to devalue by more, and that this would have imposed burdens on their borrowers (whose debts were largely fixed in terms of external currencies) at least as great as that imposed by high interest rates. (It is true, however, that any tightening of policy – whether fiscal or monetary – will have some effect in discouraging external investors, so far as either set of measures will reduce activity, and to that extent earnings on investment, there. Higher interest rates there will, however, also have some effect in making the country a more attractive place in which to place funds than will a tightening of fiscal policy, which tends to reduce interest rates there – at any given level of activity.)

On the other hand, there may in a situation of crisis be a special difficulty about trying to restore confidence by raising interest rates in the crisis-affected country. If a bank is in serious liquidity difficulties and raises its deposit rate above those of its competitors, this may be interpreted by potential and actual depositors as a signal that it is in serious difficulties. Similarly, if a country raises its interest rates at a time when it is facing a crisis of confidence that action may then have an adverse effect upon the confidence of external investors.

There are other reasons why resort to monetary policy may not be effective in restoring confidence in a currency that is thought likely to depreciate. Bensaid and Jeanne (1997) have pointed out that attempts to use monetary policy to restore confidence in a currency's parity may lead to self-fulfilling expectations of further depreciation, and illustrate their argument by reference to the crises of some European currencies in the early 1990s. For the government of the country whose currency is under suspicion will incur various costs if it raises interest rates. In particular, its servicing of the national debt will become more costly, and it runs the risk of reducing output and employment, with consequent social costs. It may also feel that the effects on the distribution of income of further rises in interest rates are undesirable, or at least politically difficult. Potential investors may see that these costs make the government reluctant to raise interest rates to the point where capital inflow will be large enough to arrest the depreciation of the currency in question. These authors say that there will always be some rate of interest that will have this effect. But as capital inflows in recent times have become increasingly dependent on earnings expectations, rather than mainly on relative interest rates, this is by no means certain to be true now or in future. For the effect of further tightening of monetary policy in reducing output, employment, and so earnings, may repel more equity capital than any additional inflow of capital that may be attracted by the higher interest rates.

3.1.1   IMF Drawings and Lines of Credit from other Central Banks

During the Asian crisis of 1997–99 there was a proposal for Asian countries themselves, including Japan, to introduce a scheme for their own mutual lines of credit. This idea appears to have been frowned on and virtually ruled out, by the IMF or its most influential member or members. The fear appears to have been that the ready availability of such funds would reduce the ability of the IMF to impose tight conditions upon drawings from the Fund by the countries affected by the crisis. In retrospect, and in view of the widespread view that the IMF probably insisted upon too tight an overall policy from some at least of the countries suffering in the crisis, this might have been no bad thing. But, in general, the availability of other lines of credit inevitably reduces the ability of the IMF to impose tight conditions on drawings from the Fund. At the same time, however, there is nothing to stop the IMF from taking into account the availability of lines of credit to a country from other sources in determining the scale of drawings that it will grant a country in a crisis situation. Moreover, the adequacy of the Fund's resources to deal with crisis situations is likely to be insufficient, so that funds from other sources – whether private or government – will almost invariably be necessary in order to meet a crisis situation.

3.1.2 Dealing with 'Contagion'

The problem of dealing with the indirect repercussions on other countries of a financial crisis in one (or more) countries is likely to require especially large flows of funds from a number of sources. For the essence of this lender-of-last-resort function is that there should be no doubt about the availability of funds on a sufficient scale to restore and maintain confidence in countries affected by the contagion. In principle, the essence of crises due to contagion is that the countries affected are not themselves the source of the problem, but are merely affected indirectly by investors (wrongly) equating them in their own mind with the country suffering the direct crisis. In this situation – provided that the assistance given merely offsets the effects of the contagion – there can (essentially by definition) be no problem of assistance from the IMF (or any other source) leading to unwise policies in the borrowing country, or to unwise investment decisions (both these dangers being forms of 'moral hazard'). At the same time, in practice, if several countries are simultaneously affected by a crisis situation, it may be difficult to say for certain which of them are affected only by contagion, and which of them are in more fundamental difficulties.

The IMF has set up two new facilities in recent years that should help to meet serious crises arising out of a heavy outflow of capital from one or more member countries. (Its role in various crises of the past is discussed in Boughton (2000).) The first new facility is the provision for a country that is already facing a serious withdrawal of capital, or other strain on its reserves or exchange rate, to borrow much more than its Fund quota in a short period to meet a crisis situation under the Supplemental Reserve Facility (SRF) – and subject to a high rate of interest. The second is the Contingent Credit Line (CCL), under which the IMF can reach agreement in advance with some individual countries after a thorough examination of their policies, and subject to their continuing to pursue policies of the agreed sort, about the automatic availability of resources to them from the Fund. In effect, the IMF can under this arrangement give external investors confidence in the policies of the country with which the agreement has been reached.

Countries may be somewhat unwilling to commit themselves in advance to detailed policies; but, on the other hand, under this arrangement they receive in return an assurance (in case of need) of funds – from the IMF, and indirectly probably also from private sources – that would not otherwise be available. This presumably reduces the likelihood of their suffering contagion from any crisis that may arise in what is widely felt to be in some sense a similar country, or one with which they have close trade or investment ties. Such arrangements may also help a country that is facing a crisis itself for reasons that are not primarily the result of policy failures on the part of its government. The desirability (or otherwise) of such arrangements naturally depends upon the sort of policies the IMF agrees with such countries. If those policies that the Fund insisted upon were excessively deflationary, however, it would be much less likely that the countries in question would agree to such arrangements. Moreover, the purpose of such arrangements is to promote the world public good of minimising the risk of contagion, as well as to minimise the risk of countries being forced to apply excessively deflationary policies in order to deal with a crisis. It would therefore be in the interests of IMF members to ensure that the policies approved as a condition of such arrangements were not so tight as to make member countries unwilling to commit themselves in advance to the policies in question. It is worth bearing in mind that when the Fund reaches such an agreement with a member, this is likely to increase the willingness of private investors to make loans and investments in that country, and presumably also to make other international institutions readier to make funds available to it.

There is, however, some risk of both borrower and lenders becoming too lax in their appraisal of fundamental factors if the IMF has reached agreement with a country for a Contingent Credit Line to be available to it. By reaching such an agreement the Fund may also have in effect put itself into a position where it will be seen as guaranteeing investments in the country in question, and thus lay itself open to criticism if that country suffers a crisis in future. Against this, the availability of CCL to a country must make a crisis less likely.

But this is an example of the virtually inevitable conflict between the risk of moral hazard and the need to maintain confidence in the financial system. This risk arises from in effect providing an incentive to both borrowers and lenders to be less careful in their actions than would be desirable, on the one hand, while, on the other, trying to maintain confidence in order to minimise contagion. Ideally, one would like the Fund to provide appropriate assistance in times of crisis, but for both borrowers and lenders to be unaware of this prospect in advance of the crisis. This might be interpreted as implying that the Fund should in a crisis make assistance available more readily, and on a larger scale, than it has suggested or promised in advance. But there is also an argument that it should try to establish confidence by creating the impression that it will make assistance available more readily than it will in fact do – in the hope that this policy will make a crisis less likely to occur – yet also less likely to give rise in future to moral hazard.

Both these courses of action are, however, open to serious risks. If the Fund stands ready to help but leads member countries to expect that it would make less available in a crisis than it would in fact, this risks precipitating a crisis unnecessarily. On the other hand, if it fails to provide the level of crisis assistance that it had led people to expect, this runs the risk of making a crisis worse – once one occurs. If the Fund tries to solve this dilemma by vagueness – 'constructive ambiguity' (which seems to be what most central banks usually do), there is a risk that borrowers or lenders (or both) may come to assume that it will do less or more than it will do in fact. This will either make crises more likely, or make them worse when they do occur.

On balance, the wisest course appears therefore to be for the Fund to be frank and open ('transparent') about the extent to which it could be relied on to help in a crisis. Probably the principle should be that it will decide what help to give to a country according to whether its policies are sound, but that it will do everything within its power and available resources to shield other countries from contagion.

3.1.3 Policies in the Rest of the World

If a financial crisis arises in one or more countries, the chances of overcoming it will be greatly influenced by the policies pursued in the rest of the world at the same time. The rest of the world may react by adopting deflationary or protectionist policies to shield these other countries from the effects on other countries' balance of payments of the reduction in imports into the crisis-affected country that will normally occur. If so, that will obviously make it harder for the latter to overcome its problems. In the face of any widespread crisis, especially one that involves contagion, it is thus important that the rest of the world should concentrate upon maintaining effective demand, especially demand for imports from crisis-affected countries. This may often involve a country in having a greater balance of payments deficit – or a weaker exchange rate, or both – than it would otherwise have chosen. This should be regarded as a useful contribution to overcoming the crisis and the contagion resulting from it. If this should lead the country in question to ask for IMF assistance, that request should be regarded favourably by the IMF. The resolution of a crisis will obviously also be easier if the remedies imposed on the crisis countries do not lead to their reducing the level of real output and employment any more than is absolutely unavoidable.

3.1.4 Exchange Rate Policy and Macroeconomic Policies

In some Asian countries the attempt to hold the exchange rate fixed at an unrealistic level was an important precipitating cause of the crisis. This has prompted a more flexible exchange rate policy on the part of many countries, and at the same time there has been discussion of restoring some sort of fixity to exchange rates. The Deputy Managing Director of the IMF suggested not long after the Asian crisis (Fischer 2000) that the choice should be between completely freely floating exchange rates, on the one hand, and complete fixity of the exchange rate on the other (the 'bipolar view'). He has, however, more recently admitted that he and other advocates of that viewpoint overstated their case. His view more recently (Fischer 2001) is that countries should not try to adhere rigidly to a fixed peg exchange rate; and that a wide range of alternative exchange rate regimes may be appropriate for different countries at different times.

These arguments will not be reviewed here in detail. But it is appropriate here to consider what bearing the choice of exchange rate arrangements will have on the problem of dealing successfully with a crisis once it has arisen.

In the context of macroeconomic policies to deal with crises, some degree of exchange rate change may be necessary. As no country could ever be sure in advance that it would never face a serious crisis, no country could therefore ever confidently commit itself to fixing its exchange rate unalterably. Nor could a country reasonably assume that some degree of exchange market intervention would not be a useful element in dealing with some future crisis; so that a commitment to a completely freely floating exchange rate would also be unwise.

In contrast to the bipolar view, therefore, the exact opposite viewpoint is likely to be a better guide to dealing with a crisis. In other words, *neither* the extreme of trying to commit a country to an unalterable exchange rate, *nor* that of leaving it entirely to the market (when bandwagon effects, and other irrational forms of behaviour often dominate exchange rates in the short run) is likely to be a useful standpoint from which to try to address an exchange rate crisis.

In any event, in a world where the exchange rates of most countries – including the major ones – are floating relative to one another, it is far from clear what a commitment to a fixed exchange rate would mean. For fixing the exchange rate in terms of one currency means in effect allowing it to float in terms of most others. Indeed, the more fixed is an exchange rate in terms of one currency the more volatile it must (by definition) be in terms of the rest. The additional certainty provided for external investors would thus really apply only to those of the country against whose currency the country borrowing the funds has decided to fix: investors in other countries would actually face additional exchange rate uncertainty.

The only sort of fixed exchange rate that could be established is therefore an exchange rate fixed in terms of one other currency – along the lines of Argentina's or Ecuador's fixing on the US dollar. Fixing in terms of some weighted average of major currencies – as has been proposed for some Asian countries – is not likely to constitute the sort of fixity that will impress external investors. For it will mean that the currency that does the fixing is in fact varying in terms of the currencies in the package, according to the weights used and the variations in the exchange rates of each of the currencies in the basket relative to one another.

In any event, a firm commitment to any sort of exchange rate fixity means subordinating fiscal and monetary policy to this one pseudo-objective of exchange rate fixity (in terms of one other currency or some weighted average of currencies). This means that in the event of a crisis arising, that country cannot use fiscal and monetary policy to achieve other objectives where they conflict with exchange rate fixity (in the sense in question). A large temporary withdrawal of capital from a country may in fact mean that some degree of depreciation will be needed – if only temporarily – as an important element in policy to deal with a crisis. To tie a country's hands in advance by saying that that remedy would never be employed therefore risks prejudicing its ability to choose the best combination of policy measures to deal with a crisis. Moreover, in order to maintain a given exchange rate in the face of a major crisis, it is likely to be necessary to bring about a degree of deflation in the crisis country that will make its problems worse (including having an adverse effect on those capital inflows that are attracted by good earnings prospects) – and to that extent also exert an additional, and unwanted, deflationary effect upon the rest of the world.

Against this, it might perhaps be argued that the confidence of external investors is less likely to be strengthened if they can count on a country's currency not depreciating in the event of some sort of crisis. But that will be true only if they have confidence that the government of the country will always keep the exchange rate fixed even in the face of a most serious crisis. Moreover, such confidence is likely to be absent if adherence to a rigidly fixed exchange rate results in severe deflation in the country in question.

The only situation in which a commitment to an absolutely fixed exchange rate may carry conviction is when the country in question has come from a situation where confidence in its currency had already sunk so low that a commitment to fixity in terms of the US dollar (for example) appears to be the only appropriate remedy – as has appeared to be the case for some Latin American countries. Even in these cases, however, it is appropriate only when a very high proportion of the country's external transactions, and of its total output, is with the country on whose currency it is fixing. For in that case the use of variations in the exchange rate is likely in any event to be a weak instrument for achieving real effects. In such cases as these, if the IMF has approved the policy of maintaining a commitment to this sort of fixed exchange rate, it would have to be prepared to make funds available on an appropriately large scale to maintain confidence in the ability of the country in question to implement this commitment in the face of a crisis situation.

At the other extreme, that of a completely freely floating exchange rate, it is also questionable whether a firm commitment never to intervene in the market, whatever the situation, makes a lot of sense. Exchange rate fluctuations may occur for essentially irrational reasons, and some degree of official intervention may often be the best way to nip a crisis in the bud. The difficulty about this is that the government or central bank of a country is not always the best judge of when some degree of intervention may be justified (whereas an outside body such as the IMF may sometimes be better able to take an objective view on this matter). Presumably it is this consideration that has persuaded some advocates of the 'bipolar' view to favour completely free floating as one of the two defensible choices for exchange rate policy.

Yet, as we have seen, neither the extreme of absolute fixity nor that of completely freely floating exchange rates is likely to be useful for dealing with crises – or indeed many other situations. It is virtually impossible to suggest simple principles for exchange rate policy. Indeed, it is best not to focus on absolute principles, but to focus instead on achieving the best combination of macro instruments – together with some degree of exchange market intervention in particular circumstances. The right exchange rate, like happiness, is most likely to be achieved not by pursuing it directly but as a by-product of doing other things well.

In short, the prescription that exchange rates should be either absolutely fixed or freely floating – can more appropriately be reversed. Both for dealing with crises and also for more normal situations, neither the extreme of free floating nor that of an absolutely fixed exchange rate is likely to be appropriate. It may be difficult to determine the appropriate degree of intervention and the appropriate mix of fiscal and monetary policy measures – especially for dealing with a crisis – but there is no simple rule of thumb that will do the job instead.

3.2   CRISES IN DEVELOPED ECONOMIES

The discussion relating to less developed countries in Section 3.1 can be applied, virtually without amendment, to crises in developed economies. But, in addition, there are various other considerations that require to be introduced if a serious crisis arises in one of the more developed economies.

In the first place, a crisis in a European country is likely to involve special factors arising out of the existence of the European Monetary System, both for those European countries that are members of the euro exchange rate system, and those that have not, but which have in practice been fixing their exchange rate on the euro.

The second, and major, element in considering crisis situations in more developed economies arises from their greater scale in terms of output and financial arrangements compared with most less developed economies. This is obviously of special importance in the event of a crisis arising in one of the two largest economies, the USA and Japan. In general, the system is most likely to be open to contagion when large countries with highly developed financial systems fall into a crisis situation. The case for IMF intervention on those grounds is thus to that extent stronger when such a case occurs than if the crisis originates in smaller countries. On the other hand, there may be alternative sources of assistance, especially inter-central bank lines of credit, that are more readily available to such countries than to smaller and less influential ones. Moreover, the SRF and CCL facilities, financed so far as necessary by the IMF's General Arrangements to Borrow and the New Arrangements to Borrow, would presumably be more readily available to developed industrialised countries, which are the contributors to the GAB and NAB arrangements.

3.2.1   Crises in Non-Euro European Countries

If a crisis should arise in one of the European countries that is not a member of the euro system, but which normally fixes its exchange rate on the euro, that country would obviously have freedom to alter its exchange rate, and so have one greater element of freedom in dealing with a crisis situation, by comparison with a European country that adheres formally to the euro. On the other hand, it would not have any reasonable expectation of any special help being made available to it from members of the euro system or from the European Central Bank, and would to that extent be correspondingly more reliant on the IMF or other countries. Here we face the difficulty that in recent decades developed countries have not in fact made use of their IMF drawing rights, and that if they were to do so (perhaps in a crisis situation) there would be correspondingly fewer IMF resources available to deal with any simultaneous crises elsewhere – or, indeed, for more normal drawings upon the Fund.

It is quite possible that a crisis situation leading to a lapse of confidence in the currency of a European country outside the euro system could have repercussions on euro members also, especially ones with close financial and trade ties with the country directly affected. Problems of contagion could thus arise within Europe. Furthermore, if flows of private capital (or of government aid) to less developed countries from the country suffering the crisis had to be cut down – perhaps because some sort of controls over capital were imposed – the repercussions could be felt in developing countries also. In any event, the danger of contagion of one sort or another would raise a presumption that the public good of the world economy as a whole would justify the provision of some degree of assistance in helping the affected country to solve its crisis. The case for assisting any countries likely to suffer contagion would be stronger, on the assumption that they were – by definition – not themselves responsible for the crisis in question.

3.2.2   Crises in Euro Countries

Additional problems arise if a crisis should affect one of the countries adhering to the euro exchange rate system. The first is that individual members of the euro system no longer have freedom to alter their exchange rate. This means that they have fewer instruments available to deal with a crisis, as they can neither intervene individually in the foreign exchange market nor use variations in their own monetary policy (which is handled for all of them as a group by the European Central Bank). The whole weight would thus be thrown upon the fiscal policy of the country suffering the crisis – at least so far as concerns macroeconomic policy. The most likely source of such a crisis would be a lapse of confidence in the banking system of a European country, and the most likely remedy would thus be some sort of tighter regulation of banks there, together with some form of assistance to those countries and institutions affected. But such remedies take time to implement, and in the meantime tighter fiscal policy would appear to be the only remedy for a euro country suffering an outflow of capital resulting from a crisis of confidence in its banking system.

It might be expected that membership of the euro system would at least help to maintain external confidence in the exchange rate crisis country – by comparison with an otherwise similar European country that was not a member. But once a point was reached where doubts began to arise about a country's continued ability to be a member of the euro system, that would clearly no longer be true. When that point was reached, other members of the euro system – and, indeed, the euro system itself – might also come under suspicion. The other members of the euro system would presumably be determined to ensure that this situation did not arise, and would on that account be ready to help the member in difficulties, though there is so far no publicly expressed intention that this should be one of the responsibilities of the European Central Bank. Indeed, the interests of the other members of the euro system in helping the crisis country – in order to prevent the whole system from unwinding – might well be so great as to raise the possibility that moral hazard could be involved. For a euro member in a crisis might be given assistance on a scale that would risk the repetition in that member country or some other of whatever deficiencies of the financial system had led to the onset of the crisis.

Some of any outflow of capital from a euro member country that faced a crisis would be to other member countries. It should not, on the face of it, be difficult to re-cycle some of the liquidity that would flow to them in such a way as to alleviate the crisis in one of their members. But the government of other euro area countries might be reluctant to do this, in case they and financial institutions within their borders might need to make use of their own liquid resources if the contagion spread to them.

But some of the capital outflow associated with the crisis in a euro county could be expected to flow to non-euro countries. With the exchange rates fixed within the euro system, this would weaken the euro as against non-euro currencies, and make it to that extent more likely that the currencies, and perhaps the financial systems, of other euro countries might fall under suspicion.

3.2.3   A Crisis in the USA

Some sort of financial crisis in the USA having international repercussions can certainly not be precluded. The Long-Term Credit Management bail-out of the mid-1990s is one example of a way in which a financial institution based in the USA can impose potential risks of crisis upon other countries. More generally, the high level of the US current account deficit, and the extent to which it has been financed by private capital inflow (both towards US private borrowers and into US government securities), much of which can be easily withdrawn, raises the real possibility of a crisis of confidence in the US dollar arising at some future time. This would present special problems for the world economy, as the international repercussions for the rest of the world would be serious. Indeed, they would probably be more serious than those for the USA, for which a depreciation of the US dollar as against other currencies might have advantages at least in the short run. For the rest of the world, however, it could have seriously adverse effects, leading to contagion and a crisis of confidence in the world financial system as a whole

The use of the IMF's resources to assist the USA would face serious obstacles, in view of the extent to which they are likely to be required to meet the needs of smaller countries. There might also be serious obstacles of a political or psychological sort within the US to resorting to the IMF. But the IMF has additional resources available to it under the General Arrangements to Borrow, and since 1998 also the New Arrangements to Borrow, to which most member countries in the developed world have contributed. These are available to meet systemic strains on the system. The presumption is that they would generally be used to meet the needs of contributing to the IMF quotas) to finance assistance to Russia and Brazil – which are not contributors.

3.3   GENERAL ISSUES AND CONCLUSIONS

One of the general issues relating to crisis management is the problem of 'bailing in' private lenders to assist in dealing with a crisis. When a country's exchange rate and financial stability fall under suspicion, there is a strong incentive for individual external lenders (and, indeed, its own residents so far as they can) to withdraw capital before the exchange rate falls further or controls are imposed over the withdrawal of capital. In the long run, however, lenders to that country have a common interest in seeing financial stability restored and unnecessary depreciation avoided. The problem is to secure agreement among lending individuals or institutions to continue to support a country through a crisis. If they know that the IMF has thrown its support behind the country and its policies, they are more likely to be willing to cooperate, and so reduce the potential scale of the crisis. It has been proposed (see, for example, Griffith-Jones and Kimmis 1999; and Miller and Lei Zhang 2000) that the IMF should have the power to 'bail in' lenders in a crisis situation: that is, to compel them to roll over their loans. For in such a situation, an individual lender will usually feel that it can benefit by standing out of the arrangement to roll over; whereas all the lenders will benefit in the long run, to some extent at least, if a rollover of the loans from all of them is agreed upon. The parallel is bankruptcy laws within countries. These have the aim of enabling a firm in difficulties to continue in operation, and this is to the benefit of its creditors if its assets are worth substantially more when held together than if they have to be sold individually to meet the debts of the firm that is facing bankruptcy.

If arrangements are made in advance to permit the IMF to enable it in a crisis to declare a standstill on payments to a country's creditors, this may have the disadvantage of discouraging lending to many countries that would have been worthy borrowers, as well as to others, as the risks of international investing would, on the surface at least, be increased. But if the standstill enables a crisis-affected economy to work its way out of crisis, with IMF assistance, in the long run all lenders will benefit. If so, the general level of international investment over a long period should not be adversely affected.

It is, however, very difficult to reach such arrangements once a crisis has arisen. For this reason various suggestions have been made for 'bailing in' lenders in advance. One suggestion (Buiter and Sibert 1999) is that it should be mandatory for countries raising debt fixed in terms of external currencies to have attached to such loans an automatic right for such loans to be rolled over when they fall due if the IMF or some other specified international body determines that disorderly conditions (in effect a financial crisis) had arisen for the borrowing country. Lenders would presumably require some additional expected return to offset this potential restriction on their freedom to withdraw their funds on the maturity of their loans. The cost of the loans to the borrowers would therefore inevitably be greater, and this might well reduce the flow of such funds to countries that might be considered a financial risk – though that might be a useful result if lenders would otherwise have been disposed to lend to it excessively. But it is difficult to imagine all countries (both private and official borrowers) – especially developed countries such as those in the USA or Europe – agreeing to take part in such a scheme. To subject itself to such a scheme might be interpreted as an acknowledgment by a country that there was a substantial risk of a financial crisis arising there. In any event, no-one can say in advance which countries are likely to be subject to a financial crisis, and it would be invidious for the IMF or any other body to presume to do so.

There appears to be little or no alternative to endeavouring to secure the cooperation of creditors by discussions when a crisis has arisen. (Ways in which this problem might be dealt with are discussed in International Monetary Fund 1999, pp. 48–51). If the IMF is the body bringing them together it has the potentially powerful instrument of conditional lines of credit that it can make available subject to the adoption of responsible policies by the crisis country's government. This means that the Fund can argue that the combination of the use of its resources with the adoption of appropriate policies in the country could, together with the agreement of lenders for their loans to be rolled over as they fall due, make recovery of the country more likely, and thereby enhance the prospects of the lenders to that country benefiting in the long run.

The problems that arise when there are crises in one or more countries, and possible remedies for dealing with them, are now more widely appreciated than before the Asian financial crisis of 1997–9. This should make it easier to deal with future crises. But each crisis is likely to have unique features, and will thus need to be dealt with ad hoc when it arises. It may facilitate international agreement over such matters if all countries – including the financial and economically most powerful – bear in mind the possibility that the next crisis may well affect them directly or indirectly.

REFERENCES

Bensaid, B. and O. Jeanne (1997), 'The instability of exchange rate systems when raising interest rates is costly', *European Economic Review*, **41** (8), 1461–78.
Boughton, James (2000), 'From Suez to Tequila: the IMF as Crisis Manager', *Economic Journal*, **110** (460), 273–91.

Buiter, W.H. and A.C. Sibert (1999), 'UDROP – a Contribution to International Financial Architecture', *International Finance*, **2** (2), 227–47.

Fischer, S. (2000), speech in Singapore, April.

Fischer, S. (2001), Exchange Rate Regimes: Is the Bipolar View Correct?, address to American Economic Association meeting, January 6, 2001, published on <www.imf.org/external/speeches/2001/01/010601A.HTM>.

Griffith-Jones, Stephany and Jenny Kimmis (1999), 'Stabilising Capital Flows', in Jonathan Michie and John Grieve Smith (eds), *The Political Economy of World Economic Governance*, London and New York: Routledge.

IMF (International Monetary Fund) (1999), *Annual Report*, Washington DC: IMF.

Miller, Marcus and Lei Zhang (2000), 'Sovereign Liquidity Crises: The Strategic Case for a Payments Standstill', *Economic Journal*, **110** (46), 335–62.

4   Economic Reforms and Constitutional Transition

Jeffrey Sachs, Wing Thye Woo and Xiaokai Yang

4.1   UNDERSTANDING ECONOMIC TRANSITION

There are two major approaches to studying economic transition. One of them, surveyed by Dewatripont and Roland (1996), McMillan (1996), Blanchard (1997), Qian (1999), Maskin and Xu (1999), and Roland (2000), uses formal models of endogenous transaction costs to analyse economic transition. This approach explicitly spells out the assumptions and predictions and has all the advantages of the formal models. Its shortcoming is that most of the formal models are partial equilibrium models that cannot figure out the complex interplay between endogenous transaction costs and the network size of division of labour.

Also, the formal models are too simple to capture the complexity of institutional changes. The core of transition is a large-scale shift of constitutional rules (Sachs and Pistor 1997). Economic transition (that is, price liberalisation and privatisation) is only part of the transition.

In a recent debate about relative merit of gradual versus shock therapy approaches to the transition, the gradualist view was overwhelmingly dominant (see Roland 2000 and Sachs and Woo, forthcoming). This is partly due to the lack of constitutional thinking among economists. Some economists who are in favour of gradualism easily jump to the conclusions by looking only at the short-term economic effects of different approaches to the transition. To understand why this is not appropriate, we may raise the question: If the transition of constitutional rules in France in the 19th century had been gradual, would the transition have been more successful and welfare improving?

We are grateful to Yingyi Qian, Ralph Thaxton, Yijiang Wang, James Wen, Jich-Min Wu, Chenggang Xu, Yongsheng Zhang, Francis Lei, Leond Chen, David Li, Wen Hai, Tim Zhu, and participants of seminars at Australian National University, Peking University, and Hong Kong University of Science and Technology for helpful discussion. The remaining errors are solely ours.

There are three difficulties in answering the question. First, the long-term effects of the changes in the constitutional rules on economic performance are not always consistent with their short-term effects. It is not easy to distinguish one from another of the two. For instance, the formation of the constitutional order in France started in the French Revolution and lasted for about one century. The short-term effect of the French Revolution on the economy was disastrous (Beik 1970). However, the Napoleonic Code and many other institutions and policies that emerged from the long transition process from the Old Regime to the new constitutional order might have had positive long-term effects on economic development in France. This transition, together with the rivalry between the UK, France, other European continental countries, and the US, generated the leap-frog of the Western Continental Europe's economic development over the UK in the second half of the 19th century (Crafts 1997). Also, the short-term economic effect of the American Independence War and American Civil War was very negative.[1] But most historians would not deny the significantly positive long-term economic effects of the two transitions of constitutional rules.

The transition from the old regime to the new constitutional order may have significant short-term negative effects on economic development for at least two reasons. First, the transition must face the well-known dilemma of powerful and legitimate state violence being essential for protecting all individuals' rights (Barzel 1997). According to Buchanan (1989), property rights emerge from the police's powerful (hence credible) and legitimate violence that can effectively enforce the penalty for theft. But such powerful state violence usually tends to violate rather than protect individuals' rights. Because of this dilemma, the short-term economic effects of the changes of constitutional rules on economic development are more likely to be negative. Second, it takes a long time to build up players' confidence in game rules. When changes in game rules occur during the transition, the lack of credibility of the new rules could create social disorder and have adverse effects on economic development.

The second difficulty in answering the above question relates to the trade off between the smooth buyout provided by gradualism and state opportunism institutionalised by the dual track approach that is associated with gradualism (Roland 2000, p. 43; and Cheung 1996). It is not easy to identify the efficient balance of the trade off, which might be different for different countries. The transition to fair, transparent, stable and certain constitutional rules is incompatible with the dual track approach, which features arbitrary and discretionary government power and unfair, unstable, uncertain, and nontransparent game rules. The former requires the credible commitment of the government to the game rules, while the latter is characterised by non-credibility of the government's commitment to the fair rules. Also, the dual track approach institutionalises the arrangements wherein the government officials are the rule maker, the rule enforcer, the referee, and the player at the same time. This is incompatible with the constitutional principle that they must be separated (see Sections 4.4 and 4.5).

If economic development is a process in which many countries conduct social experiments with various institutions in a long period of time in order to find the institutions that promote economic development, then some countries happen to be associated with an evolutionary process toward the efficient institutions and others happen to experiment with the inefficient ones. For the former, economic transition would be associated with gradual evolution of institutions. But for the latter, the inefficient institutions, old game rules, and related tradition must be discontinued and new game rules and new tradition must be created and consolidated. This transition needs a big bang to establish credible commitment by major players to giving up old game rules.

The third difficulty in answering the question raised above involves the comparison of total discounted welfare between different generations of individuals. The French Revolution intensifies the rivalry between French continental culture and British common law tradition. This might increase the generic diversity of institutional experiments and create more opportunities for welfare improvement in human society. Certainly, if such benefit exists, it goes to the younger generations in many countries at the cost of the older generations in France. Similarly, the US's Independence War increased the genetic diversity of institutions and culture within the Anglo-Saxon tradition, thereby increasing the welfare of young generations at the expense of the old ones. But we economists have no consensus about how to efficiently trade off one generation's welfare against the other generation's.

Finally, the transition of constitutional rules usually involves many stages. It is very difficult, if not impossible, to analyse the complete effects of a single stage of transition. For instance, the French Revolution had very negative immediate impact on France's economic development. It did, however, clear the way for Napoleon's big-bang transition to the new constitutional rules based on the Napoleonic Codes and equality of all men before the law, which had positive effects on France's economic development. Mao's experiments with administrative decentralisation in the absence of markets and private property rights in the 1960s and early 1970s were disastrous for China's economic development. But they generated a big shock to the central planning in China and cleared the way for Deng's regional decentralisation and other market-oriented reforms.

According to Mokyr (1990), the rivalry between Britain and France was an important driving force of the big bang transition of French institutions during and after the French Revolution. According to Yang (1994), the rivalry between Chinese and Russian communists was an important driving force of Mao's big shock to the central planning system in China in the 1060s and 1970s. Hence, it is more important to investigate the driving mechanism than to investigate the short-term economic effects of one of the many stages of transition of constitutional rules.[2]

Recently, many models of the commitment game have been used to show why, in the short-run, the dual track approach can work in China in the absence of the credible commitment mechanism to constitutional order (Qian 1999). But it is much more important to use the commitment game models to formalise North and Weingast's

(1989) ideas about why the credible commitment mechanism to constitutional order is essential for long-term economic development.

This may need evolutionary game models with information problems to explain the endogenous evolution of game rules associated with institutional changes and constitutional transition. But so far, no such models are available. The existing evolutionary game models can only explain the evolution of strategies, but not that of game rules. We cannot even predict the emergence of the simple game rule that penalises theft via criminal laws, the judiciary system, and the police. Perhaps, evolutionary game models that formalise economics of state, developed by Barzel (1997), and economics of constitution, developed by Buchanan (1989), can finally provide some tools of the trade for the economics of transition. But before that, formal models of economic transition might play a quite limited role in policy making. They are too simple and too specific to be close to real, complex, large-scale institutional changes.

Hence, another approach to the economics of transition that involves no formal models has so far been very influential in policy making. This line of research includes the meticulous documentation of changes of institutions and policies and their economic consequences, represented by Lardy (1998), and the descriptive analysis of policy and history, represented by North (1997), North and Weingast (1989), Qian and Weingast (1997), Sachs (1993), and Sachs and Woo (forthcoming).

In this chapter, we shall combine the two approaches to study transition economics. We will use the inframarginal analysis of the network of division of labour to investigate economic transition. When formal models are too simple to capture the complexity of institutional evolution, we will combine this inframarginal analysis with insights from constitutional economics, the new economic history school, and the economics of state to address problems in economic transition.

Sections 4.2 and 4.3 discuss how to use the Smithian models covered in Sachs and Yang (2000) to investigate the features of the Soviet style socialist system and the driving mechanism for economic transition. Sections 4.4 and 4.5 examine the relationship between market-oriented reforms and the transition of constitutional rules. Section 4.6 uses some formal models to analyse some transition phenomena, such as large scale output fall and financial crisis.

4.2   THE SOCIALIST SYSTEM AND EVOLUTION IN DIVISION OF LABOUR

In order to understand economic transition, we have to first address the following questions: Why has the Soviet style socialist system finally been rejected by most countries that adopted it? Why could such a system survive, spread, and even achieve short-run impressive growth performance before it was finally rejected? The second question relates to the question: What are the characteristics of the Soviet style economic system? In this section we shall address the three questions. We then draw the distinction between the Soviet style socialist system, Mao's socialist system, and Deng's socialist market system. The distinction can then be used to explain the differences in transition pattern between China, Russia, and East Europe.

The debate between Lange, von Mises, and Hayek relates to the first question. von Mises (1922) and Hayek (1940) believed that the Soviet style economic system will fail to work since it cannot obtain necessary information in the absence of the market. They argued that the calculation cost for working out an internally consistent plan is too high to be feasible. Lange and Taylor (1964) used the neoclassical general equilibrium model to argue that market socialism can solve the problem of a prohibitively high calculation cost of the economic plan. Under market socialism, markets for consumption goods are allowed, but all firms and production means are owned by the state. The central planner commands the managers of all state firms to maximise the profit for given prices and report the profit maximising quantities to him. Then he adjusts market prices according to excess demand until the markets for consumption goods are cleared. They believed that market socialism could allocate resources more efficiently than a capitalist system. Hayek (1988) and Friedman (1962) disagree. According to them, the central planner has no incentive to adjust prices to clear the market, and the managers of state firms have no incentive to maximise profit in the absence of private ownership of firms. Instead, the central planner has all reasons to keep positive excess demand, which can generate planning power and a great deal of tangible and intangible benefit for him.

According to Kornai (1980, 1992), managers will not maximise profit and will not respond to changes of prices if the budget constraint is soft. The managers have every reason to understate production capacity and overstate input requirement, so that prices cannot convey real information in the absence of private ownership of firms and factors. Hence, disequilibrium becomes chronic and resource allocation is distorted.

Some Chinese economists have developed several theories of the Soviet style economic system in the 1980s. One of them is referred to as the theory of absence of ownership. Several papers by Hua Sheng, Zhang Xuejuen, and Lo Xiaopen (1988), Yi Gang (1988), Ping Xinqiao (1988), and Men Qinguo (1988) almost simultaneously proposed a theory of absence of ownership. This theory states that the state ownership system is used to purposely divide different components of ownership of the same property between separate institutions. According to the definition of ownership in the economics of property rights, ownership consists of two components: exclusive rights to disposal of property and exclusive rights to bearing (positive or negative) earnings from property (see Furubotn and Pejovich 1974). In a socialist economy, rights to disposal of property are divided among the planning committee, the price bureau, the labour bureau, the government industrial departments, and managers of enterprises. The planning committee has a say on long-run investment and related resource allocation; the price bureau has a say on pricing; the labour bureau has a say on the assignment of personnel; the government industrial departments have a say on intermediate term investments and the allocation of crucial goods and input factors; the managers have a say on daily managerial decisions. Rights to collecting revenue or enduring losses, another component of ownership, are divided between the finance ministry and the industrial ministries. Hence, no single individual or institution has complete ownership of a single piece of state-owned property. The Chinese call this 'a system without a real boss,' or 'a system with an absence of ownership.' It was argued that any decentralisation and liberalisation reform of such a system in the absence of any substantive change in property right structure will create more problems than it solves.

One of these articles (Men Qiuguo 1988) points to the fact that such division of different components of ownership between separate institutions is a necessary sin if there are no private property rights in place. Such an institutional arrangement mimics a control system in modern corporations. It is a sort of check-and-balance mechanism. This check-and-balance system, along with substantial privileges for the top officials provides an effective control system, as well as incentives to manage this system. Zhang (1986, 1999) proposed several important propositions to highlight essential rules of privatisation in economic reforms. The major of them are several impossibility claims under the state ownership system of firms: 'it is impossible to have entrepreneurship; it is impossible to separate firms from state; it is impossible to constrain managers' behaviour via bankruptcy; it is impossible to efficiently match management with firms under the state joint stock ownership system.' He claims that the bureau of state assets is a second government which is unable to manage state assets efficiently if the original government cannot do it.

Cheung (1974) and Shleifer and Vishny (1992, 1993) develop two theories of price control. The theories are quite relevant to the theory of the Soviet style economic system. According to Cheung's theory, price control can be used to create rents, which are the difference between the official price and the market equilibrium price. Competition for the rents will create a possible social disorder that cannot stop until the rents have been dissipated. The threat to social order calls for a hierarchical social structure, which distributes rents according to individuals' social status. The hierarchy is used by the privileged class to pursue their interests at the cost of society. The theory could mean that shortage is purposely created (perhaps in the subconscious of officials) to justify a hierarchical social order. Shleifer and Vishny's theory of pervasive shortages under socialism implies that shortage is a way for government officials to extract monopoly rents, which is better than a direct monopoly price because it can be used to cover up monopoly profit, thereby reducing public resentment against monopoly rent. The theories can be used to invalidate Lange's theory of market socialism. According to Cheung and Shleifer and Vishny's theories, if the government's purpose is to make use of the shortage to justify its monopoly power in a hierarchical social structure, how can we expect it to adjust prices according to excess demand?

The debate generates the conclusion that market socialism cannot work.[3] Hungary's experiment with market socialism verifies this conclusion (see Kornai 1986). However, this conclusion has not addressed our second question. The Soviet Union did not adopt market socialism in the 1930s and 1950s. But not only did its central planning system survive, but it was also diffused to many countries after WWII. It had achieved average real GDP growth rates of 8 per cent in 1933–1940 and of 9.4 in 1948–1958, as impressive as China's growth rates in the reform era.[4] Why could von Mises and Hayek (1944) not predict the short-run impressive growth performance of the Soviet style economic system, despite their correct prediction of the long-run failure of this system? Kornai's theory of socialism and von Mises, Hayek, Friedman, Cheung, and Shleifer's analysis of socialism have not addressed the question. The answer to this question relates to the ongoing debate about shock therapy and gradualism.

Sachs (1994), Sachs and Woo (1994b), and Yang (1994) provide an answer to this question. We shall now outline this answer, which is based on the development theories generated by Smithian models of division of labour.

As shown in the Smithian models in Sachs and Yang (2000), economic development is a process with evolution in division of labour. In particular, Ng and Yang (1997; see also Sachs and Yang 2000, chapter 15) show that in a world of bounded rationality, the evolution of division of labour is determined by the interplay between organisation information acquired by society via experiments with various patterns of division of labour and individuals' dynamic decisions on the experiment patterns. The trade offs between the information gains generated by social experiments and experiment costs, and between economies of division of labour and transaction costs, imply that more patterns of division of labour will be experimented with and more organisation information will be acquired via the market, the higher the experiment and trading efficiency. Since society can only gradually learn the information about the efficient pattern of division of labour, those simple patterns of division of labour as experimented with before are the complex ones when individuals are short of organisation information. This implies that economic development involves a gradual evolutionary process from the simple pattern of division of labour to the increasingly more complex ones.

As shown in Ng and Yang (1997; see also Sachs and Yang 2000, chapter 15), however, the latecomers of economic development can mimic the efficient pattern of division of labour by jumping over many intermediate levels of division of labour if the developed countries have already found the efficient pattern by gradual social experiments. The capitalist institutions in the developed countries were conducive to a great variety of patterns of division of labour being experimented with by the market. The free organisation information created by capitalist developed countries creates an opportunity for big push industrialisation for the latecomers. It is possible that big push industrialisation can be carried out by a Soviet style socialist system that has no institutional infrastructure that is essential for discovering the efficient pattern of industrialisation. This possibility for big push industrialisation via the imitation of the industrial pattern created by capitalist institutions in the absence of the capitalist institutional infrastructure is the rationale for relatively successful industrialisation in the Soviet style socialist countries in the 1930s and 1950s. It is by ignoring this possibility that Hayek and von Mises failed to predict the survival, spread, and impressive growth performance of the Soviet style economic system in the middle of the 20th century.

To address the third question, we briefly outline the characteristics of the Soviet style socialist system as follows.

1. By keeping a low relative price of agricultural to industrial goods and controlling all firms, this system used state ownership of all firms and central planning to achieve a high profit margin of the state industrial sector. The profit of state firms was allocated to mimic the high saving and investment rates and a growth rate of the heavy industrial sector that is higher than in the light industrial sector. This pattern of industrial development was created by the capitalist industrialisation process. In terms of the Smithian model in Shi and Yang (1995; see also Sachs and Yang 2000, chapter 12), the higher growth rates of the heavy industrial sector are generated by the increases in production roundaboutness and in the income share of the sector producing producer goods, which are one aspect of the evolution in division of labour.

2. State ownership of firms and a central planning system were used to organise comprehensive industrial investment programmes, which simultaneously created many very specialised industrial firms when the markets for a great variety of industrial goods were absent. This kind of comprehensive state investment programme generated a big jump of the network size of division of labour, which implies a jump of variety of highly specialised industrial sectors. In the Soviet Union in the 1930s, this kind of comprehensive state industrial investment plan was worked out by hiring many experts from capitalist developed countries (Zaleski 1980). In China in the 1950s, this was achieved with the assistance of experts from the Soviet Union and East Europe. The comprehensive state investment programmes quite effectively utilised free organisation information about the efficient pattern of division of labour and industrial linkage network effects of division of labour. A specific case of such programmes is China's programme of 694 large projects and 156 Soviet Union-aided key projects in the 1950s, which successfully created a large industrial network of division of labour among many highly specialised firms within a short period of time, when there was no market for those highly specialised producer goods (Zhou 1984). For instance, a firm specialising in producing artificial diamonds used in the machine tools industry was established in Zhengzhou as one of the 156 key projects, with assistance from East Germany when demand for machine tools was not enough to support a large specialised firm making artificial diamonds.[5]

3. The central planning authorities quite systematically mimicked industrial standardisation, mass production, the production line, the mechanism of checks and balances between managers, treasurers, and accountants within a capitalist corporation, Taylor scientific management, and other organisation patterns and management approaches developed by capitalist firms. A mechanism of checks and balances between industrial ministries, the ministry of finance, state banks,

the planning committee, the pricing bureau, the bureau of material distribution, and other institutions was established by dividing rights to disposal and appropriation of the same properties among the institutions. This checks-and-balances mechanism established quite an effective control mechanism for the whole economy by the central planning authorities. Top government and party officials collectively claim the residual of the operation of the planning system, so that they have the incentive to run this system to maximise the residual. According to Lenin, the Soviet central planner should organise the whole economy as a large corporation. But at the top of the apparatus, there were no effective checks and balances. The monopoly in founding firms and in all sectors by the government and party apparatus is in sharp contrast to the constitutional order created in the UK in 1688 with free association (including automatic free registration of private firms) and an independent judiciary. That system establishes checks and balances at the top of the political arena. Hence, the Soviet style socialist system creates great room for institutionalised state opportunism.

4.   The central planning authorities used a set of material balance tables and an iterative procedure to match demand with supply of goods in the absence of markets for intermediate factors. The system can fairly well approximate the result generated by Leontief's input–output method.[6] However, the Leontief input–output method cannot take into account the substitution between different inputs. It is incapable of sorting out the final demand for consumption goods and of providing an effective incentive mechanism for players to reveal private information. According to Roland (2000, chapter 1), the equilibrium that is achieved via a dynamic iterative process of the central planning is inefficient.[7]

5.   However, the imitation of all successful patterns of industrialisation and internal patterns of capitalist firms was realised by destroying the capitalist institutional infrastructure that generated the successful patterns of industrialisation and organisation in the capitalist developed economy. This is the first centralised social experiment with economic institutions. The precondition for a centralised social experiment is to establish monopoly power in the sector that designs system arrangements. This was realised through violent revolution, violent infringements upon private property rights, and 'red terror' in the numerous purging campaigns.[8] The lack of fair competition in the sector that designs institutional arrangements implies that the institutional arrangements that are chosen cannot be efficient. Also, the Soviet style socialist economic system is the first system that was purposely designed by a government rather than emerging from the spontaneous evolution and from interactions of players through fair competition and the voluntary trade of property rights. According to Hayek, efficient institutional arrangements can emerge only as a result of such fair competition and voluntary trade.

As Sachs (1994) suggests, the strategy of imitating the industrialisation pattern of the capitalist developed economy, in the absence of a capitalist institutional infrastructure, can generate short-run impressive growth performance. However, as the potential for the imitation has been exhausted or as the network of division of labour becomes increasingly more complex, the long-run cost of this strategy will outweigh its short-run benefit since this system does not have an institutional infrastructure that can create its own capacity for economic development and institutional innovations.

More generally, when the latecomer to economic development tries to catch up to the developed country, it usually undergoes a reverse engineering of institutional development. It first tries to mimic the industrial pattern, then the economic institution, such as the organisation structure of private firms, then the legal system, such as corporation laws, then the political system, such as representative democracy. It may finally adopt some constitutional rules, such as checks and balances on power, and ideology and behaviour norms from the developed countries. According to North (1994) and North and Weingast (1989), the original process of economic development in the UK was the other way around. Ideology and moral code determined the prevailing constitutional order, which determined the political system and legal system, which then generated a certain economic performance. In a geopolitical environment without an overarching political power in the international political arena, the economic performance difference between countries will generate pressure for changes in ideology and constitutional rules. North believes that changes in ideology and moral codes are much slower than changes in economic structure. This, together with the fact that the latecomer has more opportunities for mimicking new technologies, implies that many latecomers are tempted to substitute technical imitation for institutional imitation. This generates short-term benefit at high long-term cost by delaying difficult as well as important constitutional transition. This is referred to by some economists as 'curse to the latecomer'.

It should be noted that Mao's socialist system is substantially different from the Soviet style socialist system. Rivalry between Chinese and Russian communists created a sort of check-and-balance in the international political arena that involves the design of institutional arrangements. Hence, Mao's political instinct, which was sensitive to the rivalry, led him to create his administrative decentralisation proposed in his 1956 speech 'On Ten Important Relationships' (Mao 1977a). The rivalry is the grand background from which the differences between the reforms in China and Russia emerge.

During the Great Leap Forward in 1958–1961 and the Cultural Revolution in 1966–1970, and since the Cultural Revolution, an effective central planning system has not existed in China. Five-year plans and annual plans were virtually only on paper. The success of the first five-year plan in China in the 1950s misled Mao to conclude that the success was due to the merit of the socialist system that was created by communists. He did not understand that the success was based on Russians' imitation of the capitalist economy. Hence, Mao tried to invent his own communist institutions, such as the commune and mass eating halls. Also, Mao had a strong anti-

Soviet Union sentiment. He advocated administrative decentralisation against central planning; self-sufficiency of each firm, each county and each province against specialisation and division of labour; a mass line against professionalism; small scale, self-sufficient communes; and brigade firms with indigenous technology against large state firms with advanced technology, and so on (see Mao 1977b). This, on the one hand, slowed down the evolution of division of labour in China and kept rural China a traditional autarchic society. On the other hand, it created a vacuum in coordination mechanisms in Mao's China: neither central planning nor the market could coordinate the division of labour developed in the first five-year plan. This vacuum was filled by quasi-private firms and collective firms during the Cultural Revolution and by commune and brigade firms, which are later referred to as township and village enterprises (TVE) after 1984, and by a decentralised bilateral and multilateral bargaining system in the 1970s. Procurement fairs that implemented decentralised bargains were developed in the Mao era. Barters were very common in the fairs and sometimes commodities in short supply were used as commodity money.[9]

As the 1996 World Development Report on the transition economies indicates:

> Despite the industrialization efforts of the 1950s and 1960s, China was very poor and largely rural at the start of its reforms. Agriculture employed 71 per cent of the work force and was heavily taxed to support industry. Social safety nets extended only to the state sector – about 20 per cent of the population. Poor infrastructure and an emphasis on local self-sufficiency led to low regional specialization and large numbers of small and medium-sized firms. The economy was far less centrally planned and administered than the Soviet economy. Local governments had greater power and developed considerable management capacity, preparing them for a more decentralized economy. Chinese industry also received subsidies, but cross-subsidization was less pervasive (than in the Soviet Union).
>
> Because the agricultural sector had been so heavily repressed, freeing it up had immediate payoffs. … China thus started transition largely as a peasant agrarian economy and with far greater scope for reallocating labour than Russia.

In the former Soviet Union, more than 85 per cent of the workforce was in non-agricultural state enterprises, compared with around 18 per cent of the workforce in China (Sachs and Woo 1999, table 6). Perhaps 99 per cent of the labour force of the former Soviet Union (including the 14 per cent of the labour force in state and collective farms) were entitled to an 'iron rice bowl' under the Soviet system as of 1985 (see Cook (1993) for extensive documentation of worker protections in the Soviet Union). Very high proportions of workers in the Eastern European economies enjoyed similar guarantees.

Yang, Wang and Wills (1992) have shown that rural China was quite an autarchic society until 1978. The degree of commercialisation was 0.3 before 1978, although the first five-year plan developed a high level of division of labour in urban China by mimicking the pattern of Soviet Union's industrialisation. This means that rural China could develop a high level of division of labour either via commercialisation or via central planning. It is easy to develop a commercialised market system from a low level of division of labour. But it is extremely difficult to develop private property rights and related markets in an economy with a high level of division of labour which was developed through central planning. Reforms were easy in rural China because of a low level of division of labour. In contrast, reforms in urban China were more difficult because of a much higher level of division of labour there established via central planning (see Byrd 1983, 1988; Byrd and Tidrick 1987; Perkins 1988; and Walder 1989). However, it was much easier in China as a whole than in Russia because the central planning system was paralysed during the Cultural Revolution. Also, Mao's industrial system was much more disintegrated and locally self-sufficient than the Soviet style socialist system.

If an economy has developed a high level of division of labour quite successfully through centralised big push industrialisation, then the centralised planning system which is not good for long-term economic growth is embodied in the high level of division of labour which contributes to long-term economic growth. Since the sophisticated input and output interdependence generated by a large network size of division of labour is coordinated by the central planning system, it is extremely difficult to separate the dismantling process of the central planning from the malfunctioning of the coordination of a large network of division of labour. There is an inertia to use central planning to coordinate the high level of division of labour if reforms take place gradually. A big push or shock therapy may be necessary to cut off the central planning coordination mechanism from the high level of division of labour. In the process, paralysis of the input–output network might be inevitable because of the high risk of coordination failure in a large, highly interdependent network of division of labour. Put another way, a well developed central planning system can be dismantled only through shock therapy, since the system itself does not have the institutional infrastructure that is necessary for discovering the efficient institutional arrangements over the transitional period from the Soviet style socialist system back to a capitalist system.

China experienced the shock process during 1958–61 and 1966–70, when the central planning system was paralysed by Mao's Great Leap Forward and the Cultural Revolution, and during 1971–76, when Mao's policy of administrative decentralisation prevailed. Mao's administrative decentralisation divided the ownership of state firms among the central, provincial, and county governments and communes. In contrast, in the Soviet Union, there was a uniform ownership of all state firms. Deng's regional decentralisation consolidated Mao's administrative decentralisation by institutionalising the fiscal relationship between the central and provincial governments. Government revenue from tax and state firm profit was divided between the central and provincial governments according a certain division rule. In the early stage of Deng's regional decentralisation, a fixed amount of provincial government revenue was delivered to the central government. In the later stage, a fixed proportion of the tax revenue was delivered to the central government. A Chinese style fiscal federalism emerges from the evolution, which provides a driving force for China's reforms in the 1990s. This fiscal federalism separates tax categories and a collection institution of local governments from that of the central government, with help from the World Bank (Qian and Roland 1998; Qian and Weingast 1997). Deng's fiscal federalism is in striking contrast with the much more centralised fiscal relationship between the federal and local governments in Russia (Zhuravskaya 1998 and Qian 1999). This partly explains the difference in reform performance between China and Russia.

But contributions of Deng's regional decentralisation and fiscal federalism to economic development should not be overstated. First, it fragments the market and promotes monopoly power of local state enterprises (Zhou 1999; He 1997, p. 206). In other words, Deng's regional decentralisation inherits the bad sides of Mao's administrative decentralisation, thereby retarding the formation of the integrated national market. Lardy (1998a, p. 204) uses the automobile sector to illustrate this point. Second, China's fiscal federalism is far away from the fiscal federalism in the US. A residential registration system which has been in place since 1954 greatly restricts the free mobility of labour and human capital. Despite recent reforms to this system, which allow migrants who have no permanent residence in large cities to obtain annually renewable temporary residency, the migrant's position in China's large cities is not as good as that of immigrants with green cards in the US. Migrants in China must pay much higher school fees for their children and a much higher price for housing than local permanent residents. In Beijing and other large cities, firms hiring migrants with no local permanent residency are heavily fined by the government.[10] Finally, China has a very centralised appointment system for leading provincial government officers. The central government regularly rotates the officers between provinces to make sure that they are absolutely loyal to the central government when local interests are in conflict with that of the central government. Hence, when Deng purposely kept a weak central government for political reasons after 1989, the fiscal federalism was more like that of the US. But when Premier Zhu moves to increase the power of the central government in the post-Deng era, the fiscal system becomes far removed from the fiscal federalism in the US.

China still had great scope for the strategy of big push industrialisation and imitation when it entered the reform era. The high income share of the traditional autarchic sector in China implies that it still has room to mimic the efficient pattern of division of labour in the capitalist developed economy in the absence of private property rights and market. But the potential benefit for this strategy had been already exhausted in the Soviet Union when it started its reform programme.

But China's impressive development performance is not only due to the potential for mimicking the old capitalist industrialisation pattern. Also, a great variety of social experiments in Japan, Hong Kong, Taiwan, South Korea, and other East Asian countries provides room for a new mimicking strategy. The newly industrialised capitalist economies provided free information on a new pattern of industrialisation of labour-intensive exports. This pattern exploits a significant differential in per capita real income between developed and less developed economies to export labour-intensive manufactured goods in exchange for capital-intensive equipment. Ethnic Chinese businessmen from Taiwan and Hong Kong bring to China human capital, entrepreneurial expertise, institutional knowledge, and capital, which are essential for the imitation of the new capitalist industrialisation pattern. The Chinese government also purposely learned from Taiwan and Hong Kong's experience. For instance, the special economic zone is certainly a direct imitation of the export process zone and the free trade zone in Taiwan and other capitalist countries. The zones significantly reduce transaction costs caused by tariff and other barriers to trade. Private rights of foreign direct investors are much better protected in the zones than in the rest of the host country. According to the theory of capital and division of labour in Yang (1999; see also Sachs and Yang 2000, chapter 16) and the theory of indirect pricing in Yang and Ng (1995; see also Sachs and Yang 2000, chapter 8), this implies that foreign entrepreneurs have a strong incentive to sell their entrepreneurial know-how indirectly to the host country via the institution of the firm.

But Deng's reform era shares two fundamental elements of Stalin and Mao's socialism: the party's monopoly of political power and the dominance of state-owned firms. According to Lardy's documentation (1998), the state sector expands in terms of level of output and employment, employment share, and level and share of financial resources that it receives during the reform era. In the largest special zone, Shengzhen, state-owned firms dominate the economy. In 1992 when many government institutions were short of revenue, they were encouraged to found lucrative businesses to subsidy their expenses. Many new government enterprises and businesses were founded very rapidly, so that 60–90 per cent of government institutions run commercial businesses (Wen 1999, pp. 319–27). The government institutions use their dual positions as regulation makers and enforcers and players in the economic arena to pursue state opportunism. For instance a local government tax bureau runs a restaurant and uses predation tax to force other local restaurants to close, and a police unit runs an enterprise producing fireworks and uses its power in issuing licences to maintain its monopoly in this business (Wen 1999, p. 321). The institutional characteristics imply institutionalised state opportunism and corruption. Economic development is still a hostage of the vested interests of the privileged class.

The most important characteristic of China's market-oriented reforms is the absence of constitutional order and the rule of law. This implies institutionalised state opportunism, self-dealing of the ruling class, and rampant corruption. We will analyse the features of the market-oriented reforms in the absence of constitutional order in Section 4.5.

In summary, China's impressive growth performance in the 1980s and 1990s can be attributed mainly to its low initial level of development (that is, the nature of its recovery from disastrous Maoism) and to the new opportunity for mimicking the new export-oriented industrialisation pattern. Deng's socialist market economy emerges and evolves from a mix of Mao's administrative decentralisation and state-owned firms, and the imitation of Taiwan and Hong Kong's new development pattern. In this sense, Deng's socialist market system is different from Lange's market socialism, from Stalin's socialism that mimics the old capitalist industrialisation pattern under central planning and the uniform state ownership of firms, and from Mao's socialism that does not copy any capitalist experience. It is possible that after the potential for mimicking has been exhausted, China's new pattern of socialism may fail to work, which is what happened to Soviet style socialism after the successful imitation of old capitalist industrialisation in the 1930s and 1950s.

Misunderstanding the initial conditions and driving forces of China and Russia's reforms generates many misleading views on the comparison between China and Russia's reforms. The first of them is the overstatement of development performance of China by some China experts. As pointed out by Sachs and Woo (forthcoming), China's broad growth performance is no better than the performance of other East Asian economies. Virtually every market economy in East Asia has grown very rapidly in the past 30 years, based on a strategy of rapid export growth of labour-intensive manufactures. During 1986–94, China averaged an annual per capita growth of around 5.6 to 6.8 per cent in PPP-adjusted GDP. Other East Asian countries also showed equivalent or even higher rates of annual per capita growth in PPP-adjusted GDP over the longer period of 1965–90, including: Hong Kong, 5.8; Korea, 7.4; Singapore, 7.4; Taiwan, 6.3; Indonesia, 4.7; Malaysia, 4.5; and Thailand, 4.6. In addition, the difference in per capita real income between China and newly industrialised countries, such as Taiwan, is still increasing.

China's official statistics overstate real growth rates too. Lardy (1998) shows that official data overstate the growth rate by at least 1–2 per cent. According to some Chinese scholars, such as Luo Shao (*Economic Highlights*, May 15, 1999, p. 1), the official data overstate growth rates by 2–3 per cent. Also, Lardy (1998) provides evidence that the Chinese government purposely hides information about bad loans of state banks and the financial state of state firms. China's actual performance in development is greatly inferior to that indicated by the official data. It can be shown that even if China's growth rates are much higher than those of Japan, Taiwan, South Korea, the US, and Germany, the difference in per capita real income between China and these countries will still increase before 2015 because of a very low absolute level of per capita real income in 1979 China. Hence, we must pay more attention to the absolute difference in per capita income level and its change than to the difference in growth rates.

Some economists argue that China's short-run impressive growth performance indicates that privatisation of state-owned firms is not necessary for a successful transition. This is equivalent to the false statement that the Soviet Union's short-run impressive growth performance in the 1930s would ensure the long-run success of the Soviet socialist system. Other economists (Qian 1999) consider China's fiscal federalism as the major explanation for impressive growth performance. This may not be very convincing, since post-communist Eastern Europe as a whole is much closer to a fiscal federalism than is China's communist centralised government system. The variety of institutional experiments in Eastern Europe is certainly much greater than in different provinces in China. If fiscal federalism is the most important determinant of the difference in transition performance, then it is Eastern Europe, rather than China, that should have better transition performance. As we discussed before, different initial conditions, different development stages, room for imitation, and inaccurate Chinese official data explain the differences in transition performance.

Economic transition is part of the transition in constitutional rules. Speed and the time path of the transition are determined by its driving mechanism. Hence, the next section will focus on the driving mechanisms for constitutional transition.

4.3 DRIVING MECHANISMS FOR TRANSITION

Many historians agree with the view that a great driving force for experiments with various institutions and diffusion and imitation of and transition to successful institutions in Western Europe is a geopolitical structure where no single overarching political power exists (Sachs and Yang 2000, chapter 1). This implies that the sizes of major countries are close, so that there is no very large country that can dominate others in Western Europe. Intensive competition between many governments in small countries is conducive for the emergence of more capable governments. This can explain why large inland countries, such as Russia and China, are slower than other countries to adopt competitive institutions. This also explains why small island countries, such as Britain, Japan, and Taiwan, are more able to quickly adopt competitive institutions.

The renaissance in Western Europe had profound and complex effects in consolidating the decentralised political structure in Western Europe. On the ideological level, mankind and the meaning of life itself were put at the centre of renewed philosophic speculation. On the economic level, the rise of competing city states in Renaissance Italy spurred the role of international trade, with the attendant market institutions of banking, contract law, shipping law, and secured transactions. Political speculations, crowned by Machiavelli's *The Prince*, explored ways for the Prince to strengthen the state in competition with other states, including the role of the state in fostering economic prosperity.

Throughout European history, innovations in economic and political life have started in one region and then spread to others on the basis of their perceived or demonstrated advantages, or through conquest, colonisation, or imperial rule. It was considerably more difficult for new European ideas and institutions to spread into Russia and China's vast continental expanse. Institutional innovations carry less well into continental, largely self-contained societies, such as China, India, and Russia than they do into small, open societies that are dependent for their very survival on international trade, international alliances, and the timely adoption of 'best practices' from abroad. Perhaps 'small is beautiful' in economic reform, if the small entity isn't simply gobbled up by a larger power.[11] In any event, it is probably no accident that Russia, China, and India have had the most difficult time of all the traditional societies in the world in adopting the new political and economic institutions from abroad, even when those institutions have an overwhelming track record of effectiveness.

Sachs and Woo (1999) and Roland (forthcoming) have provided evidence that small transition economies have greater state capacity in managing transition. They gain institutional knowledge faster and can manage rapid transition better than large transition countries (Sachs and Woo 1999, p. 14). A quite successful Eastern European-style 'big bang' in Vietnam in 1989 might be partly attributed to the small size of this country.

The post-socialist countries in Eastern Europe and the current transitional economies in Asia provide a sufficiently great genetic diversity of countries and cultures for a great variety of institutional experiments with transition from the socialist system to the capitalist one, with which human society has no previous experience. Simultaneous experiments with various patterns and speeds of transition in many countries may provide the opportunity to quickly acquire institutional knowledge about transition.

Many economists may argue that particular historical and cultural traditions of different developing countries may lead to different institutional transition paths. Asking all countries to follow the same transitional path might be criticised as an outdated imperialist attitude and a self-centred view of the western cultural tradition. The development experience in many countries seems to reject this criticism. Some countries, such as the Soviet Union and 1949–1979 China, tried to mimic capitalist industrialisation without the capitalist legal system and property right structure; and failed. Other countries, such as Taiwan and South Korea, tried to mimic the capitalist legal system and property right structure without a democratic political system before the end of the 1980s. They realised that this does not work and finally initiated the transition to a constitutional democracy at the end of the 1980s. Japan mimicked all the capitalist legal, political, and economic institutions from Britain and Germany, but kept the Emperor's substantive power. It enjoyed very successful economic development in the absence of real constitutional checks and balances of the Emperor's power. Then it entered WWII, acting aggressively towards China and other countries and bringing disaster to the Japanese, Chinese, and other Asian peoples. Even after the big-bang constitutional transition under the American military occupation, Japan still maintained some of the 'Asian behaviour norms' in the relationship between the government and private business, which caused the troubles in the 1990 financial crisis.

All this experience suggests that there is a universal institutional core that is essential for long-term successful economic development. Hence, the transition is a harmonisation process of the institutions in ex-socialist countries with global capitalist institutions, rather than a process to create institutional innovations that are substantially different from the capitalist institutions (Sachs and Woo 1999).

4.4 MARKET-ORIENTED REFORMS ASSOCIATED WITH THE TRANSITION OF CONSTITUTIONAL RULES

There are two patterns of transition. One has been adopted by Eastern Europe and Russia, in which market-oriented reforms are just a small part of the transition of constitutional rules. The other has been adopted by China and Vietnam, in which market-oriented reforms are implemented under communist game rules (that is, a communist monopoly of political power). We consider first in this section the former pattern of transition.

Example 1: Russia's Constitutional Transition

As Sachs and Pistor (1997, pp. 3–5) indicate, the tradition to the rule of law in Russia has been absent. In the first stage of the transition from January 1992 to October 1993, reforms were implemented under the old communist regime. During this period, economic reforms were launched consisting of three major pillars: price and trade liberalisation, stabilisation, and privatisation. From the very beginning, all of these measures remained incomplete, and indeed some of them failed during this period. The record of stunted reforms is linked to the absence of constitutional order in several ways. First, the government often lacked the political and constitutional means to implement reforms, especially in the face of entrenched opposition from the communist-era Supreme Soviet. Equally important, the government lacked constitutional restraints on its own behaviour, so that many opportunities for reform were squandered by official abuse and corruption.

The failure of stabilisation, for example, can be traced proximately to the behaviour of the Russian Central Bank, which issued massive and inflationary credits to the economy. The explosion of credits mainly followed the appointment of Mr Viktor Gerashchenko, the Communist-era head of Soviet Gosbank, as chairman of the Central Bank in June 1992. During 1992 and 1993, the Russian Central Bank transferred a very large proportion of national income (perhaps as much as 40 per cent of GDP in 1992, and 20 per cent of GDP in 1993) to key pressure groups, political favourites of the Government and the Bank, and various cronies of leading officials, with the transfers being financed by the inflation tax imposed on the society at large. The Bank's books were unauditable, with large flows of untraceable money.

The common denominator of all these distortions to the reform process was the absence of rule of law in government decision making and executive authority. Procedures were ad hoc, non-transparent, and often corrupt. Civil society was too weak to offer important countervailing pressures, so that abuses went largely unchecked. Decision making was not guided by general legal norms evenly applied, but was rather individualised to particular enterprises and pressure groups.

The first phase of reforms saw the eruption of political power struggles that brought the country to the edge of a civil war. The second phase, which started in October

1993 and is still continuing saw the consolidation of political and economic power by those who had gained the most during the first phase. This consolidation was accompanied by governance of more orderly rules, if not always by formal law. The state Duma operated under the new rules, and elections were held as scheduled in December 1995. In addition, presidential elections were held on schedule at the end of Yeltsin's five-year term. At the same time, many deep constitutional problems remained. Struggles over executive power continued in a new though less dramatic guise, between the government and various parts of the presidential apparatus. After 1992, the presidential apparatus grew to enormous proportions outside constitutional constraints or public oversight.

Whether the rule of law has taken hold in Russia is a difficult question to answer. Countries that respect the rule of law usually share the following features: they 'divide the powers of government among separate branches; entrench civil liberties (notably, due process of law and equal protection of law) behind constitutional walls; and provide for the orderly transfer of political power through fair elections' (Sachs and Pistor 1997). The subjection of the sovereign to predetermined legal constraints affects public and private law development in a given country. Where this is the case, arbitrary state interference is minimised, and state action – as a regulator, tax administrator, or contract enforcer – becomes impartial and predictable.

It takes time to reform the judicial system, to train and/or to replace its personnel, and to replace existing laws with new ones. Nevertheless, it is important to assess whether the commitment to the rule of law, as opposed to personal fiat, however well intentioned, is apparent. Indicators for such a commitment include the division of powers, civil liberties, independent judiciary, and the orderly transfer of power.

Before 1991, hardly any of these features were established in Russia. As of 1996, a number of important achievements have come about. A new Constitution is in place which, despite some doubts about the validity of the procedure by which it was adopted, has apparently found widespread legitimacy. Two parliamentary elections have been held under this Constitution. Most importantly, perhaps, presidential elections have been held and the unsuccessful contender accepted them.

These achievements are significant, indeed remarkable, but we should also note that Russia has not yet experienced an orderly transfer of political power, so that the hardest test of the new constitutional order has not yet been seen.

The new constitution acknowledges the separation of powers, but a closer examination reveals the limits of these nominal commitments. In particular, the division of power between the legislature and the executive is blurred. This is most visible in the legislative powers allocated to the President. The President may rule by decree, and his decrees are binding as law.

It is worth noting that most provisions of the Constitution would not hold water if legally contested. The liberal idea that civil rights are natural-law rights and shall be used as a defence against the state seems alien to the Russian Constitution. In its language, the state grants these rights to its subjects. But what the state grants, it may also take away again. In addition, the Constitution lacks the crucial procedural safeguards to ensure the effectuation of civil liberties, including equal protection of the law. 'Special' laws designed for a particular person or entity, as opposed to general laws addressed to an anonymous or only generally defined target group, have been rampant in Russia. They provide the legal basis for tax exemptions, special privatisation rules, and allocation of rights to those with the best access to the President's decree power. As a result, the state retains ample scope for arbitrariness, which not only creates uncertainty, but also provides a breeding ground for corruption.

Gray and Hendley (1997) set out three basic conditions for law-based private transacting, which are good laws, sound supportive institutions, and market based incentives that create a demand for law and legal institutions. Drawing from a comparison with commercial law development in Hungary, they suggest that the development of effective judicial and administrative support institutions is the most difficult task to accomplish, not only in Russia, but also in other transition economies. However, Russia still falls short of providing the first conditions for law-based transactions: good laws that reduce transaction costs and enable private actors to mobilise their own rights. Pistor (1997) discusses the implications of the lack of a comprehensive corporate law at the outset of privatisation for the development of property rights and corporate governance post-privatisation. She traces the nature and quality of legal rules issued in post-socialist Russia, not only to Russia's legal tradition, but also to policy choices made by reformers during the course of economic reform. She argues that comprehensive legal reform was delayed in favour of speedy economic reforms based on ad hoc decision making and decrees with detrimental consequences for the development of property rights and governance structures.

As indicated by Sachs and Pistor (1997), the roots of Russian exceptionalism in the rule of law and in the lack of economic freedom, in comparison with the rest of Europe – are deep. The exceptionalism far predates the 1917 Bolshevik Revolution, and indeed was already dramatic in the mid-19th century, when Alexander II launched his attempts at the Great Reforms (described by Owen 1997). The exceptionalism can be traced back several centuries, plausibly to the start of the Muscovite state.

Following the emergence of Moscovy from more than two centuries of Mongol domination (1240–1480), law has played a conspicuously less important role than in Western Europe. The great formative stages of Western European law – the application of Roman Law by medieval Europe; the struggle of the Princes and the Papacy over political authority and legitimacy; the Renaissance and the Enlightenment – touched Russia only indirectly. Perhaps equally important, after the 16th century, the Russian Orthodox Church was subsumed in state power. The Tsar was both the head of state and the head of the Russian Orthodox Church. This dual role eliminated one of Western Europe's key bulwarks against the concentration of power in the hands of a single ruler. Medieval Europe's prolonged struggle between Church and State over sovereign authority, natural law, and political legitimacy played a fundamental role in fostering law-bound state power and bolstering standards of political morality; in Russia, by contrast, the struggle ended in a dominant state and a politically subservient Church.

The trade-off between the benefit of constitutionalism and the demand for flexible and great executive power (Hellman 1997), which was the focus of the debate among Russian economists and policy makers, is similar to the trade off between the reduction of resistance from the vested interests and institutionalisation of state opportunism of the dual track approach in China. Shleifer (1998) has made an argument in support of Russia's shock therapy. According to him, corruption, which is associated with evolutionary approach to reforms, is a way to buy out the monopoly power of the privileged class. However, he goes on, corruption is not an effective method of reform for two reasons. First, the implicit contracts based on corruption are not easy to enforce because the entitlement for selling government officials' control rights is not legally well defined. Second, tolerance of corruption will generate incentives for creating more government officials' control rights. Hence, the most efficient way to initiate reforms is to remove government officials' control rights through the kind of privatisation reform seen in Eastern Europe and Russia. But as Sachs and Pistor (1997) suggest, the success of liberalisation and privatisation reforms is dependent on the transition to constitutional order.

Hellman (1997, p. 58) provides empirical evidence for a positive correlation between growth performance and the passage of constitutions in East and Central Europe. The result is not convincing, since the transition of constitutional rules is a very complicated and long process. Compared to short-term negative effects of the transition of constitutional rules in the American Independence War and Civil War on economic growth, the current difficulties in Russia's transition are not unusual and cannot be attributed to the shock therapy approach. But because of the lack of any tradition of rule of law in Russia, Russia's transition might be more difficult than were American and French transitions in the 17th and 19th century. It took one century for France to undergo the transition from the Old Regime to the new constitutional order. Russia is a large and mainly inland country, with a history that is more unfavourable to transition. It is likely that Russia's transition from communism to the new constitutional order is as difficult as was France's transition in the 19th century.

Many scholars attribute Russia's poor transition performance to weak enforcement of laws. However, as Pistor (1997) points out, the weak enforcement is due to bad laws and state opportunism. A comparison between 18th century Britain and France also suggests that a great state taxation and law enforcement capacity in Britain was due to fair constitutional order and weak state capacity for taxation and law enforcement in France's old regime was due to state opportunism and to the absence of fair constitutional rules. The Chinese case provides another support for this view, since the Chinese communist party's monopoly of political power institutionalises state opportunism that uses laws (which are often bad laws) to pursue interests of party apparatus at the expenses of society at large. This 'rule by laws,' distinguished from the rule of law, makes the law enforcement in China very weak. Many court rulings cannot be enforced in the 1990s (He 1997).

4.5   MARKET-ORIENTED REFORMS IN THE ABSENCE OF CONSTITUTIONAL ORDER

China's dual track approach is representative of the market-oriented reforms in the absence of constitutional order. China's Constitution (http://www.quis.net/chinalaw) is similar to other socialist constitutions that give the Communist Party a monopoly of political power and the notions of division and of checks and balances of power. One of the differences between China's Constitution and that of the Soviet Union is that in its preamble, the ideology of Marxism, Leninism, and Mao thoughts are taken as the source of the legitimacy of the power structure in China. Although Western scholars of law consider the preamble as having no legal implication, its notion on the source of power is similar to the old notion of the origin of power being Divine, rather than from contract and the consensus of the ruled. Western constitutionalists, such as Pilon (1998), would pay particular attention to the three features of the Chinese Constitution. First, it is programmatic. It sets up a specific agenda for building socialism. Hence, it is more like the bylaws of China, Incorporated. Second, in the Chinese Constitution, there are no genuine provisions for popular ratification. It gives no indication of how citizens join or consent to so far-reaching a programme. It thus raises fundamental questions about the legitimacy of the Chinese Constitution. Finally, all citizens' rights are given by the state and party apparatus, but monopoly of power by the state and party apparatus is given from the 'Divine' – the ideology of Marxism, Leninism, and Mao Thoughts, which needs no justification. Hence, Pilon (1998, p. 355) calls the Chinese Constitution 'a program for unlimited government'.[12]

So far, no influential movement to reject the Constitution has been developed in China. The sense of crisis among Chinese people is not strong enough. This, together with the large size of China, implies that pressure for the transition of constitutional rules is too weak for serious consideration of such a transition. Hence, China's market-oriented reforms can be conducted only within a 'bird cage' of communist game rules. It is not surprising that reforms are hijacked by the vested interests of the party apparatus.

The arrangements in which the rule maker, the referee, the rule enforcer, and the player are all the same party apparatus institutionalise state opportunism, which pursues the party's interests even if social welfare is sacrificed. The state opportunism is illustrated by the government's control of the entry of private firms into the important sectors and state predation of private firms. There is a list of sectors in which domestic private firms are not allowed to operate. The sectors include the banking sector, post and telecommunications, railroads, airlines, insurance, the space industry, petroleum chemistry, iron and steel, publications, wholesale business, news, and others. In addition to the thirty sectors, private firms are restricted from operating in another dozen sectors, including automobile manufacturing, electronic appliances, and travel agencies (Huang 1993, p. 88). In addition, a stiff licensing system for international trade, wholesale and retail distribution networks, publication, and many other businesses eliminates many lucrative opportunities for private business, generating trade conflict with the US and other developed countries. In particular, all government institutions which have power to issue licences have vested interests in the sector where licensees operate. For instance, the licence for international trade is issued by the Trade Ministry, which is the largest owner of trade companies in China. The licence for the wholesale and retail distribution network is issued by the local government committee which owns local state distribution networks. Of course, the principle for issuing a licence is to promote the monopoly interest of the government institutions.

Mueller (1998) documents the adverse effects of state monopoly of the telecommunications sector on economic development. This monopoly implies that the regulator of this sector, the major player, and the referee who enforces the regulation are the same state organisation. State opportunism is then institutionalised and retards economic development. Also, China has a very strict government approval system of founding firms. There is neither free association nor automatic registration of a company except in the Hainan Province (Mao 1999; Pei 1998). Also, there are arbitrary and often very high registration capital requirements for founding firms. This, together with the residential registration system and the state monopoly in the housing and banking sectors, provides many effective control methods that can be used to pursue state opportunism. As Pilon (1998) points out, all the self-dealing is, of course, supported by the fundamental game rules in China's Constitution.

State predation of private firms started in political campaigns in the early 1950s. According to Bai, et al. (1999), it has continued in the reform era. One persistent cause is the ideological discrimination against private businesses amid power struggles and ideological debates within the government. As Bai, et al. (1999) document, another form of state predation in the reform era was simply revenue grabbing. Governments of different levels tended to impose various kinds of taxes and fees in order to grab as much of the observable revenue from their business jurisdiction as possible. A 1988 study of private firms in Liaoning Province found that taxes and subcharges alone would take away 63 per cent of the observed enterprise profits. When the scores of different fees were also taken into account, the tax burden was even higher. Such a tax burden made it hard for private firms to survive, unless they evaded taxes and fees by hiding their transactions and revenue (*China Economic Almanac* 1989, p. 107). Ten years later, a 1998 study of private firms in the Anhui Province reported that gross profits for many products were about 10 per cent of total revenue, whereas total taxes and fees added up to more than 10 per cent. There were more than 50 types of fees imposed on a private business, and some types of these fees are prohibited by the government's own publicised regulations and rules. This study reached the conclusion that 'owners who do not want to close down their businesses had no choice but to evade taxes' by hiding revenue (*Jilin Daily*, 30 May 1998). Peasants in the rural areas were major victims of excessive taxes and fees. Throughout the reform period, the government made countless promises to reduce extortive levies and the discretionary tax on peasants, but extortive levies and discretionary taxation continued to be widespread. In some places, 61 different types of fees were charged (Ding, Yan, and Yang 1995).

China started to mimic western style laws in the 1990s. But under the communist constitutional rules, the laws, such as the Corporation Law passed in 1994, and the Anti-Unfair Competition Law passed in 1993, cannot be implemented. The incompatibility between Corporation Law and the communist constitutional rules is noted by Yang (1998) and that between the state monopoly in the telecommunications sector and Anti-unfair Competition Law is noted by Mueller (1998, p. 200). It might be concluded that imitation of many Western style laws would not work within the communist constitutional rules. The constitutional constraint implies that China's reforms can only follow the dual track approach. This approach generates long-term costs that likely outweigh its short-term benefit of buying out the vested interests of the privileged class. We will use several examples to illustrate this point.[13]

Example 2: China's Rural Reform and Land System

The first example is China's rural reforms and land system (see Yang, Wang and Wills 1992; Sachs and Woo 1999, p. 30; and Wu 1998). In China's rural reforms, rights to the use of land that is collectively owned by villagers were given to farmers in the end of the 1970s. The sale of land was strictly prohibited in the 1980s, though transfer of use rights has been permitted under tight regulations since 1984 (Yang, Wang and Wills 1992, p. 18). Village cadres control reallocation of land according to changes in village population. The data suggest that the impressive agricultural growth in the early years of agriculture reform was a one-shot improvement in productivity that followed the liberalisation of the agricultural sector and the introduction of the household responsibility system for land tenure. A simple extrapolation exercise indicates that the big achievement of the 1978 agriculture was to return rice and wheat yields to their underlying trends that were suppressed by the stringent collectivist agriculture practices of the 1958–77 era.[14]

Growth of the agricultural sector slows down after 1985 due to three factors. The first factor was farmers' uncertainty about future land use rights. Despite the 1984 government decision that farmers could get leases up to fifteen years long, Prosterman, Hanstad and Li (1996) found in their field work the following fact:

> Local officials have not implemented this policy to any significant degree... [In] many villages, representatives from the collective take back all the land in the village every three to six years and reallocate the plots to adjust for changes in household size. The result is that farmers have refrained from making many small long-term improvements (for example, digging wells and small feeder drains, applying more organic fertiliser) in the land that would have increased grain yield.[15]

Johnson (1994) pointed out that some of the government's policy responses to the post-1985 slowdown increased farmers' concerns about land security, and hence reduced farmers' work efforts and investments in the land. For example, the government announced in late 1990 that some farming operations, such as ploughing, fertilising and harvesting, would be re-collectivised in order to reap economies of scale from mechanisation.

The second important factor for agriculture stagnation is that the state monopoly of the procurement and distribution network of grain has been strengthened since 1994 (Lin 1998, p. 68). The monopolised distribution system causes an appallingly large scale of corruption and waste. When the state decided to clamp down on inflation in late 1993, grain procurement quotas were re-introduced and price controls were put on 27 agricultural commodities. Worse yet, whenever credit was tightened to fight inflation (1985, 1989 and 1992), the government would pay for part of its grain procurement with coupons (IOUs) instead of cash (Sachs and Woo 1999). This also explains the flagging growth in grain production.

A third factor contributing to the post-1985 slowdown in agricultural productivity growth has been the large reductions in investment in agricultural infrastructure (for example, irrigation works) in the years after 1979. The level of real investment in agricultural infrastructure in 1994, for example, was only 58 per cent of the 1979 level. It appears, however, that in many rural areas the decline of state investment in agricultural infrastructure was accompanied by a reduction in state efforts to develop human resources. This can be explained by the absence of a land market and related contracts. Even in the absence of state investment, the agricultural infrastructure can be developed by land-related contracts. But within the institutional constraint, project contracts based on land entitlement are not feasible. Also, in the absence of land trade, local governments cannot raise revenue through property tax and sales tax on land. Local government must use profit from township and village enterprises, expropriate tax, and discretional fees to raise enough revenue for retaining the friendship of local officers, and for infrastructure construction. But this institutionalises corruption and other opportunism by local officers, thereby restricting government fund-raising capacity.

According to Wu's documentation (1998), this dual track approach to land ownership generates a dilemma between the efficient commercial use of land and social justice. Many local officers in coastal provinces divide village-owned land into two parts: land that can be leased to foreign or private companies for commercial use and land used by villagers for household farming. Under the 'dual land system', village officers gain control rights to commercial land and grab rents from it. In exchange, villagers claim priority rights to employment in the firms leasing land. But the difference between the rents and employment income is huge. Hence, the effect is that the local officers steal rents from villagers who collectively own land. Since this stealing is so unjust, many farmer protests have taken place. The central government was forced to prohibit the practice of the dual land system. This prohibition slows local industrialisation and eliminates many socially beneficial business opportunities.

In summary, the institutional constraint imposed by the communist Constitution generates dilemma between justice and efficiency. The dual track approach developed under market-oriented reforms in the absence of constitutional order institutionalises corruption and opportunistic behaviour by government officers and creates more obstacles to constitutional transition. Yang, Wang and Wills (1992) estimate the degree of transferability of rural land in China and estimate the potential gains of privatisation of land ownership. According to their econometric model of the relationship among per capita real income, the degree of commercialisation (level of division of labour), and efficiency indices of specifying and enforcing property rights, Chinese peasants' per capita real income would increase by 30 per cent if free land trade were allowed in 1987. This again verifies Sachs and Woo's claim that despite (rather than 'because of') the dual track approach, China's agricultural sector has had quite an impressive development performance. But if the dual track approach were replaced by a transition to complete private ownership of land as in pre-1949 China, China's economic performance would be even better and the current agricultural stagnation would not occur.

Example 3: China's Township–Village–Enterprise

The second example of the dual track approach is China's township–village–enterprise (TVE). As Sachs and Woo (1999) indicate, there are two common usages of the term TVE that can be potentially confusing: the official usage in statistical collection and the academic usage in discussion of ownership-type. The official statistical meaning has broadened over time. Prior to 1984, TVE referred to township-owned or village-owned, and from 1984 onward, TVE statistics also include joint-owned (by several persons or families) and individual-owned (by one person or family hiring less than seven employees). The present official statistical usage gives the impression of TVEs being overwhelmingly private in nature, because 87 per cent of TVEs in 1994 were individual-owned. Individual-owned TVE produced less than 27 per cent of TVE output, and less than 19 per cent of industrial TVE output.[16]

However, most academic discussions on the ownership structure of TVEs implicitly use a narrower definition that covers only the enterprises that are registered formally (and increasingly falsely, in our opinion) as township-owned and village-owned. This implicitly narrow definition explains why Naughton (1994a) categorically described TVEs as 'local government-owned'. Unless otherwise noted, we will adhere to this narrow definition of TVEs as public-owned in the following analysis on the 'ownership nature of TVEs'.

The TVE is hardly innovative, since such local government or collectively owned firms were experimented with in many countries, such as Japan and Qing Dynasty China, in the end of the 19th century. But under a constitutional order that protects private rights of firms, such firms and collectively owned firms are not competitive in most cases. The TVEs operate entirely outside of the state plan, and with rather hard budget constraints (receiving few subsidies from the state budget of the central and provincial governments, and only rarely from local government). Without question, local governments have viewed the TVEs as an important potential source of revenues for local budgets (Oi 1992). In the early 1980s, the central government introduced the explicit tax contract, a system of fiscal contracts where the central government negotiated a revenue quota with each province. This fiscal contract arrangement is replicated at each level of government down to the township level. This revision in fiscal relations makes the local governments the residual claimants of income generated by any firms established by them at the local level. 'As a result, local governments use every method possible, including many which straddle the boundaries of legality, to promote rural industry, at the same time milking it to supplement their government budgets' (Zweig 1991).

Some economists view TVEs as an important and highly successful institutional innovation, melding market incentives with public ownership. Others, by contrast, view them as a partially successful half-way house on the way to real private ownership. While the former emphasise the special fit of the TVEs with China's undeveloped economic conditions, the latter emphasise the serious institutional constraint and problems ahead unless China moves now to real privatisation of the TVEs (Sachs and Woo 1999).

The foundation for collective-owned rural industrial enterprises was laid during the decade-long Cultural Revolution, when the official emphasis on self-reliance and the breakdown of the national distribution system caused the rural communes to expand their non-agricultural activities. These commune-brigade enterprises were relabelled as TVEs when the commune system began to dissolve in 1979. The concern for rural underemployment and local development has led to steady liberalisation of the rules governing the formation of TVEs; and since 1984, the terms of approval and supervision of TVEs have varied greatly across regions.

Given the varieties of TVEs, the vagueness about their ownership and control, and their evolving nature, it is therefore natural that different authors have emphasised different 'basic' characteristics of the TVEs, often without acknowledging their great diversity over time and space. For example, Nee (1996) regards TVEs as informal joint ventures between the state and the private sector, often with 'extensive informal privatisation of collective-owned assets and firms', whereas others view TVEs as a form of public ownership no different from the large urban state sector. Peng (1992) emphasises the 'semi-private' nature of TVEs to explain their operational autonomy, while Oi (1995) accents a state-centred view in which TVEs are the production units in 'a large multi-level corporation' managed by the county–township–village hierarchy.[17] The terminological haze has thickened in the 1990s with the additional easing of restrictions on the registration of firms as TVEs, making the co-existence of true TVEs and red-capped private enterprises a common phenomenon in many places, as stressed by Ronnas (1993).

The TVE system in the reform era inherits many advantages as well as disadvantages of Mao's commune and brigade firms. It distorts the geographical location of firms, retards efficient urbanisation, relocates resources from large state firms with advanced technology to local firms with inferior technology, and creates a Chinese style dualism: the coexistence of flexible TVEs with inferior technology and rigid, large state firms with superior technology.[18] This dualism implies a dilemma between the exploitation of technology and location efficiency and the exploitation of X efficiency. Hence, impressive growth of the TVEs has its cost too. Under a free enterprise system, many TVEs might be replaced by large private firms located in the urban areas, which are more competitive than large state firms in urban areas. Hence, from this view, a very high growth rate of TVEs might be inefficient. Alwyn Young (1998) provides empirical evidence for the distortions generated by TVEs and related regional decentralisation. Wen, et al. (2000), Jefferson, et al. (1999), and Murakami, et al. (1994) have found empirical evidences that private firms are more efficient than collective firms including TVEs, which are more efficient than state-owned firms.

TVE shares all the common flaws of the enterprise system under local government control. It generates unfair game rules since the rule maker, the referee, and the player are the same local government. It institutionalises state opportunism and corruption. Hence, game rules are not stable, transparent, and credible. The adverse effects of the TVE on economic development have not received enough attention, while many China specialists have paid a great deal of attention to its advantage compared to the Soviet style system of state firms under the complete control of the central government. The TVEs have a harder budget constraint than do state firms owned by higher levels of government. They as a whole are more competitive than state-owned firms. According to Wu's excellent field work (1998), the TVE, together with the half-way house approach to reforms of the land ownership system and with the residential registration system, generates a very peculiar Chinese style feudal system. In this system, local government officers' territory jurisdiction power, judiciary and enforcement power, control rights to land, official position in the party apparatus, rights to founding firms, rights to raising money, and control rights to the TVE are not separable, just like in a feudal system in Europe in the Middle Ages. The case of Daqiuzhuang illustrates the characteristics of the feudal system (He 1997). Party head Yu Zuomin in the village of Daqiuzhuang blocked the state police's enforcement of the court order in a murder case. Yu is the leading government officer, party head as well as the president of all TVEs of this village. He controls the local paramilitary force and has de facto judicial power. Many media reports also indicate that local government officers use the TVE as a vehicle for predation. They force village folk to contribute to funds for setting up a TVE and to take on all the risk of the venture. Revenue from the venture is then grabbed by the officers (He 1997).

Under the Chinese style feudal system, people are ranked as different groups with different rights. The local party officers are first-class citizens who have all rights and privilege to pursue their vested interests at the cost of others. The second class of citizens are village folks who have local residency. They can get good jobs in the TVEs and claim part of the welfare fund of the village. The third class of citizens are migrants who do the dirtiest job in the TVEs and cannot receive any part of the welfare benefits. This is similar to a feudal system, for the following two reasons. First, local residents will lose their claims to land ownership which is not tradable if they migrate to another location permanently (Ye 1999). An individual's social and economic position is determined by her political and residential stature rather than by her income and her constitutional rights. The Chinese style communist-feudal system, together with low labour mobility caused by the residential registration system and the state housing system in cities, explains why local government and collectively owned firms boom in rural China, while they are not as competitive as capitalist firms in the capitalist economies, where individuals have personal freedom and can freely trade labour, capital, land, and other properties. The feudal system and low labour mobility imply that community members expect to remain in the same place indefinitely and the common interests of residents in the same local community are quite stable. Hence, they have more incentive to contribute to the TVEs than they would in a free market system.

This new feudal system not only distorts the matching between managers and firms, the geographical location pattern of firms and resource allocation, and retards urbanisation, it also generates social injustice that may cause social unrest.

The TVE ownership structure is highly unusual by international standards. In most East Asian countries with rural industry, such as Indonesia and Thailand, ownership of small enterprises is private, often within a family. By contrast, TVE ownership is collective, at least officially. Some scholars have argued that collective ownership reflects deep Chinese cultural patterns (Weitzman and Xu 1994). However, this 'cooperative culture' hypothesis would appear to be called into question by the dominance of small private enterprises in rural Taiwan, as well as by the prevalence of small, Chinese-owned private firms throughout East Asia. If there is any cultural affinity regarding small business, it would seem to be for private, family-owned businesses rather than collectively owned businesses.

Other scholars have said that collective ownership is an effective way to raise capital funds for rural enterprise and to reduce the principal-agent problem by shortening the supervision distance (Oi 1995). They use these reasons to interpret the TVE ownership structure as a good adaptation to market failures caused by China's underdeveloped markets for factors of production. According to Naughton (1994a),

> Banks are ill-equipped in the early stages of transition to process small-scale lending applications and assess risks. Local government ownership in China played a crucial role in financial intermediation. Local governments could better assess the risks of start-up businesses under their control ... and serve as guarantors of loans to individual TVEs.

Some economists have even interpreted the TVE record as definitive proof against the conventional wisdom that private ownership is the natural ownership form of small-scale enterprises, and argued that what mattered for efficiency is not ownership, but competition in product and factor markets (Nolan 1993).

Sachs and Woo (1999) are sceptical of this functionalistic explanation of TVE ownership form, especially of its emphasis on the state's superiority in financial intermediation. Taiwan's small and medium private enterprises exhibited dynamic growth in the 1960–85 period even though they were heavily discriminated against by the wholly state-owned banking system. The informal financial markets (curb markets) appeared 'spontaneously' to cater to their needs (Shea and Yang 1994). The power of market forces (when tolerated by the local authorities) to induce financial institutional innovations was also recently seen in Wenzhou city in Zhejiang Province when economic liberalisation began in 1979. Liu (1992) reported that:

> Ninety-five per cent of the total capital needed by the local private sector has been supplied by 'underground' private financial organizations, such as money clubs, specialized financial households and money shops ...[19]

An adequate general theory for TVE ownership structure should be based on two main considerations. First, private ownership was heavily regulated and discriminated against in many areas until recently. While individual ownership was given constitutional protection in 1978, private ownership, which is considered different from individual-ownership in China was given constitutional protection only in 1987. Therefore, (registered) collective ownership of rural industry arose as the primary response to the profitable niches created by central planning because of the severe disadvantages faced by enterprises registered as privately owned. Zhang (1993), using 'non-collective TVEs' to refer to partnerships and individual and private enterprises, reported that:

> ... in virtually all aspects relating to local governments, the non-collective TVEs tend to be unfavorably treated ... (compared to) their collective counterparts. Areas in which local governments appear to have discriminated against non-collective TVEs include access to bank credits, to larger production premises, to government allocation of inputs and energy, to government assistance in solving technical problems and for initiating joint ventures and so forth. In the field of taxation and profit distribution, there is evidence that non-collective TVEs run a greater risk of being excessively levied, and that local governments tend to treat the non-collective TVEs more arbitrarily than they do the collective ones.

In short, the 'market failures' identified by some China experts are not caused by inefficiencies intrinsic to a private market economy (like externalities and public goods). These so-called market failures are actually created by ideologically motivated constraints imposed by the state. Specifically, the banks have extended more loans to TVEs than to private enterprises because of state directives, and not because of the TVEs being intrinsically more efficient or because of the local banks' recognition that the local governments were better assessors of risks than they themselves (Chang and Wang 1994).

There is general assent that the TVEs face stronger market incentives (including harder budget constraints) than do the state-owned enterprises (SOEs). As shown in Sachs and Woo (1999), two of the three types of TVEs, the Jiangsu and Zhejiang types are fairly similar in essence to the red-capped private enterprises. The local officials have the private incentive to maximise the profits of TVEs because 'the careers and salaries of officials at the county, township and village levels are directly affected by the performance and growth of their rural enterprises' (Oi 1995), and because neither local residents nor workers have access to legal, formal channels to exercise their ownership rights. In short, informal privatisation by local officials has reduced the principal-agent problem and rendered the TVEs more efficient than the SOEs.[20] This private-incentive (informal privatisation) hypothesis would explain why Peng (1992) found that the wage determination process was the same for rural public enterprises and rural private enterprises.

If this interpretation of 'informal privatisation' is valid, then continued TVE efficiency is possible only if the group cohesion of local officials does not degenerate into individual efforts at asset-stripping. We see the key to the group cohesion in Jiangsu and Shandong in the 1980s to be the heavy discrimination against private enterprises in these regions. The resulting lack of economic space in these regions to hide looted assets diminished the incentive for individual officials to rob the TVEs they oversaw. Without the strong legal discrimination against private property, asset-stripping would have occurred more freely, and the inefficiency normally observed with informal privatisation would have become more prevalent.

If this view is correct, the crucial implication is that gradual growth in the relative size of the private sector and in labour mobility will eventually undermine the group cohesion among local officials against individual asset-stripping (by providing secured hiding places for looted property), and thereby damage TVE performance.

With the further reduction in discrimination against private ownership since early 1992, intended to ameliorate the rural unemployment caused by the 1989–91 austerity policies, many TVEs have been taking off their 'red hats' – albeit with difficulties in many cases.

As China heads toward a market economy, an increasing number of private companies are no longer feeling the need to register as 'red cap' or collectively owned ventures because the difference in preferential treatment between private and public units has been narrowed. But there is a problem. The collective units are now arguing that private firms could not have developed without their help. As the so-called 'owners' of the companies, the party apparatus usually asks for high compensation for the 'divorce' or asks the companies to merge with state firms. ('Private firms jump to take 'red caps' off,' *China Daily*, 4 November 1994.)

Example 4: China's State Firm Reform and Price Liberalisation

The third example of the dual track approach is China's state firm reforms and price liberalisation (Sachs and Woo 1999, p. 17). By 1983, a de facto contract responsibility system (CRS) of the SOE had emerged. An SOE would sign an individually negotiated contract with its supervising agency specifying the annual amount of revenue (tax-cum-profit) to be turned over to the state, thereby supposedly giving the firm the incentive to maximise its financial surplus. However, SOEs remained subject to a soft budget constraint, being absolved of the responsibility of paying the contracted amount if the financial outcome was poor. Managers and workers colluded to strip state assets in the form of bonus and employee benefits in kind. As a result, the state found the decline in revenue expressed as a percentage of GDP to be much larger than anticipated.

In 1983, the state began to replace the CRS with an income tax. This income tax system was short-lived, however, because it not only failed to arrest the decline in revenue–GDP ratio, but state firms tried to bargain with the government over tax terms and to claim that the government determined prices, rather than their management, taking responsibility for low profit. By 1986, SOEs were reverting to an expanded CRS. Under this system, many managers set up collective firms to transfer valuable assets to them and leave all bad debt to the state firms contracted. Also, many contractors cannot honour their contracts (see Qiye Jingji, *Enterprise Economy* 1995, No. 7, p. 45). This is not surprising, since according to the economics of property rights (Alchian and Demsetz 1972), nobody has the incentive to find good contractors and to enforce contracts efficiently if nobody claims the residual rights of the state firms. The CRS was again replaced by an income tax in January 1994. As shown in Yang and Ng (1995; see also Sachs and Yang 2000, chapter 8), claims to private residual rights of a firm are essential for indirectly pricing entrepreneurial services which involve prohibitively high direct pricing costs. Hence, privatisation of the SOE is essential for successful reforms. Whether China's experience of state firm reform confirms this depends on empirical evidence.

As reported in Sachs and Woo (1999, pp. 19–28), the productivity performance of the SOEs remains a highly contentious issue. Some researchers see improvements, while others do not. But most writers have two important points of agreement: (1) SOE productivity growth, if any, has been lower than non-state firm productivity growth; and (2) improvements in total factor productivity (TFP), if any, are associated with quickly deteriorated financial performance of the SOEs during the reform period.

According to Bai, Li and Wang (Bai, et al. 1999), TFP improvements (if any) have not increased economic welfare in China, and this is why the Chinese general public and Chinese leaders have continued to see SOE reform as a failure. Bai, et al. (1999) pointed out that TFP growth is a good index of welfare improvement only 'in the context of profit-maximising and market-oriented firms. However, for SOEs under reform, these conditions are not satisfied. In fact, this is the very reason for SOE reform. One of the important non-profit objectives of the managers is their excessive pursuit of output.'

When both output and profits were included in the objective function of SOE managers, Bai et al. (1999) found that 'a higher productivity as measured by the TFP growth may actually lead to lower profitability and therefore, in many cases, lower economic efficiency.' The image of some Chinese SOEs producing undesired goods, but with greater efficiency, finds some support in the aggregate data on inventories. Inventory investment in China averaged 7 per cent of GDP in the 1980–93 period, compared to an average of 2 to 3 per cent for the OECD countries. Only some Eastern European countries prior to 1990 had such high inventory investment rates. These high inventory levels suggest considerable production that is simply not marketable. In particular, the unsold inventory is counted as output of SOEs in China. Hence, estimates of TFP based on the output data are clearly overstated. Lardy (1998, p. 206) also documents the correlation between a mountain of unsold inventories and increasing numbers of bad loans to SOEs.

Even if one believes that SOE managers in China are mainly maximising profits, technical innovations comprise only one method of maximising an SOE's profits. It may be financially even more rewarding for an SOE manager in China to spend time developing good relations with the state bureaucracy than increasing production efficiency. Until the 1990s, the large and medium-sized SOEs had to fulfil their production quota at below-market prices, and they received subsidised inputs in return. If the amount of subsidised inputs was high, the quota system would generate a positive rent to the enterprise. Li (1994) estimated that an SOE that made positive market profits on its above-quota production in the 1986–88 period received a rent that was 2.7 times that of its market profit. Bureaucratic haggling was vastly more profitable than competing in the market. Li's rent estimate may be the lower bound, because it did not include the rent that an SOE received from tax bargaining, a practice so pervasive that an SOE paid an effective income tax rate of 33 per cent instead of the legal rate of 55 per cent then in force.

Economists have a consensus about the financial performance of SOEs. There has been a steady increase in SOE losses since additional decision-making powers were given to SOE managers in the mid-1980s. The situation stabilised in the 1990–91 period when the state attempted to recover some of the decision-making power devolved to the SOEs. In 1992, decentralising efforts accelerated at the initiative of local leaders after Deng Xiaoping called for faster economic reforms in order to avoid the fate of the Soviet Union. The unexpected result was that faster economic growth was accompanied by larger SOE losses. About two-thirds of the Chinese SOEs ran losses in 1992 when output growth in that year was 13 per cent. These enterprise losses cannot be blamed on price controls, because price controls covered only a small proportion of SOEs in 1992. State enterprise losses have continued to accelerate since then. In the first quarter of 1996, the entire SOE sector slid into the red for the first time since the establishment of the People's Republic of China in 1949. It reported a net deficit of 3.4 billion yuan.[21]

Some economists emphasise the 'spontaneous appropriation' of firm profits by managers and workers as the most important cause for the general decline in SOE profits. With the end of the central plan and the devolution of financial decision-making power to the SOEs, the key source of information to the industrial bureaus regarding the SOEs were reports submitted by the SOEs themselves. This reduction in the monitoring ability of the state in a situation of continued soft budget constraints meant that there was little incentive for state-enterprise managers to resist wage demands, because their future promotion to larger SOEs was determined in part by the increases in workers' welfare during their tenure.[22]

One of the earliest attributions of the erosion of SOE profits to the decentralising reforms was a 1986 report by the China Economic System Reform Research Institute, which pointed out the emerging tendency of SOEs to over-consume and over-invest through various bookkeeping subterfuges.[23] Woo, Hai, Jin and Fan (1994), and Fan and Woo (1996) used various samples and national data to show that the sum of direct income (wages and bonuses) and indirect income (for example, subsidies and in-kind distribution) increased more than labour productivity growth. Minami and Hondai (1995) found that since 1988, the labour share of output in the machine industry started rising with the acceleration of decentralised reforms in 1985 and exceeded the estimated output elasticity. Bouin (forthcoming) calculated that the marginal product labour of industrial SOEs increased by 5 per cent in 1989–93, while the product wage of industrial SOE workers rose by 7 per cent. Meng and Perkins (1996) studied the determinants of wage and labour demand in 149 industrial SOEs and 139 non-state firms in Guangzhou, Xiamen, Shenzhen, and Shanghai (four coastal economies that are marked by more intense market competition) in the 1980–92 period. Meng and Perkins found that the SOEs under decentralisation reforms were maximising income per employee (by dipping into profits) like labour-managed firms, while non-state firms were maximising profits like capitalist firms.

Naughton (1994b) was sceptical of the excessive compensation explanation, because 'the SOE wage bill, including all monetary subsidies, has remained approximately unchanged at about 5 per cent of GNP since 1978'. There are two difficulties with this point of view. The first is that the correct test for the excessive compensation hypothesis is to normalise the SOE wage bill by value-added in the SOE sector and not by economy-wide GDP. The second difficulty is that direct cash income is only a part of the total package of labour compensation, and that the main categories of direct cash compensation have been under strict state regulation in order to control inflation and embezzlement. The wage and bonus regulations have forced the SOEs to increase workers' income through indirect means like better housing, improved transportation, new recreational facilities, benefits in kind, and study tours.[24]

The financial weakness of SOEs has destabilised the macroeconomy by increasing money creation through three channels. The first channel is the monetisation of the growing state budget deficits caused by the declining financial contribution from the SOE sector. SOEs paid income taxes that amounted to 19.1 per cent of GDP in 1978, 6.6 per cent in 1985 and 1.7 per cent in 1993; and they remitted gross profits of 19.1

per cent, 0.5 per cent and 0.1 per cent respectively. The second channel for money creation is the financing of mounting SOE losses by bank loans. The third channel is the disbursement of investment loans to the SOEs to make up for their shortage of internal funds to finance capacity expansion and technical upgrading.

Some economists claim that SOEs take care of social welfare for the government, and new nonstate firms have younger employees and have little burden of pension payments and other welfare benefits. Hence, a deteriorated financial performance of SOEs is understandable as the size of the private sector relative to the state sector increases.

Lardy (1998, pp. 53–7) documents the fact that the SOEs have been expanding in terms of levels of output and employment and in terms of employment share and finance share, although its output share decreases and financial performance deteriorates. In particular, most of the loans made by the monopolised state bank system go to the SOEs, and other inputs into the SOEs have been increasing. As he shows, the financial performance of state firms has deteriorated despite increasing competition and continuous market liberalisation in the past two decades. The rise in liabilities relative to assets of state-owned firms, reaching an average of 85 per cent in 1995, is perhaps the most conclusive evidence. According to Lardy (1998, p. 119), China's four major state banks as a group have a negative net worth and thus are insolvent. This potential financial crisis is mainly caused by the deteriorating financial performance of the SOE. He indicates that the combination of a rising savings rate and significant seignorage have provided the central government with financial resources that it has used to temporarily paper over deeply rooted structural problems. Contrary to Bai, et al. (1999), this view implies that anonymous banking in China, which encourages an unusually high saving rate, is a source of a potential financial crisis rather than a driving force of China's growth.[25]

It is notable that the original demands of the 1989 Tiananmen demonstrators were for reduction of inflation and corruption. We therefore think that the oft-given justifications for the absence of privatisation in China on the grounds of preserving social stability may be overlooking the social tensions being created by the asset-stripping, corruption, and macroeconomic instability caused by the unreformed ownership structure of the SOEs. (Of course, corruptly managed privatisation, as in the case of natural resources in Russia, can also lead to profound inequities and social instability). He (1997, pp. 71–240) documents the large scale of corruption caused by the dual track approach to the land market, state firm reforms, and price reforms. According to her, the large scale of corruption has been so pervasive that immorality and opportunism have spread into every aspect of society. According to many Chinese whom we contacted, resentment against social injustice caused by this large-scale corruption may cause a popular rebellion against the regime. But this serious potential consequence of the dual track approach has not received its deserved attention from economists outside China.

Reports since 1995 indicate that full-scale sales of small and medium SOEs have occurred all over China. The best known example is Zhucheng city in Shandong province, which started privatising SOEs in 1992 when two-thirds of its SOEs were losing money or just breaking even.[26] Almost 90 per cent of county-supervised SOEs in Zhucheng have already been privatised. The acceleration in the SOEs' conversion to joint-stock companies reflects the leadership's opinion that partial privatisation through public offerings in the stock markets and through joint ventures with foreign companies would be an improvement over the contract responsibility system. However, the corporatisation of state firms in the absence of formal privatisation created large-scale corruption.

The relationship between the dual track approach and corruption is best illustrated by He's documentation of two types of spontaneous privatisation in China. He (1997, pp. 101–38) documents the partial privatisation of state firms via joint stock companies in China during 1987–1993.[27] Under the game rules wherein the rule maker, the referee, and the player are the same government agent, this spontaneous privatisation involves a large scale of corruption. She identifies four types of corruption in this government insider-controlled process. The first mode of corruption is to directly allocate shares of state-owned joint stock companies to government officers who have the approval power for setting up and regulating such companies, and who have the power to allocate land, bank loans, and other important resources (He 1997, p. 55). In the second mode, private companies are set up in Hong Kong or overseas as partners or subsidiaries of the state joint stock company. Then, via various dealings between the two firms with peculiar terms (for instance, selling at a low price and buying at high prices), state assets are transferred from the latter to the former (He 1997, p. 60, p. 69). In the third mode, private shareholders bribe the government representatives in such joint stock companies to transfer the government shares free of charge to the former via various restructuring schemes of ownership (He 1997, pp. 57–60). In the fourth mode, the government representative in the joint venture between the state firm and a foreign company purposely understates the value of the state asset, then gets paid by the foreign partner under the table. Finally, many real private joint stock companies have emerged during this period. But the owners of the companies must pay a very high bribe to get them registered and keep them going (that is, getting land and other essential inputs and all kind of official approvals and permissions to avoid government expropriation and restriction of private business). A very strong patronage relationship between government officers and private firms is essential for the survival of private firms in China.[28] He (1997) and other Chinese scholars hold that partial privatisation of state firms via joint-stock ownership was a failure. Performance of most new joint stock companies has not improved. The principle of 'one share one vote' in China's Company Law is not implemented in partial privatisation even after 1994 when China's Company Law was passed. Shares owned by the government have more voting rights. Insider trading and corruption are rampant. Many cases of spontaneous privatisation of this kind of state holding companies, documented in He (1997), involve capital flight to overseas.[29] This pattern of companies becomes a vehicle for insiders stealing state-owned assets.

He (1997, pp. 71–100), also documents many cases of spontaneous privatisation of use rights of land under the dual track approach to state ownership of land and trade of land use rights. According to her, this is a large scale corruption process in which government officers who have approval power for procuring land sell their approval documents for money. Most of the money used to purchase land was from state banks. Hence, in this large scale of China's enclosurement during 1988–1994, many state bank officers who have approval rights to loans, and their supervisors were involved in corruption. Again, the dual track approach creates the market for use rights of land on the one hand, and institutionalises corruption and state opportunism on the other.

In the 1995 ranking by Transparency International of the seriousness of corruption within 41 countries, China ranked second in the extent of corruption (Sachs and Woo 1999). Continuing corruption and misuse of state assets will further undermine public support for the existing political institutions. The adverse effect of the dual track approach may well outweigh its positive effect on raising constituencies for the reforms via buying out the vested interests.

In addition, the dual track approach generates very unequal income distribution, which is associated with inefficiency. Discrimination against rural residents institutionalised by the residential registration system creates anti-efficiency unequal income distribution between the urban and rural areas. Discrimination against inland regions institutionalised by trade privileges granted to a restricted set of coastal regions creates anti-efficiency unequal income distribution between coastal and inland regions. The growing income gap between coastal and inland provinces, documented in Jian, Sachs, and Warner (1996), and an increasing Gini coefficient not only restrict the extent of the market and slow down the evolution of division of labour, but also generate popular and strong resentment against the regime, which has caused a lot of protests and might cause large-scale rebellions.[30]

It seems to us that China's experience with the dual track approach does not provide much new information that institutional experiments in the rest of the world did not already provide. It just verifies again that successful economic development needs not only markets, but also constitutional order and the rule of law to protect individuals' rights and to provide effective checks and balances of government power. Appropriate moral codes, behaviour norms, and breaking political monopoly of the ruling party are essential for the formation of the constitutional order.

4.6 TRADE-OFFS BETWEEN RELIABILITY AND THE POSITIVE NETWORK EFFECTS OF DIVISION OF LABOUR AND BETWEEN INCENTIVE PROVISION AND STABILITY

Output fall during transition in Eastern Europe and Russia is a phenomenon that many economists did not expect. Roland (2000, p. 202) reports the surprising scale of such output fall. Poland's growth rates of real GDP were −11.6 and −7.6 in 1990 and 1991. Hungary's were −3.5, −11.9, −3.0, and −0.9 in 1990, 1991, 1992, and 1993, respectively. Czech's corresponding figures were −0.4, −14.2, −6.4, −0.9, respectively. Russia's growth rates of real GDP were −13, −19, −12, −15 in 1991, 1992, 1993, 1994, respectively. In this section, we use the models developed in Lio (1998) and Sachs and Yang (2000, chapter 10) and a cobweb model similar to the one of Aghion, Bacchetta, and Banerjee (1998) to explain the output fall phenomenon.

The Lio model (1996, 1998) shows that complete insurance can increase reliability of the network of division of labour, thereby increasing the equilibrium level of division of labour and related aggregate productivity. Prior to the reforms, the Soviet Union and other socialist countries established a large network of division of labour by mimicking the capitalist industrialisation pattern. Each state in the socialist bloc specialising in a sector supplied to all the other states and bought goods from each of the other specialised sectors in other states. For instance, Ukraine specialised in producing grain, Czech specialised in producing locomotives and other engines, and East Germany specialised in producing machine tools. This large network of division of labour would have very low reliability in the absence of insurance. Hence, an implicit complete insurance system was developed in the socialist countries. There was complete employment insurance, pension insurance, medical insurance, trade insurance, and so on. Each state firm was insured for all goods it produced in the sense that the central planner would buy all of them. Although this complete insurance generated a great deal of moral hazard, it provided reasonably high reliability of the large network of division of labour.

As the Soviet Union broke down, the complete trade insurance between the ex-socialist countries disappeared. The reliability of the large network of division of labour established by the central planning system in the 1950s, of course decreased exponentially in the new reform era before the market for insurance was developed. As Roland (2000) suggests, the major reason for output fall is the break of the trade connection between ex-socialist countries. From the model in Yang and Ng (1993, chapter 11), we have learned that there is a trade off between deepening the relationship with the incumbent trade partner and broadening potential trade connections. Under a socialist system, the transaction cost coefficient for broadening potential relationships is extremely great because of the rigid hierarchical structure of the central planning system. Hence, there is not much room for trading off a large number of potential partners against a deep incumbent relationship in order to increase the reliability of the network of division of labour. As the break-up of the Soviet Union and the socialist bloc cut the incumbent trade connection between many highly specialised firms, the entire network of division of labour of course failed to work. According to Lio's theory, it would be very surprising if there were no such mass output fall after the break-up of the Soviet Union and the socialist bloc.

The Lio model (1996; see also Sachs and Yang 2000, example 10.6) shows that there is a trade off between incentive provision, which can be increased by incompleteness of insurance, and reliability gains of the network of division of labour, which can be increased by insurance. This trade off implies that focusing on incentive provision and ignoring the positive contribution of the implicit insurance to the network reliability of division of labour may not achieve the efficient balance of the trade off. The development of various insurance markets is essential for the success of privatisation reforms.

The recent Russian financial crisis was correlated with high international capital mobility. Aghion, Bacchetta, and Banerjee (1998) develop a cobweb model to explain why great capital mobility in a developed international financial market may decrease market stability. Their story runs as follows. If there is a time lag between economic performance and financial signals, there would be a trade off between incentive provision, which can be increased by sensitivity of feedback between signals and players' actions, and stability of the feedback process, which will be decreased by increasing the sensitivity. A feedback system that is not sensitive to signals (as in a socialist system) would fail to provide enough incentive for economic development. But a too-sensitive feedback process will generate nonconvergent fluctuation, an explosion, or a chaotic process. In the model of Aghion, et al., the degree of feedback sensitivity is represented by a feedback sensitivity coefficient in a difference equation that relates signals to players' actions via a time lag between the two variables. High capital mobility in a developed international financial market is associated with a large value of the coefficient. This high mobility implies that any trivial positive signal can attract capital from all countries in the world, and thereby create a huge inflow of capital within a very short period of time. Any trivial negative signal can have a huge opposite effect, which can generate a panic flight of capital (explosion or chaos in the nonlinear difference equation).

This trade-off between incentive provision and stability implies that it is not efficient to have an extremely high power incentive. Russia liberalised its capital account prior to privatisation reforms. This significantly increased the sensitivity of the feedback mechanism. Privatisation reforms further increased the sensitivity, which is good for providing incentives, but not good for stability. Of course, corruption and money laundry were the source of negative signals. Without the moral hazard caused by opportunism, sensitive feedback itself may not make trouble, just as in the highly developed financial market in Taiwan and in Western Europe. But moral hazard itself is not enough to explain Russia's and South Korea's financial crises, since moral hazard in China, which was not greatly affected by the Asian financial crisis, is even greater than in Russia and South Korea. Some economists explain the financial crises in Russian and Asia using the conventional models of moral hazard. But the models cannot explain why the crises occurred when liberalisation and privatisation were implemented. Lio's models (1996, 1998) and the model of Aghion et al. show that the trade offs between reliability, transaction costs, and economies of division of labour and between incentive provision, sharing risk, and stability can explain the crises better. In the rest of this section, we use a cobweb model to illustrate the story behind the model of Aghion et al.

Example 5: A cobweb model with the trade off between sensitive, incentive and stability

Consider the Smithian model in Sachs and Yang (2000, example 4.2). An individual's decision problem based on the CES utility function is:

Max:	$u = [(x^c)^\rho + (y^c)^\rho]^{1/\rho}$	(utility function)
s.t.	$x^c \equiv x + kx^d \qquad y^c \equiv y + ky^d$	(definition of quantities to consume)
	$x + x^s = l_x^a \qquad y + y^s = l_y^a$	(production function)
	$l_s + l_y = 1$	(endowment constraint)
	$p_s x^s + p_y y^s = p_s x^d + p_y y^d$	(budget constraint)

where x and y are respective amounts of the two goods self-provided, x^s and y^s are respective quantities of the two goods sold, x^d and y^d are respective quantities purchased, l_i, the quantity of labour allocated to the production of good, p_i, is the price of good, i, which is a given parameter in a Walrasian regime. The optimum decisions in the various configurations are summarised in Table 4.1.

We now introduce the discrete time dimension into the model. There is a one-period time lag between changes of the relative number of individuals choosing

Table 4.1
Corner Solutions in Four Configurations

Config-uration	Quantities self-provided	Supply functions		Demand functions	Indirect utility function $u(p)$
A	$x = y = 0.5^a$	0		0	$2(1-\rho a)/\rho$
(x/y)	$x = [1+(k/p)^{\rho/(1-\rho)}]^{-1}$	$x^s = [1+(p/k)^{\rho/(1-\rho)}]^{-1}$		$y^d = x^s/p$	$[1+(k/p)^{\rho/(1-\rho)}]^{(1-\rho)/\rho}$
(y/x)	$y = [1+(kp)^{\rho/(1-\rho)}]^{-1}$	$y^s = [1+(kp)^{\rho/(1-\rho)}]^{-1}$		$x^d = py^s$	$[1+(kp)^{\rho/(1-\rho)}]^{(1-\rho)/\rho}$

where $p \equiv p_y/p_x$ and $r \in (0, 1)$. Configuration A is autarky where each individual self-provides x and y. Configuration (x/y) denotes that an individual produces and sells good x and buys good y. (y/x) denotes that an individual produces and sells good y and buys good x. The corner equilibrium relative price in structure D consisting of configurations (x/y) and (y/x) is $p = 1$, given by the utility equalisation between the two configurations.

professional occupations (x/y) and (y/x) in response to the difference in utility between the two occupations. Hence,

(1) $\quad M_x(t) - M_x(t-1) = \beta[u_x(t-1) - u_y(t-1)]$

where t denotes the time period and β is the sensitivity coefficient of changes in the number of specialist producers of x in response to the difference in utility between two occupation configurations. $M_i(t)$ is the number of specialist producers of good i in period t. The indirect utility function u_i for a specialist producer of good i is given in the above table. Since $M_x(t) + M_y(t) = M$ where population size M is a given parameter, changes in $M_x(t)$ are proportional to changes in $M_y(t)$ in the opposite direction. For simplicity, we assume that $M = 1$. Further, there is a one-period time lag between changes of relative price of good y to good x in response to changes in excess demand for good y. Hence,

(2) $\quad p(t+1) - p(t) = \alpha[M_x(t) y^d(t) - M_y(t)y^s(t)]$

where $M_y(t) = 1 - M_x(t)$ and $y^d(t)$ and $y^s(t)$ are given in Table 4.1. α is the sensitivity coefficient of changes of relative price in response to excess demand for good y. The (1) and (2) constitute a second order nonlinear system of difference equations in p and M_x. Assume that the initial state of the system is given by $M_x(0) = M_0, p(0) = p_0$, and $p(1) = p_1$. Then, the dynamics and comparative dynamics of this system can be given by simulations on the computer. Figure 4.1(a) gives the results of the simulations for $\alpha = 0.6$, $\beta = 0.2$, $\rho = 0.6$, $k = 0.6$, $M_0 = 0$, $p_0 = 0.2$, and $p_1 = 0.21$. In panel (b), α is increased to 1.61 and other parameters are unchanged. In panel (c), α is increased to 1.62 and other parameters are unchanged. In panel (d), all parameter values are the same as in panel (a) except that β increases from 0.2 to 0.3. In panel (e), all parameter values are the same as in panel (a) except that k increases from 0.6 to 0.601.

A comparison of the time paths of relative price p and the numbers of x specialists M in panels (a) and (b) shows that as the feedback sensitivity parameter α increases from 0.6 to 1.61, the convergence of the feedback process to the static equilibrium (steady state, $p = 1$ and $M_x = 0.5$) becomes faster. Panel (c) shows that as the sensitive coefficient a reaches the threshold level, 1.62, the number of specialist producers of x becomes negative after several rounds of feedback. A comparison between panels (b) and (d) shows a similar result of an increase of value of sensitivity parameter of β from 0.2 to 0.3 with unchanged $\alpha = 1.61$. The negative number of specialists in an occupation is not feasible. Hence, this implies a breakdown of the division of labour and all individuals have to choose autarky, even if the static equilibrium is the division of labour (utility in the structure with the division of labour is higher than in autarky). This panic rush of individuals from the occupation configuration producing x to that producing y as M_x tends to 0 looks like the panic rush of investors from one country to the other in a highly integrated world market with a very high level of international division of labour. A comparison between panels (b) and (e) shows that an increase in

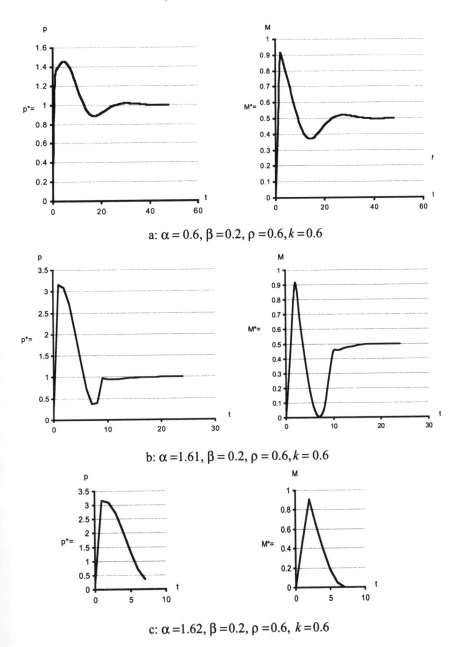

a: $\alpha = 0.6,\ \beta = 0.2,\ \rho = 0.6, k = 0.6$

b: $\alpha = 1.61,\ \beta = 0.2,\ \rho = 0.6, k = 0.6$

c: $\alpha = 1.62,\ \beta = 0.2,\ \rho = 0.6,\ k = 0.6$

Figure 4.1   Trade-off Between Sensitive, Incentive and Stability of Feedback Mechanism

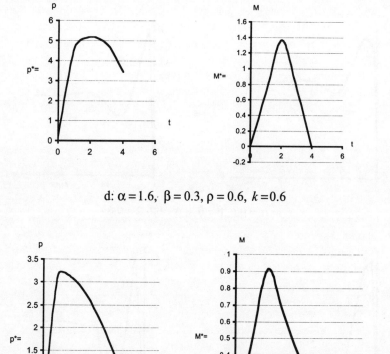

d: $\alpha = 1.6,\; \beta = 0.3, \rho = 0.6,\; k = 0.6$

e: $\alpha = 1.6,\;\; \beta = 0.2, \rho = 0.6, k = 0.601$

Figure 4.1   Trade-off Between Sensitive, Incentive and Stability of Feedback Mechanism (continued)

the trading efficiency coefficient k has the same effect of an increase in feedback sensitivity parameters. Also, as k reaches a threshold, the system will overshoot and never reach the steady state.

The results are very intuitive. If the system starts from a non-equilibrium state, then an occupation generates more utility than the other, so that individuals will shift from the latter to the former. This will adjust aggregate demand and supply of a traded good and thereby excess demand for this good. The relative price will change in response to the change in excess demand. The indirect utility functions in different occupations will change in response to this change in relative price. This will again cause changes in the relative number of specialists in the two occupations if the steady state is yet to be achieved. In this feedback process, the more sensitive the feedback, the faster the convergence of fluctuations toward the steady state. But if the feedback is too sensitive, the system may overshoot, so that the steady state can never be reached. A larger trading efficiency coefficient has an effect similar to that of a larger feedback sensitivity coefficient. It can speed up the convergence of the feedback before a threshold is reached. A very high trading efficiency may generate overshoot that paralyses the feedback mechanism.

This model can be used to explain fluctuations of excess demand for professionals, such as lawyers and accountants, with a time lag between education and professional work. Also, it can explain the financial crisis caused by liberalisation reforms that increased sensitivity coefficients or trading efficiency by raising the mobility of capital, goods, and labour.

Liberalisation and privatisation reforms will increase feedback sensitivity coefficients or the trading efficiency coefficient. This will make the convergence of the economic system toward equilibrium faster, but will also increase the risk of overshoot that reduces the realised level of division of labour and related trade. It can be shown that for the same feedback sensitivity coefficient and trading efficiency, the larger the initial difference between value of price and its static equilibrium level, the more likely the feedback system may break down by overshoot. This explains why Taiwan was not greatly impacted by the Asian financial crisis.

Taiwan implemented liberalisation and privatisation reforms of its financial sector before liberalising its capital account. This ensured a low moral hazard caused by state monopoly of the financial sector. This implies that the initial difference between prevailing market price and its static equilibrium level was not great when feedback sensitivity was raised by liberalisation reforms. China had very high moral hazard. But since it had a very small feedback sensitivity coefficient due to the government's tight control of the capital account, it was not greatly affected by the Asian financial crisis either. In contrast, South Korea liberalised its capital account before great moral hazard in its state monopolised financial system was significantly reduced. Hence, the initial difference between market price and its static equilibrium level, which relates to moral hazard, and the feedback sensitivity and trading efficiency coefficients, which relate to the openness of the financial market, are two major determinants of the trade off between incentive provision and stability. Hence, the different cases of Taiwan, China, and South Korea can all be explained by the cobweb model. The story suggests that the sequence of liberalisation and privatisation reforms makes a difference. In the literature of engineering, the degree to which the feedback system achieves the efficient balance of the trade off between feedback sensitivity and stability is referred to as feedback quality. The major task in macroeconomic policy-making is to raise feedback quality.

4.7   CONCLUDING REMARKS

This chapter investigates the relationship between economic reforms and constitutional transition, which has been neglected by many transition economists. It is argued that assessment of reform performance might be very misleading if it is not recognised that economic reforms are just a small part of the large scale of constitutional transition. Rivalry and competition between states and between political forces within each country are the driving forces for constitutional transition. We use Russia as an example of economic reforms associated with constitutional transition and China as an example of economic reforms in the absence of constitutional transition to examine features and problems in the two patterns of transition. It is concluded that under political monopoly of the ruling party, economic transition will be hijacked by state opportunism. The dual-track approach to economic transition may generate a very high long-term cost of constitutional transition that might well outweigh its short-term benefit of buying out the vested interests.

NOTES

1   The negative short-term economic effect of the American Independence War is documented in Nettels (1962, p. 50), Nussbaum (1925), Taylower (1932), Philips (1929, pp. 115–19), Deane and Cole (1967, p. 48). The negative short-term economic effect of the American Civil War is documented in Woodward (1951, pp. 120–40).

2   The debate between gradualism and shock therapy has a long history since the debate between Edmund Burke (1790) and French revolutionaries. Olson (1982) was a recent supporter of big bang institutional transition. He argued that a stable constitutional order institutionalises rent seeking, and that a big bang to the existing order can break institutionalised rent seeking. Hayek (1944, 1960) was a recent supporter of Burke's view of spontaneous order and gradual evolution of institutions. It might be fair to say that the coexistence of British gradualism and French big bang is better than either one of them alone.

3   Recent criticisms of and defences for market socialism can be found from Bardhan and Roemer (eds) (1993).

4   See Mitchell (1998, pp. 912, 919) for the growth rates in terms of constant prices in the Russia during the two periods. This was a surprise to von Mises and Hayek. Because of this impressive growth performance, Samuelson and many other economists could not even sense the pending fall of the Soviet economic system when the disintegration of the Soviet Union was about to occur (see Skousen 1997).

5   Such state investment programmes are quite consistent with the theory of big push industrialisation discussed in Ng and Yang (1997). The documentation of the mimicry of capitalist industrial pattern and big push industrialisation in the

Soviet Union can be found from Zaleski (1980). Lenin (1939) outlined his understanding of the features of capitalist industrialisation, which Soviet planners mimic later on. The documentation of China's big push industrialisation can be found from Fang (1984).

6   For the operation of the material balance process in a Soviet style economic system, World Bank (1984) provides detailed documentation.

7   The early literature of the socialist economy focuses on feature (4) of the socialist system and has paid too little attention to features (2), (3), and (5). In fact, the comprehensive state investment programme is much more important than balance of daily production plans in a socialist system. Kornai's theory of the soft budget constraint focuses on feature (5).

8   Riskin (1987) and World Bank (1984) document the process to establish a Soviet style socialist system.

9   Qian (forthcoming) documents Mao's two administrative decentralisation movements in 1958–60 and in 1969–75. Also, the features of the evolution of institutional arrangements from Mao's China to the reform era can be identified by putting information from the following sources together. Bruun (1993), Granick (1990), Liu (1992), Nee and Sijin (1993), Oi (1986), Perkins, ed. (1977), Riskin (1971; 1987), Schurmann (1968), Solinger (1992), Vogel (1989), Walder (1986, 1992), Wank (1993), Wong (1985, 1986a, b).

10 For a meticulous documentation of the evolution of China's residential registration system, see Cheng (1991). An updated version of this thesis, which covers recent changes of the system, is available from Cheng. According to him, urban residents have more voting rights than rural residents in China.

11 Pipe (1999, p. 153) attributes the rise of parliamentarism in Britain and its decline in Spain and France in the middle ages to the small size of Britain relative to that of Spain and France.

12 For history of the Constitution of People's Republic of China and its recent amendments, see Pilon (1998), Yang (1994), and Qian (1999).

13 See Roland (2000, p. 15, p. 198) for the cost of dual track approach.

14 Specifically, the 1982–91 yield levels for rice and wheat lie on the straight lines extrapolated from the 1952 yield levels using the yield growth rates of the 1952–57 period.

15 To us, this finding of widespread uncertainty about future land use rights explains the long time puzzle why rural land markets in China have been surprisingly inactive despite the legality of lease transfers. For another case-study, see 'No Rights Mean No Incentive for China's Farmers,' *New York Times*, 15 December 1996.

16 Data are from the *1992 TVE Yearbook*. Li (1999) documents a case of spontaneous privatisation of TVE via the transformation to public holding companies in Shunde county of Guangdong province. According to him, a long spontaneous privatisation process since the end of the 1980s has already transformed most TVEs in this county to joint stock companies. At the end of

the 1990s, private firms become dominant players in this county though corruption, predation, and other state opportunism are rampant.

17   According to Oi, the county government was corporate headquarters, the township governments were regional headquarters, and the villages were companies.

18   China's degree of urbanisation is much lower than in capitalist economies with similar per capita real income (He 1997, p. 275).

19   Despite the great contributions of local private banks to economic development, the government still follows the regulation that prohibits private banking business and closes many local private banks (Lardy 1998, pp. 53–7).

20   Although Walder (1995) does not accept the 'private incentive' hypothesis, he acknowledges its plausibility: 'It has sometimes been documented, and is even more widely suspected, that significant numbers of village-run, and perhaps even township-run enterprises are in effect operated as family business, in which there is no clear distinction between officials' income and village revenue. This can occur when village officials grant rights to operate public industrial assets to themselves or family members or other partners on contracts that give them fixed percentage of the enterprises' profits after contractual payments to the government are made. This may also occur through embezzlement and the abuse of expensive accounts ... Unfortunately there are no reliable estimates of how widespread such "hidden privatisation" is ...'

21   'Record loss suffered by state sector,' *South China Morning Post International Weekly*, 29 June 1996.

22   This SOE tendency to over-reward workers received official acknowledgment in 1984 when the government introduced a progressive bonus tax to control the generous dispensation of bonuses that began in 1979. An annual bonus of up to 4 months of basic wages was exempted from the bonus tax; but a fifth month bonus would require the SOE to pay a 100 per cent bonus tax; a sixth month bonus would be subject to a 200 per cent bonus tax, a seventh month bonus would be subject to a 300 per cent bonus tax, and so forth.

23   This report has been published in English as Reynolds (1987).

24   These indirect transfers are listed under either production costs or investment expenditure financed from depreciation funds. The ingenuity of disguising extra compensation can be quite impressive. Chen (1994) reported that 'in some enterprises, [workers'] shares, with promised interest rate higher than bank deposit rates in addition to fixed dividend payment, are simply a device to raise the level of wages and bonuses which have been regulated by the government to control inflation.'

25   The anonymous banking can protect private properties against state predation; it also protects money laundering and associated corruption. Because of institutionalised state opportunism, the Chinese government's tax collection capacity is rapidly weakening as the private sector develops. Hence, Bai, et al. (1999) considers the anonymous banking, combined with control of interest

rates, as an effective way for government to tax residents indirectly. But this again generates a dilemma between efficiency and injustice caused by tolerance of corruption.

26 'China City Turns Into a Prototype for Privatization,' *Wall Street Journal*, 10 June 1995. See also 'Heilongjiang puts 200 firms on the block,' *China Daily*, 7 June 1996.

27 There were 3800 joint stock companies in China in October 1993 (He 1997, p. 53).

28 Chen and Zhou (1996) document many cases of large private companies that emerged in this period and state predation of private firms.

29 According to Xing (1999), enormous values of errors and missing items in China's international income balance reflect the huge amount of capital flight. This item was $9.8, $17.8, $15.6, and $16.9 billion in 1994, 1995, 1996, and 1997, respectively.

30 China's Gini coefficient increased from 0.2 in 1978 to 0.433 in 1994 (He 1997, p. 257). According to He, the official Gini coefficient in 1994 understated inequality because of the hidden illegal income of the rich. She cites one nonofficial estimate of the Gini coefficient as 0.59 in 1995. In contrast, Taiwan's Gini coefficient decreased from 0.53 in the 1950s to 0.33 in the 1970s during the takeoff stage of economic development.

REFERENCES

Aghion, P., P. Bacchetta and A. Banerjee (1998), 'Capital Markets and the Instability of Open Economies', working paper presented at Harvard University and MIT Growth and Development Seminar.

Alchian, A. and H. Demsetz (1972), 'Production, Information Costs, and Economic Organization', *American Economic Review*, **62**, 777–95.

Bai, Chong-En, David D. Li, and Yingyi Qian, Yijiang Wang (1999), 'Anonymous Banking and Financial Repression: How Does China's Reform Limit the Government's Predation without Reducing Its Revenue?', mimeo, Stanford University.

Bardhan, P. and J. Roemer (eds) (1993), *Market Socialism, the Current Debate*, Oxford: Oxford University Press.

Barzel, Y. (1997), 'Property Rights and the Evolution of the State', mimeo; and 'Third-party Enforcement and the State', mimeo, Department of Economics, University of Washington.

Beik, Paul H. (ed.) (1970), *The French Revolution*. New York: Harper & Row.

Blanchard, Olivier (1997), *Economics of Post-Communism Transition*, Oxford: Oxford University Press.

Bouin, Olivier (forthcoming), 'Financial Discipline and State Enterprise Reform in China in the 1990s', in Olivier Bouin, Fabrizio Coricelli and Francoise Lemoine (ed.), *Different Paths to a Market Economy: China and European Economies in Transition*, Paris: OECD.

Bruun, O. (1993), *Business and Bureaucracy in a Chinese City*, Chinese Research Monographs No. 43. Berkeley, Institute of East Asian Studies, University of California.

Buchanan, James M. (1989), *Explorations into Constitutional Economics*, College Station: Texas A&M University Press.

Burke, Edmund (1790), *Reflections on the French Revolution*, edited by W. Alison Phillips and Catherine Beatrice Phillips, Cambridge: Cambridge University Press, 1912.

Burtless, Gary (1995), 'International Trade and the Rise in Earnings Inequality.' *Journal of Economic Literature*. **33**, 800–16.

Byrd, W. (1983), 'Enterprise-Level Reforms in Chinese State-Owned Industry', *American Economic Review*, **73**, 329–32.

Byrd, W. (1988), 'The Impact of the Two-Tier Plan Market System in Chinese Industry', *Journal of Comparative Economics*, **11** (3), September 1987, 295–308. Reprinted in Bruce L. Reynolds, *Chinese Economic Reform: How Far, How Fast?*, London: Academic Press.

Byrd, William (1991), *The Market Mechanism and Economic Reforms in China*, New York: M.E. Sharpe.

Byrd, W. and G. Tidrick (1987), 'Factor Allocation and Enterprises Incentives', in Gene Tidrick and Jiyuan Chen (eds), *China's Industrial Reform*, New York: Oxford University Press.

Chang, Chun, and Yijiang Wang (1994), 'The Nature of the Township Enterprises.' *Journal of Comparative Economics*, **19**, 434–52.

Che, Jiahua (1999), 'From the Grabbing Hand to the Helping Hand', working paper, Department of Economics, University of Notre Dame.

Chen, Aimin (1994), 'Chinese Industrial Structure in Transition: The Emergence of Stock-offering Firms', *Comparative Economic Studies*, **36** (4), Winter, 1–19.

Chen, Yinan and Zhiren Zhou (eds) (1996), *Chuangye Zhifu Bushi Mong (It is not a Dream to Make a Fortune from Entrepreneurship)*, Hainan International News Center.

Cheng, T. (1991), 'The Present and Future of China's Residential Registration System', PhD dissertation, Department of Sociology, North-East University.

Cheung, S. (1974), 'A Theory of Price Control', *Journal of Law and Economics*, **17**, 53–71.

Cheung, Steven N. S. (1996), 'A Simplistic General Equilibrium Theory of Corruption', *Contemporary Economic Policy*, **14**, 1–5.

Cook, Linda (1993). *The Soviet Social Contract and Why It Failed: Welfare Policy and Workers' Politics from Brezhnev to Yeltsin*, Cambridge, MA: Harvard University Press.

Crafts, N. (1997), 'Endogenous Growth: Lessons for and from Economic History', in D. Kreps and K. Wallis (eds), *Advances in Economics and Econometrics: Theory and Applications*, Vol. II. Cambridge: Cambridge University Press.

Deane, Phyllis and William Cole (1967), *British Economic Growth*, Cambridge: Cambridge University Press.

Dernberger, Robert (1988), 'Financing China's Development: Needs, Sources and Prospects', in Robert Dernberger and Richard Eckaus, *Financing Asian Development 2: China and India,* Lanham MD: University Press of America, pp. 12–68.

Dewatripont, Mathias, and Gérard Roland (1996), 'Transition as a Process of Large Scale Institutional Change', in David Kreps and Kenneth Wallis (eds), *Advances in Economics and Econometrics: Theory and Applications*, Cambridge: Cambridge University Press.

Ding, Guoxiang, Qingzeng Yan and Xun Yang (eds) (1995), *Zhongguo Nongchun Gaige Jishi (A Bibliographical Record of Events in China's Rural Reform)*, Shanxi Economic Publishing House.

Fan, Gang and Wing Thye Woo (1996), 'State Enterprise Reform as a Source of Macroeconomic Instability', *Asian Economic Journal*, November.

Fang Weizhong (ed.) (1984), *Jinji Dashi Ji (Major Economic Events in the People's Republic of China, 1949–1980)*, Beijing: Chinese Social Science Press.

Friedman, M. (1962), *Capitalism and Freedom*, Chicago: The University of Chicago Press.

Furubotn, E. and S. Pejovich (eds) (1974), *The Economics of Property Rights*, Cambridge, Mass.: Ballinger Publishing Company.

Granick, D. (1990), *Chinese State Enterprises: A Regional Property Rights Analysis*, Chicago: University of Chicago Press.

Gray, Cheryl, and Kathryn Hendley (1997), 'Developing Commercial Law in Transition Economies: Examples from Hungary and Russia', in J. Sachs and K. Pistor (eds), *The Rule of Law and Economic Reform in Russia*, Boulder: Westview Press.

Hayek, F. (1940), 'Socialist Calculation III: The Competitive 'Solution', *Economica*, **7**, 125–49.

Hayek, F. (1944), *The Road to Serfdom*, Chicago: University of Chicago Press.

Hayek, F. (1960), *The Constitution of Liberty*, Chicago: University of Chicago Press.

Hayek, F. (1988), *The Fatal Conceit: The Errors of Socialism*, Chicago: University of Chicago Press.

He, Qinglian (1997), *The Primary Capital Accumulation in Contemporary China,* Hong Kong: Mirror Book.

Hellman, Joel (1997), 'Constitutions and Economic Reforms in the Post-Communist Transitions', in J. Sachs and K. Pistor (eds), *The Rule of Law and Economic Reform in Russia*, Boulder: Westview Press.

Hua, Sheng, Xuejuen Zhang and Xiaopen Lo (1988), 'Ten Years in China's Reform: Looking Back, Reflection, and Prospect', *Economic Research*, **9**: 11–12.

Huang, Z. (1993), 'Current Development of the Private Firms in the Mainland China', *Economic Outlook*, **8** (32), 87–91.

Jefferson, G., I. Singh, J. Xing and S. Zhang (1999), 'China's Industrial Performance: A Review of Recent Findings', in G. Jefferson and I. Singh (eds), *Enterprise Reform in China: Ownership, Transition, and Performance*, Oxford: Oxford University Press, pp. 127–52.

Jian, Tianlun, Jeffrey Sachs and Andrew Warner (1996), 'Trends in Regional Inequality in China', *China Economic Review*, **7** (1), Spring, 1–21.

Jin, Hehui, and Yingyi Qian (1998), 'Public vs. Private Ownership of Firms: Evidence from Rural China', *Quarterly Journal of Economics*, **113** (3), August, 773–808.

Johnson, D. Gale, (1994), 'Does China Have a Grain Problem?', *China Economic Review*, **5** (1), 1–14.

Kornai, J. (1980), *Economics of Shortage*, Amsterdam: North-Holland.

Kornai, J. (1991), *The Road to a Free Economy*, New York: Norton.

Kornai, J. (1992), *The Socialist System: The Political Economy of Communism*, Princeton: Princeton University Press.

Kornai, Janos (1986), 'The Hungarian Reform Process: Visions, Hopes, and Reality', *Journal of Economic Literature*, **24**, December, 1687–1737.

La Porta, R., F. Lopez-de-Silanes, A. Shleifer and R. Vishny (forthcoming), 'The Quality of Government', *Journal of Law, Economics and Organization*.

Lange, J. and F. Taylor (1964), *On the Economic Theory of Socialism*, New York: McGraw Hill.

Lardy, Nicholas (1998). *China's Unfinished Economic Revolution*, The Brookings Institution.

Lau, L., and D-H. Song (1992), 'Growth versus Privatization: An Alternative Strategy to Reduce the Public Enterprise Sector: The Experience Taiwan and South Korea', working paper, Department of Economics, Stanford University.

Lenin, V. (1939), *Imperialism, the Highest Stage of Capitalism*, New York: International Publishers.

Li, David (1994), 'The Behavior of Chinese State Enterprises under the Dual Influence of the Government and the Market', University of Michigan, manuscript.

Li, Junhui (1999), 'Shunde de Zhuangzhi (The Transformation of the Ownership System in Shunde County)', *Economic Highlights*, **36**, 3.

Li, Wei (1997), 'The Impact of Economic Reform on the Performance of Chinese State Enterprises, 1980–1989', *Journal of Political Economy*, **105** (5), 1081–1106.

Lin, J.Y. (1998), 'The Current State of China's Economic Reforms', in James Dorn (ed.), *China in the New Millennium: Market Reforms and Social Development*, Washington, DC: CATO Institute.

Lio, M. (1996), 'Three Essays on Increasing Returns and Specialization: A Contribution to New Classical Microeconomic Approach', PhD dissertation, Department of Economics, the National Taiwan University.

Lio, M. (1998), 'Uncertainty, Insurance, and Division of Labor', *Review of Development Economics*, **2**, 76–86.

Liu, Yia-Ling (1992), 'Reform From Below: The Private Economy and Local Politics in the Rural Industrialization of Wenzhou', *China Quarterly*, **130**, 293–316.

Luo, Xiaopeng (1994), 'Gaige yu Zhongguo Dalude Denji Chanquan (Reforms and Property Rights based on Ranking in Mainland China)', *Modern China Studies*, **41**, 31–45.

Mao, Yushi (1999), 'Zhengfu Ruhe Bangzu Qiye He Bangzu Jiuye (How Can the Government Assist Firms and Employment)?', *Economic Highlights*, **37**, 1.

Mao, Zedong (1977a), *Selected Works of Mao Zedong*, Volume 5, Beijing: People's Press.

Mao, Tse-tung (1977b), *A Critique of Soviet Economics*, translated by Moss Roberts, annotated by Richard Levy, with an introduction by James Peck, New York: Monthly Review Press.

Maskin, Eric and Chenggang Xu (1999), 'Soft Budget Constraint Theories: From Centralization to the Market', working paper, Department of Economics, Harvard University.

McMillan, John (1996), 'Markets in Transition', in David Kreps and Kenneth Wallis (eds), *Advances in Economics and Econometrics: Theory and Applications*, Cambridge: Cambridge University Press.

Men Qinguo (1988), 'On the Ownership Structure of Modern Corporation', *Young Economists Forum*, no. 4, Tianjin.

Meng, Xin, and Frances Perkins (1996), 'The Destination of China's Enterprise Reform: A Case Study from a Labor Market Perspective', Australian National University, August.

Minami, Ryoshin, and Susumu Hondai (1995), 'An Evaluation of the Enterprise Reform in China: Income Share of Labor and Profitability in the Machine Industry', *Hitotsubashi Journal of Economics*, **36** (2), December, 125–43.

Mitchell, B.R. (1998), *International historical statistics : Europe, 1750–1993*, London: Macmillan Reference; New York, NY: Stockton Press.

Mokyr, Joel (1990), *The Level of Riches: Technological Creativity and Economic Progress,* New York: Oxford University Press.

Mokyr, Joel (1993) (ed.), *The British Industrial Revolution, An Economic Perspective*, Boulder: Westview Press.

Mokyr, Joel (1993), 'The New Economic History and the Industrial Revolution', in J. Mokyr (ed.), *The British Industrial Revolution: An economic perspective,* Boulder and Oxford: Westview Press.

Mueller, M. (1998), 'China's Telecommunications Sector and the WTO: Can China Conform to the Telecom Regulatory Principles?' in James Dorn (eds), *China in the New Millennium: Market Reforms and Social Development*, Washington, DC: CATO Institute.

Murakami, Naoki, Deqiang Liu and K. Otsuka (1994), 'Technical and Allocative Efficiency among Socialist Enterprises: The Case of Garment Industriy in China', *Journal of Comparative Economics*, **19**, 410–33.

Naughton, Barry (1994a), 'Chinese Institutional Innovation and Privatization from Below', *American Economic Review*, **84** (2), May, 266–70.

Naughton, Barry (1994b), 'What is Distinctive about China's Economic Transition? State Enterprise Reform and Overall System Transformation', *Journal of Comparative Economics*, **18** (3), June, 470–90.

Nee, V. and S. Sijin (1993), 'Local Corporatism and Informal Privatization in China's Market Transition', working paper on Transitions from State Socialism, no. 93-2. Einaudi Center for International Studies, Cornell.

Nee, Victor (1996), 'Changing Mechanisms of Stratification in China', *American Journal of Sociology*, **101** (4), January, 908–49.

Nettels, Curtis (1962), *The Emergence of a National Economy, 1775–1815*, New York.

Ng, Y-K. and X. Yang (1997), 'Specialization, Information, and Growth: a Sequential Equilibrium Analysis', *Review of Development Economics*. **1**, 257–74.

Nolan, Peter (1993), *State and Market in the Chinese Economy: Essays on Controversial Issues*, London: MacMillan.

North, D. (1994), 'Economic Performance through Time', *American Economic Review*, **84**, 359–68.

North, Douglass, and Barry Weingast (1989), 'Constitutions and Commitment: The Evolution of Institutions Governing Public Choice in Seventeenth-Century England', *Journal of Economic History*, **XLIX**, 803–32.

North, Douglass (1997), 'The Contribution of the New Institutional Economics to an Understanding of the Transition Problem', *WIDER Annual Lectures*, March.

Nussbaum, Frederick (1925), 'American Tobacco and French Politics, 1783–1789', *Political Science Quarterly*, **40**, 501–503.

Oi, J. (1986), 'Commercializing China's Rural Cadres', *Problems of Communism*, **35**, 1–15.

Oi, Jean (1992), 'Fiscal Reform and the Economic Foundations of Local State Corporatism in China', *World Politics*, October, **45** (1).

Oi, Jean (1995), 'The Role of the Local Government in China's Transitional Economy', *China Quarterly*, **144**, 1132–49.

Olson, Mancur (1982), *The Rise and Decline of Nations: Economic Growth, Stagflation, and Social Rigidities*, New Haven: Yale University Press.

Owen, T. (1997), 'Autocracy and the Rule of Law in Russian Economic History', in J. Sachs and K. Pistor (eds), *The Rule of Law and Economic Reform in Russia*, Boulder: Westview Press.

Pei, M. (1998), 'The Growth of Civil Society in China', in James Dorn (ed.), *China in the New Millennium: Market Reforms and Social Development*, Washington DC: CATO Institute.

Peng, Yusheng (1992), 'Wage Determination in Rural and Urban China: A Comparison of Public and Private Industrial Sectors,' *American Sociological Review*, **57** (2), April, 198–213.

Perkins, D. (1988), 'Reforming China's Economic System', *Journal of Economic Literature*, **XXVI**, 601–45.

Perkins, D. (ed.) (1977), *Rural Small-Scale Industry in China*, Berkeley: University of California Press.

Perkins, Frances, Zheng Yuxing and Cao Yong (1993), 'The Impact of Economic Reform on Productivity Growth in Chinese Industry: A Case of Xiamen Special Economic Zone', *Asian Economic Journal*, **7** (2), 107–46.

Philips, Ulrich (1929), *Life and Labor in the Old South*, Boston: Little, Brown, and Company.

Pilon, Roger (1998), 'A Constitution of Liberty for China', in *China in The New Millennium: Market Reforms and Social Development*, Washington DC: CATO Institute.

Ping, Xinqiao (1988), 'The Reform of the Ownership System, Property Rights, and Management'.

Pipe, R. (1999), *Property and Freedom*, New York: Alfred Knopf.

Pistor, K. (1997), 'Company Law and Corporate Governance in Russia', in J. Sachs and K. Pistor (eds), *The Rule of Law and Economic Reform in Russia*, Boulder: Westview Press.

Prosterman, Roy, Tim Hanstad and Ping Li (1996), 'Can China Feed Itself?', *Scientific American*, November, pp. 90–96.

Qian, Y. (1994a), 'Incentives and Loss of Control in an Optimal Hierarchy', *Review of Economic Studies*, **61** (3), 527–44.

Qian, Y. (1994b), 'A Theory of Shortage in Socialist Economies based on the "Soft Budget Constraint"', *American Economic Review*, **84**, 145–56.

Qian, Y. (forthcoming), 'The Process of China's Market Transition (1978–98): The Evolutionary, Historical, and Comparative Perspectives', *Journal of Institutional and Theoretical Economics*.

Qian, Yingyi (1999), 'The Institutional Foundations of China's Market Transition', paper delivered at Annual Bank Conference on Development Economics.

Qian, Yingyi, and Barry R. Weingast (1997), 'Federalism As a Commitment to Preserving Market Incentives', *Journal of Economic Perspectives*, **11** (4), Fall, 83–92.

Qian, Yingyi, and Roland Gérard (1998), 'Federalism and the Soft Budget Constraint', *American Economic Review*, **88** (5), December, 1143–62.

Qian, Yingyi, Roland Gérard and Chenggang Xu (1999), 'Coordinating Changes in M-form and U-form Organizations', mimeo, Stanford University.

Rawski, Thomas (1986), 'Overview: Industry and Transport', in US Congress, Joint Economic Committee, *China's Economy Looks Toward the Year 2000: Volume 1. The Four Modernizations*, May.

Reynolds, Bruce (ed.) (1987), *Reform in China: Challenges and Choices*, New York: M.E. Sharpe.

Riskin, C. (1971), 'Small Industry and the Chinese Model of Development', *China Quarterly*, **46**, 245–73.

Riskin, C. (1987), *China's Political Economy: The Quest for Development Since 1949*,

Studies of the East Asian Institute of Columbia University, Oxford University Press.

Roland, Gérard (2000), *Politics, Markets and Firms: Transition and Economics*, Cambridge, MA: MIT Press.

Ronnas, Per (1993), 'Township Enterprises in Sichuan and Zhejiang: Establishment and Capital Generation', paper delivered at National Workshop on Rural Industrialization in Post-Reform China, Beijing, China, October.

Sachs, J. (1993), *Poland's Jump to the Market Economy*, Cambridge, MA: MIT Press.

Sachs, J. (1994), 'Notes on the Life Cycle of State-led Industrialization', *Japan and World Economy*, **8**, 153–74.

Sachs, J. and K. Pistor (1997), 'Introduction: Progress, Pitfalls, Scenarios, and Lost Opportunities', in J. Sachs and K. Pistor (eds), *The Rule of Law and Economic Reform in Russia*, Boulder: Westview Press.

Sachs, J.and W.T. Woo (1994a), 'Understanding the Reform Experiences of China, Eastern Europe and Russia', *Journal of Comparative Economics*, **18** (3), June.

Sachs, Jeffrey, and Wing Thye Woo (1994b), 'Structural Factors in the Economic Reforms of China, Eastern Europe and the Former Soviet Union', *Economic Policy*, **18** (1), April, 102–45.

Sachs, J. and W.T. Woo (forthcoming), 'Understanding China's Economic Performance', *Journal of Policy Reforms*.

Sachs, J. and X. Yang (2000), *Development Economics: Inframarginal versus Marginal Analyses*, Cambridge, MA: Blackwell.

Schurmann, H. (1968), *Ideology and Organization in Communist China*, Berkeley: University of California Press.

Shea, Jia-Dong and Ya-Hwei Yang (1994), 'Taiwan's Financial System and the Allocation of Investment Funds', in Joel Aberbach, David Dollar and Kenneth Sokoloff (eds), *The Role of State in Taiwan's Development*, Armonk, NY: M.E. Sharpe, pp. 193–230.

Shi, H. and X. Yang (1995), 'A New Theory of Industrialization', *Journal of Comparative Economics*, **20**, 171–89.

Shleifer, A. and R. Vishny (1992), 'Pervasive Shortages Under Socialism', *RAND Journal of Economics*, **23**, 237–46.

Shleifer, A. and R. Vishny (1993), 'The Politics of Market Socialism', working paper, Department of Economics, Harvard University.

Shleifer, Andrei (1998), 'State versus Private Ownership', *Journal of Economic Perspectives*, **12**, 133–50.

Skousen, Mark (1997), 'The Perseverance of Paul Samuelson's *Economics*', *Journal of Economic Perspectives*, **11**, 137–53

Solinger, D. (1992), 'Urban Entrepreneurs and the State: The Merger of State and Society', in A. Rosenbaum (ed.), *State and Society in China: The Consequences of Reform*, Boulder: Westview Press, pp. 121–42.

Taylower, George (1932), 'Wholesale Commodity Prices at Charleston, South Carolina, 1732–1792', *Journal of Economic and Business History*, **4**, 367.

Vogel, E. (1989), *One Step Ahead in China: Guangdong Under Reform*, Cambridge: Harvard University Press.

von Mises, L. (1922), *Socialism: An Economic and Sociological Analysis*, Indianapolis: Liberty Classics, reprinted in 1981.

Walder, A. (1986), 'The Informal Dimension of Enterprise Financial Reforms', in Joint Economic Committee, US Congress, *The Chinese Economy Toward the Year 2000*, Washington DC: US Government Printing Office, pp. 630–45.

Walder, A. (1989), 'Factory and Manager in an Era of Reform', *The China Quarterly*, **118**, June, 242–64.

Walder, A. (1992), 'Local Bargaining Relationships and Urban Industrial Finance', in K. Lieberthal and D. Lampton (eds), *Bureaucracy, Politics, and Decision Making in Post Mao China*, Berkeley, University of California Press, pp. 308–33.

Walder, Andrew (1995), 'China's Transitional Economy: Interpreting its Significance', *China Quarterly*, **144**, December, 963–79.

Wang, J. (1992), 'The Third Way of the Chinese Economic Reform: Establish an Institution of Competition', *The Chinese Intellectual*, **7**, 8–24.

Wank, D. (1993), 'From State Socialism to Community Capitalism: State Power, Social Structure, and Private Enterprise in a Chinese City', unpublished PhD dissertation, Department of Sociology, Harvard University.

Weitzman, Martin, and Chenggang Xu (1994), 'Chinese Township Village Enterprises as Vaguely Defined Cooperatives', *Journal of Comparative Economics*, **18**, September, 121–45.

Wen, Mei, Dong Li and Peter Lloyd (2000), 'Ownership and Technical Efficiency: A Cross-section Study on the Third Industrial Census of China', working paper, Division of Economics, RSPAS & APSEM, Australian National University.

Wen, Ming (1999), *Report on China's Property Owners (Zhongguo Youchanzhe Baogao)*, Beijing: China United Business Press.

Wong, C. (1985), 'Material Allocation and Decentralization: Impact of the Local Sector on Industrial Reform', in E. Perry and C. Wong (eds), *The Political Economy of Reform in Post Mao China*, Cambridge, Harvard University Press.

Wong, C. (1986a), 'The Economics of Shortage and Problems of Reform in Chinese Industry', *Journal of Comparative Economics*, **10**, 363–87.

Wong, C. (1986b), 'Ownership and Control in Chinese Industry: The Maoist Legacy and Prospects for the 1980s', in Joint Economic Committee, US Congress, *The Chinese Economy Toward the Year 2000*, Washington DC: US Government Printing Office, pp. 571–602.

Woo, Wing Thye, Wen Hai, Yibiao Jin and Gang Fan (1994), 'How Successful Has the Chinese Enterprise Reform Been?', *Journal of Comparative Economics*, **18** (3), June, 410–37.

Woodward, C. (1951), *Origins of the New South, 1877–1913*, New York.

World Bank (1984), *World Development Report,* various issues, Washington, DC: World Bank.

Wu, Jieh-min (1998), 'Local Property Rights Regime in Socialist Reform: A Case Study of China's Informal Privatization', PhD dissertation, Department of Political Science, Columbia University.

Xing, Yujing (1999), 'Renminbi Ziben Xiangmo Keduihuan (Is Liberalization of Capital Account of China Urgent)', *Economic Highlights*, **38** (2).

Yang, X. (1994), 'Endogenous vs. Exogenous Comparative Advantages and Economies of Specialization vs. Economies of Scale', *Journal of Economics*, **60**, 29–54.

Yang, X. (1998), *Dangdai Jingjixue He Zhongguo Jingji (Contemporary Economics and Chinese Economy)*, Beijing: Publishing House of China's Social Sciences.

Yang, X. and Y-K. Ng (1993), *Specialization and Economic Organization, a New Classical Microeconomic Framework*, Amsterdam: North-Holland.

Yang, X. and Y-K. Ng (1995), 'Theory of the Firm and Structure of Residual Rights', *Journal of Economic Behavior and Organization*, **26**, 107–28.

Yang, X. and R. Rice (1994), 'An Equilibrium Model Endogenizing the Emergence of a Dual Structure between the Urban and Rural Sectors', *Journal of Urban Economics*, **25**, 346–68.

Yang, X. and H. Shi (1992), 'Specialization and Product Diversity', *American Economic Review*, **82**, 392–98.

Yang, X., J. Wang and I. Wills (1992), 'Economic Growth, Commercialization, and Institutional Changes in Rural China, 1979–1987', *China Economic Review*, **3**, 1–37.

Ye, Xingqing (1999), 'Another Detriment of Urbanization', *Economic Highlights*, **365**, December, 1.

Yi, Gang (1988), 'The Efficiency of the Market and the Delimiting of Property Rights', *China: Development and Reform*, No. 12, Beijing.

Young, Alwyn (1998), 'Growth without Scale Effects', *Journal of Political Economy*, **106**, 41–63.

Zaleski, E. (1980), *Stalinist Planning for Economic Growth, 1933–1952*, University of North Carolina Press.

Zhang, Gang (1993), 'Government Intervention versus Marketisation in China's Rural Industries: The Role of Local Governments', paper delivered at the National Workshop on Rural Industrialization in Post-Reform China, Beijing, China, October.

Zhang, Weiying (1986), *Research Report on Economic System Reforms*, No. 30.

Zhang, Weiying (1999), *The Theory of the Firm and China's Enterprise Reforms (Qiye Lilun Yu Zhongguo Qiye Gaige)*, Peking: Peking University Press. See also

Zhou, Taihe (ed.) (1984), *Dangdai Zhongguo de Jingji Tizhi Gaige (Economic System Reforms in Contemporary China)*, Beijing: China Social Science Press.

Zhou, Qiren (1999), 'Ba Chuangye Huangdao Diyiwei Lai, Ba Jiuye Huangdao Dierwei Qu (Put Founding Firms before Finding Jobs)', *Economic Highlights*, **37** (1).

Zhuravskaya, Ekaterina (1998), 'Incentives to Provide Local Public Goods: Fiscal Federalism, Russian Style', mimeo, Harvard University.

Zweig, David (1991), 'Rural Industry: Constraining the Leading Growth Sector in China's Economy', in Joint Economic Committee, US Congress, *China's Economics Dilemmas in the 1990s: The Problems of Reforms, Modernization, and Interdependence*, April, Washington DC.

5 Thailand's Financial and Economic Crisis – Evaluating Alternative Policies for Economic Recovery

Wilai Auepiyachut and Charles Harvie

5.1 INTRODUCTION

The recent financial and economic crisis that afflicted a number of economies in East Asia led to considerable debate and controversy over appropriate macroeconomic policy responses to alleviate the adverse impacts arising during the period of the crisis itself, as well as those most likely to bring about a rapid and sustained recovery of these economies. Thailand is largely credited with having triggered the crisis due to the abandonment of its currency peg in early July 1997. As a consequence a rapid subsequent loss of confidence in the currency quickly spread to the currencies of its regional neighbours. The focus of this chapter is upon the development of a macroeconomic model for Thailand that can be utilised to identify the impact upon the macroeconomy arising from financial shocks, and can also be used, through the conduct of a numerical simulation analysis, to compare and contrast the economic outcomes from the implementation of alternative policy options in response to such shocks.

The chapter proceeds as follows. In Section 5.2 a brief overview of the build up to and factors contributing to the financial crisis in Thailand is conducted. Section 5.3 outlines the macroeconomic model for Thailand. Section 5.4 presents the parameter values of the model utilised for simulation purposes and well as the simulation scenarios conducted. Section 4.5 outlines the results obtained from simulation of the model for these scenarios, and Section 4.6 highlights important policy implications. Finally, Section 4.7 presents a summary of the major conclusions to be derived from this chapter.

5.2 OVERVIEW OF THE FINANCIAL CRISIS IN THAILAND

The major factors underlying the financial crisis in Thailand in 1997 arose from changes in the world economic environment and rapid domestic capital account liberalisation. Changes in the external environment, such as the decline of asset yields in the major industrial economies from the early 1990s, made Asian, including Thai, markets an increasingly attractive investment opportunity. Financial liberalisation policies undertaken in Thailand during the late 1980s and early 1990s were used to stimulate capital inflows and to sustain economic growth. This occurred without a commensurate improvement in the institutional structure of domestic financial markets. The weak financial sector was hidden by unprecedented rapid economic growth. However, with the slow-down in economic growth, especially in the export sector in 1996, together with increasing international financial integration, the weakness in domestic financial markets became exposed.

Before the onset of the crisis the country had experienced, for several years, rapid output and export growth with generally modest inflation and fiscal surpluses. In the first half of the 1990s current account deficits were generally in excess of 5 per cent of GDP, reaching 8 per cent of GDP in 1995 and 1996. This could only remain sustainable as long as export growth remained strong and large capital inflows continued. In 1996, however, total exports declined by 1.8 per cent, compared to increases of over 20 per cent per annum in the two previous years (see Table 5.1). The rapid deceleration in export growth was attributable to several factors. Firstly, cyclical factors such as reduced demand by major trading partners and reduced world trade volume. Secondly, Thailand structurally still depended on labour intensive industries in which it had rapidly declining international competitiveness. Thirdly, an appreciation of the currency contributed to a further loss of competitiveness. The latter partly reflected higher rates of inflation relative to its trading partners. In addition, as the US dollar strengthened against other currencies, and in particular the Japanese yen, the Thai currency, mainly tied to the US dollar, appreciated accordingly. This reduced the country's competitiveness in the export sector and, of particular significance, in its second largest export market – Japan.

These difficulties were aggravated by monetary mismanagement emanating from the Bank of Thailand. The radical and rapid liberalisation of the capital account, and the introduction of the Bangkok International Banking Facilities (BIBF), created a heavy inflow of foreign capital, especially during the period 1993–1996. Net capital inflows increased from about 8 per cent of GDP in 1990 to 14 per cent of GDP in 1995. By 1995 the BIBF accounted for around 39 per cent of net private capital inflows. The massive capital inflows also contributed to rapid growth in the country's outstanding foreign debt. The total outstanding external debt increased from 34.3 per cent of GDP in 1990 to 60 per cent of GDP by 1996. Most of the increase in debt was generated by the private sector. Within less than four years private debt through the BIBF rose quickly from being negligible to US$32.2 billion by the end of 1996, over

Table 5.1

Macroeconomic Indicators for the Thai Economy: 1990–2000 (in % of GDP unless otherwise stated)

	1990	1991	1992	1993	1994	1995	1996	1997	1998	1999	2000
Real sector											
Real GDP growth	11.2	8.6	8.1	8.4	9.0	8.9	5.9	−1.7	−10.2	4.2	4–4.5
Inflation (CPI)	5.9	5.7	4.1	3.4	5.1	5.8	5.9	5.5	8.1	0.3	na
Public sector											
Central Government fiscal											
balance (% of GDP)	4.8	4.3	2.6	1.9	2.7	3.0	1.0	−0.3	−2.8	−3.3	na
External sector (US$ billion)											
Exports	22.9	28.3	32.2	36.6	44.7	55.7	54.7	56.7	52.9	56.8	67.9
(% change)	(15.1)	(23.6)	(13.8)	(13.7)	(22.1)	(24.6)	(−1.8)	(3.7)	(−6.8)	(7.4)	(19.6)
Imports	32.7	37.8	40.1	45.1	53.5	70.4	70.8	61.3	40.6	47.5	62.4
(% change)	(29.8)	(15.6)	(6.1)	(12.5)	(18.4)	(31.8)	(0.6)	(−13.4)	(−33.8)	(16.9)	(31.3)
Trade balance	−9.8	−9.5	−7.9	−8.5	−8.7	−14.7	−16.1	−4.6	12.2	9.3	5.5
Current account balance	−7.1	−7.4	−6.1	−6.1	−7.8	−13.2	−14.4	−3.1	14.3	12.5	9.2
(% of GDP)	(−8.3)	(−7.5)	(−5.5)	(−4.9)	(−5.4)	(−7.9)	(−8.1)	(−0.9)	(−12.8)	(−10.0)	na
Net capital movement	9.7	11.3	8.1	10.5	12.2	21.9	19.5	−4.3	−9.8	−7.9	−9.5
International reserves	14.3	18.4	21.2	25.4	30.3	37.0	38.7	27.0	29.5	34.8	32.7
Total external debt											
outstanding:	29.3	37.9	43.6	52.1	64.9	100.8	108.7	109.3	105.1	95.6	80.2
Public debt	11.5	12.8	13.1	14.2	15.7	16.4	16.8	24.1	31.1	36.0	33.8
Private debt	17.8	25.1	30.5	37.9	49.2	84.4	91.9	85.2	74.0	59.6	46.4

(continued)

Table 5.1 (continued)

Macroeconomic Indicators for the Thai Economy: 1990–2000 (in % of GDP unless otherwise stated)

	1990	1991	1992	1993	1994	1995	1996	1997	1998	1999	2000
Exchange rate (baht per US$)	25.59	25.52	25.40	25.32	25.15	24.92	25.34	31.37	41.37	37.84	43.09
Monetary sector											
M2 growth	26.7	19.8	15.6	18.4	12.9	17.0	12.6	16.4	9.5	2.1	3.7
Domestic credit growth	26.9	5.5	18.0	22.7	28.9	22.9	13.9	34.5	–1.2	–4.2	–7.4
Interest rate, year end (prime rate)	16.25	14.0	11.5	10.5	11.75	13.75	13.0–13.25	15.25	11.5–12.00	8.25–8.50	7.5–8.25
Stock market price	612	711	893	1682	1360	1280	831	372	337 *	435 *	269 *
Property sector											
Property index 1995=100	na	na	75.1	85.6	103.1	100	100.3	76.1	42.0	34.3	na
Property registration (millions of baht)	na	na	11812	13795	16800	16339	13633	8191	4543	950	na

* December

Sources: IMF, *International Financial statistics*, various issues; IMF, 'World economic outlook interim assessment', December, 1997; Asian Development Bank, 'Key Indicators of Developing Asian and Pacific Countries', 2000; Bank of Thailand, Macroeconomic Section, <www.bot.or.th>.

half of total private external debt. This led to a rapid increase in the share of short-term debt to total foreign debt, which increased from 35.5 per cent in 1990 to 55.6 per cent in 1995. These excessive short-term and unhedged foreign borrowings supported high levels of investment, often in real estate where there were property price bubbles, giving rise to substantial maturity mismatches that exposed the borrowers to liquidity risk. Additionally, an enormous amount of non-performing loans held by financial institutions arising from the collapse of the asset price bubble, both in the real estate sector and in the stock exchange market, became very apparent in 1996 (See Table 5.1). Finance and securities companies, in particular, were much affected because their exposure to the real estate sector was substantial, with credits extended to this sector accounting for 25–30 per cent of their total credits.

All of these negative developments contributed to lower confidence of the international financial markets in the Thai economy. Speculative attacks against the value of the Thai currency started during 1996 and occurred on several occasions thereafter, but did not become significantly aggressive until May 1997. The Thai authorities failed to stem the speculative onslaughts by raising interest rates and instead intervened heavily in the foreign exchange market. They finally broke the peg to the US dollar on 2 July 1997 and eventually asked the IMF for assistance. This represented another policy mistake of the Thai government, with their retention of a fixed exchange rate regime alongside the liberalisation of the capital account.

The structural weakness of the domestic financial system was the root cause of the financial and economic crisis in Thailand. Institutional developments in the financial sector lagged behind real sector developments. The structural weakness in domestic financial markets distorted investment incentives. Weak supervision of the financial sector resulted in: lax regulatory standards; poorly managed financial liberalisation; inadequate corporate governance; and a general lack of transparency. This allowed problems to grow by encouraging over-borrowing and over-investment in non-productive and highly risky investments. Given the lack of developed securities markets, investment was financed mostly through the banking system, with banks borrowing heavily in foreign currencies and mostly short-term. These large currency positions were unhedged as firms and banks expected the fixed exchange rate to be maintained or that they would be bailed out when things went wrong. When things did go wrong a rapid reversal of capital inflows occurred, as domestic and international investors panicked and caused a sharp decline in share prices and in the value of the domestic currency. Hence a currency and financial crisis emerged.

A key issue, however, is whether these problems added up to the magnitude of the Thai crisis, and indeed that for the region, which took place in late 1997 and 1998. Radelet and Sachs (1999) argue that these problems were not severe enough to warrant complete collapse of the currencies in the region, a total breakdown of the banking system, and the depth and severity of the economic contraction. Instead they argue (see Radelet and Sachs 1998a, 1998b, 1999) that the crisis was mainly the result of a self-fulfilling panic by investors. Others argue that a build up of pressure from country-specific problems, in particular a serious weakness in financial systems, corporate governance, and poor economic policies in the region, led to the crisis (Corsetti, et al. 1998; Dornbusch 1998; Krugman 1998a),[1] as well as the International Monetary Fund (IMF).

5.3   MACROECONOMIC MODEL FOR THAILAND

This section outlines the model developed and utilised for simulation purposes[2]. The equations of the model are categorised under the headings of product market equilibrium, asset market equilibrium, wage-price nexus and aggregate supply, and definitions. All equations and variables in the model, except the domestic nominal interest rate and the world interest rate, are presented in log-linear form (See Table 5.2), and the macroeconomic variables are defined in Table 5.3. Overall equilibrium in the model depends upon equilibrium in the product market, asset market and external balance.

Equilibrium in the product market is discussed first. Equation (1) describes aggregate demand for real output (y^d) as comprising private consumption, private investment, government consumption, government investment, and the trade balance. Equations (2)–(8) describe the determinants of these components of aggregate demand. Specifically, private consumption expenditure (c^p) depends positively on the level of real income[3], and real private sector wealth. Total private investment consists of two components: productive (i^{pp}) and non-productive (i^{np}) investment. Non-productive investment, that is investment which does not increase the productive capacity of the economy, depends positively on real private sector wealth and net short-term capital inflows. Productive investment is positively related to Tobin's q ratio and long term capital inflows. Public sector consumption and investment spending are exogenously determined policy variables. Finally, the trade balance depends positively upon the real exchange rate, the nominal exchange rate deflated by the domestic price level, negatively on domestic aggregate demand, and positively on world real income.

Asset market equilibrium conditions are described by equations (9)–(16). The basic presumption is that the three non-money assets are imperfect substitutes due to differences in their perceived risk. With free capital mobility, arbitrage between them continuously ensures the same expected rate of return adjusted for the risk premium. An expected domestic currency appreciation or increase in the risk premium on domestic assets will raise the proportion of domestic money in wealth portfolios.

Equation (9) represents money market equilibrium where the supply of real balances, the nominal money supply deflated by the domestic price level, equates to its demand, which depends positively on the level of aggregate demand and negatively on the domestic nominal interest rate. Equation (10) describes the real return on private capital as depending positively on the level of real income, negatively on the private corporate capital stock due to diminishing returns, and positively on the public capital stock. The latter holds since the public and private capital stock are assumed to be

Table 5.2
The Model: Flexible Exchange Rate with Imperfect Capital Mobility

Product market

$$y^d = \alpha_1 c^p + \alpha_2 i^{tp} + \alpha_3 c^g + \alpha_4 i^g + \alpha_5 t \tag{1}$$

$$c^p = c_1 y^s + c_2 w^p \tag{2}$$

$$i^{tp} = \xi_1 i^{pp} + (1 - \xi_1) i^{np} \tag{3}$$

$$i^{np} = h_1 \dot{w}^p + h_2\, st_f \tag{4}$$

$$i^{pp} = \dot{k}_{\underset{-}{p}} = q + h_3\, lt_f \tag{5}$$

$$c^g = \bar{c}^g; \tag{6}$$

$$i^g = \dot{k}^g \tag{7}$$

$$t = t_1(e - p) - t_2 y^d + t_3 y^* \tag{8}$$

Asset markets

$$m = p + \sigma_1 y^d - \sigma_2 r \tag{9}$$

$$R = \varepsilon_1 y^s - \varepsilon_2 k^p + \varepsilon_3 \bar{k}^g \tag{10}$$

$$\dot{e} = r - r^* - rp^b \tag{11}$$

$$\dot{q} = \delta_3^{-1}[q - \delta_1 R + \delta_2(r - \pi - rp^b + rp^q)] \tag{12}$$

$$w^p = \gamma_1(f + e - p) + \gamma_2(k^p + q) \tag{13}$$

$$\dot{f} = \mu_1 t + \mu_2 r^* f - (1 - \mu_2)(e - p) \tag{14}$$

$$\dot{st}_f = -\beta \dot{f} \tag{15}$$

$$\dot{lt}_f = -(1 - \beta)\dot{f} \tag{16}$$

Price/wage nexus

$$p = \chi w + (1 - \chi)e \tag{17}$$

$$\dot{w} = \phi_1(y^d - y^s) + \phi_2 \pi \tag{18}$$

$$y^s = \lambda_1 k^p + \lambda_2 \bar{k}^g - \lambda_3(w - p) + \lambda_4 y' \tag{19}$$

$$\dot{\pi} = \pi_1(p - \pi) \tag{20}$$

(continued)

Table 5.2 (continued)
The Model: Flexible Exchange Rate with Imperfect Capital Mobility

Definitions

$$c = e - w \qquad\qquad (21)$$

$$l = m - w \qquad\qquad (22)$$

Table 5.3
List of Symbols Used in the Model

Endogenous Variables

y^d	Aggregate demand for real output
c^p	Private consumption
i^{tp}	Total private investment
i^{pp}	Productive investment
i^{np}	Non productive investment
t	Trade balance
y^s	Aggregate supply of output
w^p	Real private sector wealth
k^p	Private capital stock
q	Tobin's q
p	Domestic price level
e	Nominal exchange rate
c	Real exchange rate
l	Real money balances
R	Real profit stream derivable from capital services
r	Domestic nominal interest rate
π	Inflationary expectations
f	Foreign asset stocks
$\dot{st}_f$	Net short-term inflows (short-term capital outflows minus short-term capital inflows)

$\dot{lt}_f$	Net long-term inflows (long-term capital outflows minus long-term capital inflows)
w	Domestic nominal wage

Exogenous variables

c^g	Government consumption
i^g	Government investment
$\bar{k}^g$	Public capital stock
y^*	World real income
y^l	Aggregate supply of output
m	Nominal money supply (exogenous only where there is a flexible exchange rate)
r^*	World nominal interest rate
rp^b	Risk premium on holding domestic bonds relative to foreign bonds
rp^q	Risk premium on holding domestically owned equities

complementary in nature, hence productivity of private capital increases as the government provides more public infrastructure (see Aschauer 1989).

Equation (11) is the risk inclusive uncovered interest parity condition. An increase in the risk premium on domestic bonds relative to foreign bonds requires domestic bonds to generate a higher return in order to compensate investors. Equation (12) describes the change in Tobin's q ratio. This is derived from the risk adjusted arbitrage condition equating the returns on domestic and foreign bonds and equities. Equation (13) defines private sector wealth as depending positively on the real domestic currency value of domestically held foreign assets, and on the value of the private capital stock. Equation (14) defines the current account of the balance of payments, which is equivalent to the change in domestic holdings of foreign assets, as the sum of the trade balance, net interest income and the real exchange rate.

Equations (15) and (16) indicate the composition of the foreign asset stocks, in terms of their term structure. The larger is the parameter b, the larger the proportion of short-term foreign assets accumulated. Both short-term flows, equation (15), and long-term capital flows, equation (16), are assumed to adjust to changes in the current account balance but with the opposite sign.

Equations (17)–(19) define the wage-price nexus and aggregate supply. The domestic price level, equation (17), is a weighted average of domestic nominal wages and the world price of the imported good. Nominal wage adjustment is generated by an expectations augmented Phillips curve, as given by equation (18). Aggregate supply, equation (19), is endogenously determined and is derived from the economy's aggregate production function, depending positively on the private physical capital stock, public capital stock, negatively on real wages, and upon exogenous aggregate supply shocks. Inflationary expectations, equation (20), adjust adaptively to changes in the actual rate of inflation.

Finally, equations (21)–(22) define respectively the real exchange rate and real money balances.

5.4   PARAMETER VALUES AND SIMULATION SCENARIOS

The objective of this section is to identify the parameter values of the model and to outline the simulation scenarios conducted.

5.4.1   Parameter Values

In order to identify the steady state properties of the model arising from exogenous shocks, as well as the adjustment process towards long run steady state, it is necessary to specify the numerical values of the parameters of the model. The relevant parameter values utilised were obtained from econometrically estimated coefficients using cointegration and error-correction techniques, and well as values imposed to ensure model stability. Table 5.4 summarises the numerical values of the parameters utilised.[4]

5.4.2 Simulation Scenarios and Pattern of Shocks – Base Case, IMF and Radelet and Sachs (RS) Policy Approaches

Simulation scenarios

The financial and economic crisis in Thailand that erupted in July 1997 sparked a vigorous debate as to what the most appropriate macroeconomic policy response should be. The Thai government was bound to implement the IMF reform package and to announce publicly its commitment to it in order to receive financial assistance. The financial and economic crisis produced a massive contraction of domestic supply and demand that was much larger than expected. This raised serious doubts in Thailand about the IMF's role in policy management. The IMF suggested that a tightening of monetary policy in the initial stage of the crisis was required in order to stabilise the exchange rate and slow down capital outflows. The IMF package added public sector contraction, by requiring a budget surplus equivalent to 1 per cent of GDP. Moreover, at a time when confidence in the financial sector was essential the IMF required that problem financial institutions be closed.[5] Given the circumstances at the time this requirement seemed to lead to: more financial panic; business and financial institution insolvencies and bankruptcies; and hence an unnecessarily harsher economic contraction in the Thai economy. Radelet and Sachs (RS) (1998a, 1999) argued that the crisis in East Asia was mainly the result of a shift in investor confidence, policy mismanagement at the onset of the crisis by Asian governments, and poorly designed IMF supported programmes, which turned a moderate adjustment into a deep and severe economic contraction. RS argued that fiscal contraction may not be an appropriate policy in dealing with such a crisis in the early stage because fiscal policy had been fairly prudent in Thailand, and hence budget profligacy was not the source of the crisis. A temporary loosening of fiscal policy would seem to have been more appropriate. They also argue that efforts to prevent a collapse in aggregate supply, brought about through financial and corporate sector insolvencies, should have been initiated.

Table 5.5 summarises the three simulation scenarios conducted, and the pattern of shocks for each is contained in Tables 5.6–5.8 respectively.

5.4.3 Pattern of Shocks in Each Simulation – Scenarios A, B and C

Scenario A – Base case

Scenario A, which is the base case, represents two important aspects of the Thai crisis: the collapse of aggregate supply brought about through financial and corporate sector insolvencies and bankruptcies, and a jump in the risk premium on domestic bonds and equities. In the base case aggregate supply is assumed to decline by 4 per cent from its base value in the impact period and then to gradually recover over the next three years. The risk premium on bonds and equities is assumed to rise by 20 per cent in the impact period, and again gradually declines and dies away over the next three years. The pattern of these shocks is presented in Table 5.6.

Table 5.4
Parameters Utilised for the Simulations

Equation	Parameters	Long run estimated co-efficients (a)	Short run estimated co-efficients (b)	Confidence intervals (c)		Chosen parameter value from (a) or (b) for simulation	Imposed parameter for simulation	Sources for imposed parameter values
(1)	α_1						1.0	(A)
	α_2						0.1	(AMCMD)
	α_3						0.1	(AMCMD)
	α_4						0.1	(A),(C),(D)
	α_5						0.1	(AMCMD)
(2)	c_1	0.4900	0.4738	0.1892	0.7584	0.5		
	c_2	0.5237	−0.4290	−0.9012	0.0432	0.5		
(3)	ξ_1					0.8		Author's calculation
(4)	h_1	0.1585	0.5759	−1.0088	2.1606	0.2		
	h_2	0.5744	0.0633	−0.0077	0.1343	0.6		
(5)	η	0.3751	0.2345	0.0643	0.4047	0.4		
	h_3	0.1331	0.0953	0.0105	0.1801	0.1		
(7)	t_1	−1.1304	0.7342	−1.7491	3.2175	0.7		
	t_2	−1.9906	−2.8990	−11.019	5.2212	2.9		
	t_3	−	3.6489	0.1196	7.1782	3.6		
(8)	σ_1	0.2238	−2.4215	−2.2858	0.5019	0.2		
	σ_2	−0.2022	−0.0061	−0.0237	0.0181	0.2		
	σ_3	0.7133	1.7216				0.2	(C),(D)
(9)	ε_1						0.5	(A),(B)
	ε_2						0.5	(A),(B)
	ε_3						0.5	(A),(B)
(10)	δ_1						0.5	(A),(B)
	δ_2						0.5	(A),(B)
	δ_3						0.5	(A),(B)
(11)	v_1	−0.6436	−0.0762	−0.2322	0.0798		0.5	(C),(D)
	v_2	0.1988	0.0272	0.0008	0.0536		0.5	(C),(D)
(12)	μ_1	1.6339	−0.0618	−0.3437	0.2201	1.6		
	μ_2							(C),(D)
		−0.0136	−0.0050	−0.0095	0.0400		1.0	(C),(D)

(continued)

Table 5.4 (continued)
Parameters Utilised for the Simulations

Equation	Parameters	Long run estimated co-efficients (a)	Short run estimated co-efficients (b)	Confidence intervals (c)		Chosen parameter value from (a) or (b) for simulation	Imposed parameter for simulation	Sources for imposed parameter values
(13)	β						0.5	Author's calculation
(14)	χ						0.7	(A)
(15)	ϕ_1						0.7	(A)
	ϕ_2						1.0	(A)
(16)	ϕ_1	–	0.4749	0.2310	0.7188	0.5		
	ϕ_1	1.8472	0.1275	–0.3948	0.5498	0.5		
	ϕ_1	–1.8743	0.0419	–0.2935	0.3773	0.16		
(17)	π						0.5	

Notes:
(a)   Estimated coefficients obtained from a cointegration analysis.
(b)   Estimated coefficients obtained from an error-correction analysis.
(c)   Confidence Interval (95%) based on a t-distribution (t-value = 1.980)
(A)   Harvie C. (1993), 'The Macroeconomic Effects of Oil Shocks under Fixed and Flexible Exchange Rates – a Comparison', *OPEC Review*, Autumn.
(B)   Harvie C. and Kearney, C. (1994), 'Public Infrastructure Capital and Private Investment', Research Paper, The University of Wollongong.
(C)   World Bank and The National Economic and Social Development Board (NESDB), 'SIAM1 Model', 1982.
(D)   Thailand Development Research Institute (TDRI), 'Computable General Equilibrium Macroeconomic Model Construction and Calibration under SAMLIB for Macroeconomic and Energy Model Training Program', 1992.

Scenario B: IMF Approach

Scenario B represents the IMF approach in response to developments as identified for Scenario A, the base case. The policies implemented by the IMF in response to the Thai crisis, as assumed here, are as follows:

First, a tightening of monetary policy by assuming a temporary decline in the monetary growth rate by 1 per cent in the impact period, and a further decline to 2 per cent and then 1 per cent from its base value in periods 4 and 6 respectively and returning to its baseline in period 8.

Second, tightening fiscal policy by assuming a temporary change in public

Table 5.5
Summary of the Differences Between the Three Simulation
Scenarios A, B and C

Scenario A: **Base case**	**Exogenous** **shocks**	• Jump in risk perceptions • A collapse in aggregate supply	
Scenario B: **IMF**	**Exogenous** **shocks**	• Jump in risk perceptions • A collapse in aggregate supply	
	Policy **response**	• Monetary contraction • Fiscal contraction	
Scenario C: **Radelet and** **Sachs**	**Exogenous** **shocks**	• Jump in risk perceptions • A collapse in aggregate supply	**Note**: the RS policy approach, as assumed here, has no exogenous effects on aggregate supply due to the presumed success of the policy response in preventing this.

	Policy
	response
		• maintaining the
		  monetary growth rate at
		  the base value
		• a temporary loosening
		  of fiscal policy
		• efforts to prevent a
		  collapse in aggregate
		  supply	

investment spending. Public investment spending is assumed to decrease by 1 per cent below baseline on impact, and this remains so until period 6 when it rises to 1 per cent above baseline. It remains so until period 12 at which time it returns to its base level. The public sector capital stock falls by 1 per cent on impact and declines further to be 2 per cent lower than baseline in period 4, and then 1 per cent lower than baseline in period 6 and returning to its baseline in period 8. The pattern of shocks analysed in this Scenario is presented in Table 5.7.

Table 5.6
Pattern of the Shocks: Scenario A (the Base Case) (% Change)

Exogenous shocks						
The pattern of shock: risk premium on bonds	0	20	18	10	5	0
The pattern of shock: risk premium on equities	0	20	18	10	5	0
The pattern of shock: aggregate supply	0	–4	–3	–2	–1	0
Policy shocks: not applicable in Scenario A						
Transition times for such shocks	0	0'	4	6	8	12

Scenario C: Radelet and Sachs (RS) Approach

Scenario C represents the RS approach in response to the developments as identified for Scenario A, the base case. The policies assumed in response to the Thai crisis in this scenario are as follows. First, maintaining the existing monetary growth rate at its base rate. Second, loosening fiscal policy by assuming a temporary increase in public investment by 1 per cent above its base level on impact and remaining at this level until period 6, when it is then reduced below base level by 1 per cent until period 12 at which time it returns to its base level. The public capital stock increases on impact to 1 per cent above base level then to 2 per cent above base level in period 4. It is assumed to remain at this level until period 6 when it declines to 1 per cent above base level. By period 8 it is assumed to have returned to its base level. Thirdly, a jump in the risk premium on domestic bonds and equities similar to that for Scenarios A and B, but no effects arising from the collapse on aggregate supply. The latter arises due to a presumed government response to maintain banking and corporate sector solvency. The pattern of such shocks is represented in Table 5.8.

5.5 SIMULATION OUTCOMES FOR THE THREE SCENARIOS A, B AND C

The objective of this section is to identify outcomes using the base model outlined in Section 3 for the three simulation scenarios identified in the previous section[6]. The analysis focuses upon the adjustment of six key macroeconomic variables which are: the real exchange rate, foreign asset stocks, private capital stock, aggregate supply, trade balance and q ratio,[7] with the objective of comparing and contrasting the IMF and Radelet and Sachs (RS) policy approaches to the crisis.

Table 5.9 summarises the long run steady state properties of each variable under

Table 5.7
Pattern of the Shocks: Scenario B (the IMF Approach) (% Change)

Exogenous Shocks						
The pattern of shock: risk premium on bonds	0	20	18	10	5	0
The pattern of shock: risk premium on equities	0	20	18	10	5	0
The pattern of shock: aggregate supply	0	–4	–3	–2	–1	0
Policy Response						
The pattern of shock: monetary growth rate	0	–1	–2	–1	0	0
The pattern of shock: public investment	0	–1	–1	1	1	0
The pattern of shock: public capital stock	0	–1	–2	–1	0	0
Transition times for such shocks	0	0'	4	6	8	12

Table 5.8
Pattern of the Shocks: RS Approach (Scenario C) (% Change)

Exogenous shocks						
The pattern of shock: risk premium on bonds	0	20	18	10	5	0
The pattern of shock: risk premium on equities	0	20	18	10	5	0
The pattern of shock: aggregate supply	0	0	0	0	0	0
Policy response						
The pattern of shock: monetary growth rate	0	0	0	0	0	0
The pattern of shock: public investment	0	1	1	–1	–1	0
The pattern of shock: public capital stock	0	1	2	1	0	0
Transition times for such shocks	0	0'	4	6	8	12

consideration, in percentage deviation terms, from the initial base value for each of the three scenarios. It also identifies the percentage deviation from base line for the variables identified at various stages during the adjustment process. The dynamic adjustment process involved for each scenario is contained in Figure 5.1. The vertical axis for each diagram measures the percentage deviation of that variable from the base line, its starting value, while the horizontal axis measures the time period. Each diagram breaks the adjustment process into four distinct periods as follows. The impact period is that arising immediately on the announcement of the policy, or the time at which an exogenous shock occurs. The short run is described as that occurring over a period of two years, the medium run that occurring from two to four years and the long run from four years onwards.[8]

Scenario A: Base Case

The impact of an instantaneous sharp rise in the risk premium on bonds and equities, in conjunction with a sharp decline in aggregate supply, is an immediate effect upon the asset markets. The q ratio immediately declines sharply, by 8.7 per cent below its

Table 5.9
Simulation Results (% Deviation from the Baseline)

	Variables					
	f	k^p	q	c	y^s	t
Instantaneous impact						
Scenario A	0	0	−8.6742	15.5585	−1.2221	12.3494
Scenario B	0	0	−8.0267	13.8559	−1.8072	12.3284
Scenario C	0	0	−8.9168	16.4084	1.3204	9.5127
Short-run impact						
Scenario A	83.6249	−11.5639	0.4200	2.9377	−6.1351	−1.8014
Scenario B	81.9689	−13.4570	−0.3566	−18.1747	−8.1373	−2.6697
Scenario C	83.4786	−10.7254	1.0188	24.3426	−4.1456	0.4287
Medium-run impact						
Scenario A	19.1160	0.2007	0.1386	−7.4243	−0.2709	−5.8457
Scenario B	24.6118	−2.8299	0.3118	−19.2947	−2.3797	−5.4902
Scenario C	17.5464	3.0183	0.1561	5.0607	1.7621	−6.7887
Long-run impact						
Scenario A	0	0	0	0	0	0
Scenario B	0	0	0	0	0	0
Scenario C	0	0	0	0	0	0

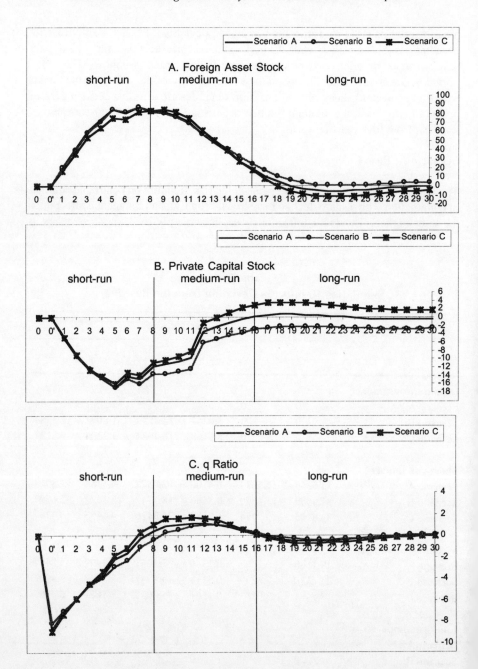

Figure 5.1   Comparison Between the IMF and Radelet and Sachs Approaches

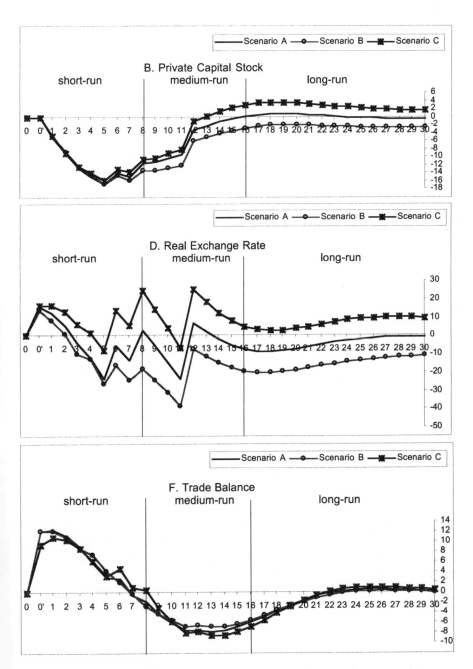

Figure 5.1   Comparison Between the IMF and Radelet and Sachs Approaches
(continued)

base value, resulting in a sharp fall in equity prices and thereby decreasing the market valuation of the capital stock relative to its replacement value. This, consequently, also implies a significant decline in the market valuation of the Thai corporate sector. The nominal and real exchange rate depreciates, contributing to a sharp increase in the nominal interest rate (by 18 per cent from its base value) to maintain the uncovered interest parity condition. The trade balance instantaneously improves by 12 per cent above its base value, resulting from the depreciation of the real exchange rate by 16 per cent above its base value.

During the first year of the short run period the initial decline in the q ratio has an adverse effect on private sector investment, with a resulting decline of private capital stock. The private capital stock declines substantially by 14 per cent below its base value at the end of the first year. Aggregate supply also declines substantially resulting from the decline of the private capital stock, by 9 per cent, for the same period. Inflation initially declines on impact before gradually rising throughout the first year of the short run period. The increased inflation is due to an increase in money wage growth, resulting from aggregate demand decreasing less than aggregate supply.

External developments during the first year of the short run period indicate an appreciation in the real exchange rate. The trade balance, which initially improves on impact, deteriorates thereafter, but remains above its base value due to developments in the real exchange rate. The substantial improvement in the trade balance during the first year of the crisis is consistent with the change in the current account balance. The accumulation of foreign asset stocks reflects current account surpluses. During the remainder of the short run period the q ratio increases continuously. Initially, after the first year, this is insufficient to stimulate sufficient investment so as to increase the overall private capital stock. By year 2, however, there is a recovery of the private capital stock which then stimulates a recovery of aggregate supply. As for external developments the major change relates to an appreciation and then depreciation of the real exchange rate. Although the depreciation of the real exchange rate in the second year increases the country's international competitiveness, the trade balance deteriorates further arising from a recovery of aggregate demand. The effect of this offsets the former effect. The increase in aggregate demand results from an increase in private consumption. Private consumption increases noticeably due to an increase in aggregate supply and real private sector wealth (not shown here), reflecting a recovery of the economy. The current account remains in continual surplus throughout the short run period, assisted by an improvement from baseline in the trade balance. While the trade balance deteriorates throughout after the impact effect it has still improved relative to its base level for most of the short-run period.

Over the medium run the q ratio continuously increases from its level during the short run and becomes positive, above its base value, at the end of the first year of the medium run period, declining thereafter to the long run steady state. This further stimulates an increase in private capital stock and aggregate supply towards its long run steady state, where they have returned to their base value. An increase in private consumption further stimulates an increase in aggregate demand which achieves its highest level at the end of the first year of the medium run period by being 4 per cent above its base value.

Thereafter, both private consumption and aggregate demand decline continuously to the long-run steady state. External developments are characterised by an appreciation of the real exchange rate before depreciating towards long-run equilibrium. This is consistent with the developments in the trade balance. The trade balance moves into a large deficit, bottoming out at some 8 per cent below its baseline at the end of the first year of the medium run period, before improving to the steady state where it has returned to its base level. Foreign asset stocks further decline to the steady state where they have returned to their base level.

Scenario B: the IMF Approach, and Scenario C: the RS Approach

For the whole adjustment process the effects in scenarios B and C are very similar in direction to those identified for scenario A. However, the magnitude of adjustment for some variables in each scenario is very different. On impact the real exchange rate depreciation is largest for scenario C, by 16 per cent from its base value, and smallest for scenario B, by 14 per cent from its base value. The nominal interest rate also increases most in scenario C, by 21 per cent from its base value, and increases least for scenario B, by 16 per cent from its base value, on impact. The trade balance also initially improves for all scenarios, although in scenario C the improvement is less than that for scenarios A and B. The improvement in the trade balance is due to a depreciation of the real exchange rate and a decline in aggregate demand. The improvement of the trade balance in scenario C is less, due to the decline in aggregate demand being noticeably smaller than that for the other cases. Only in scenario C does aggregate supply increase on impact, while the other cases indicate a decline on impact of aggregate supply. In scenario C the increase in aggregate supply arising from the additional public capital stock, due to an increase in public investment spending, is large enough to offset an increase of the real wage rate.

For scenarios A and B the initial decline in aggregate supply mainly results, apart from the exogenous decline itself, from the increase in the real wage rate due to a decline in the inflation rate. A larger decrease in the inflation rate is apparent in scenario B, where a contractionary monetary policy is implemented in response to the crisis. As a result the decline in aggregate supply is greater in scenario B in comparison to that of scenario A on impact.

During the first year of the short run period developments in the private capital stock are very similar in direction and magnitude for all scenarios, with a sharp decline of around 14 per cent below base value apparent. The remainder of the short run period sees an initial further decline in all scenarios before recovering, but the pace of recovery is noticeably different. Recovery is most noticeable in scenario C, with the private capital stock 10 per cent below its base value by the end of the short run (or second year). Scenario B shows the smallest improvement, being 14 per cent below its base value by the end of the short run. Aggregate supply in all scenarios decreases sharply to the lowest level in the first quarter of the second year of the short run period, before increasing thereafter to the end of the short run period. However, with scenario C there is a smaller decline both in the private capital stock and aggregate supply during the first year of the crisis, and a larger improvement throughout the remainder of the short run period.

Aggregate demand and private consumption also show a similar adjustment pattern over the short run. Private consumption[9] declines substantially throughout the end of the first quarter of the second year of the crisis before recovering. A larger decline and a smaller recovery are apparent in scenario B. In scenario B the decline in private consumption is more noticeable, bottoming out at some 6 per cent below its base value in the first quarter of the second year of the short-run period. It is only 2 per cent below base value in the case of scenario C for the same period. During the remainder of the short run period private consumption recovers slightly to be 2 per cent below its base value in scenario B, and has noticeably recovered in scenario C to be 5 per cent above its base value. Based upon the results presented here, therefore, implementing the IMF approach is likely to lead to the largest contraction of domestic demand, with private consumption and investment spending declining dramatically.

In terms of external developments the real exchange rate as a whole is subject to a larger depreciation in scenario C relative to scenarios A and B. For all scenarios the real exchange rate experiences a sharp initial depreciation on impact, then appreciation for a period thereafter, and towards the end of the short run a further depreciation occurs. In scenario B the tightening of monetary policy during the crisis period produces a smaller depreciation of the real exchange rate on impact and a larger appreciation thereafter relative to scenarios A and C.

The adjustment of the trade balance and foreign asset stock during the adjustment period is not much different in both direction and magnitude for all three scenarios. A sizeable initial improvement of the trade balance is apparent on impact before deteriorating throughout the remainder of the short-run. The foreign asset stock improves continuously throughout the short run period, being around 80–83 per cent higher than baseline by the end of it.

In the medium run, for all three scenarios, there is a further recovery of the economy, with the largest recovery being most apparent for scenario C for domestic demand (both in private investment and consumption), the private capital stock, and aggregate supply. During this period investment spending is enhanced primarily due to the recovery of the q ratio, and additional private consumption spending occurs as a result of the increase in real income and private sector wealth. Inflation rises continuously to steady state, where it has returned to its base rate, due to the sizeable increase of aggregate demand offsetting the increase of aggregate supply.

As for external developments the major change relates to a continuous appreciation of the real exchange by the end of the third quarter of the third year of the crisis (period 11), before depreciating again by the end of the crisis period. After the crisis period, period 12, the real exchange rate gradually appreciates throughout the remainder of the medium run period. The appreciation of the real exchange rate causes a deterioration of the trade balance, which deteriorates further throughout the remainder of the crisis period. After this it experiences a gradual improvement over the remainder of the adjustment process until the steady state. The foreign asset stock deteriorates continually throughout the medium-run, indicating current account deficits, and also for a period of time to long run steady state.

In sum, for all scenarios, the exogenous, including policy, shocks have contributed to a large volatility of the real exchange rate throughout the adjustment process. For all scenarios the real exchange rate appreciates (sharp appreciation in scenario B) before depreciating (sharp depreciation in scenario C) throughout the short-run period. The real appreciation is most noticeable with scenario B, by 20 per cent below its base value at the end of the short-run period, while the depreciation is most apparent in scenario C by 25 per cent above its base value at the same period. Over the medium run period, for all scenarios, the real exchange rate experiences a sharp initial appreciation, then depreciation thereafter, and by the end of this period has appreciated. Again the real appreciation is most noticeable with scenario B by 20 per cent below its base value at the end of the medium run period, while a larger depreciation is apparent in scenario C. A prolonged and oscillatory adjustment to the long run steady state is apparent in both scenarios B and C, where a macroeconomic policy response is adopted, while the steady state is achieved much more quickly and with less volatility in scenario A.

5.6   POLICY IMPLICATIONS

The simulation results contain a number of interesting implications for the conduct of policy. First, implementing the IMF approach leads to the largest contraction of domestic demand because private consumption and investment spending decline dramatically. In addition, it results in the slowest recovery of the economy relative to the other two scenarios. However, under the IMF approach a tightening of monetary and fiscal policy during the crisis period results in a smaller depreciation of the real exchange rate on impact and a larger appreciation thereafter. On the other hand, the RS approach produces more favourable outcomes for aggregate demand, both private investment and consumption, the private capital stock, and aggregate supply during the initial phase of the crisis. In addition, it produces the most rapid recovery thereafter. However, in terms of external developments the RS approach results in a larger depreciation of the real exchange rate on impact and a smaller appreciation thereafter.

The IMF approach appears to produce more favourable external developments, while the RS approach brings about more favourable effects upon domestic demand and supply. Fiscal and monetary contraction, as advocated by the IMF, will achieve both a stronger nominal and real exchange rate in the short run but at the cost of a more protracted decline in output, private capital stock, which is bad for long term growth, and aggregate demand. The simulation results suggest that adopting the RS approach could alleviate a severe contraction in domestic demand and supply during the crisis period. In addition, adopting the RS approach can produce the largest recovery thereafter. However the cost of adopting this approach is that the depreciation of the real exchange rate is larger than that for the IMF approach. This implies that Thai enterprises and banks exposed to overseas borrowing would be particularly vulnerable, because their loan obligations would be increased in proportion to the devaluation. Debt servicing obligations would also be increased severely. In addition to that the cost of importing raw materials, energy and machinery would increase. Import businesses would be severely affected. On the positive side, export industries would benefit because of increased competitiveness arising from the depreciation of the real exchange rate. Tourism and related services would also benefit from this. These positive effects would assist the Thai economy to rebound quickly.

A second implication is related to the management and rehabilitation of the Thai financial system. Without question there were macroeconomic imbalances, weak and fragile financial institutions, and inadequate legal foundations in Thailand. A restructuring of the Thai financial sector is therefore a high priority. However from the simulation results, specifically the effects arising from an exogenous shock to aggregate supply from business and banking insolvencies and bankruptcies, it can be suggested that, unlike the IMF approach, a structural reform of the financial system should be implemented over a longer period. Moving too quickly on financial sector reforms, such as abruptly shutting down financial institutions and forcing banks to recapitalise during times of widespread economic distress, can lead to a more severe credit crunch, increased distress for the corporate sector, and a substantial decline in aggregate supply. A poorly-thought-out approach for the recovery of the financial sector can therefore lead to an unnecessarily harsher economic contraction in the real economy. The RS approach might, therefore, be the better policy option in the short-term for dealing with the panic phase of the crisis.

Thirdly, a prolonged and oscillatory adjustment of the key macroeconomic variables to the long run steady state is apparent in both scenarios B and C, where a macroeconomic policy response is adopted, while the steady state is achieved much more quickly and with less volatility in scenario A. This implies that without the adoption of macroeconomic policies, in response to the developments of exogenous shocks, the Thai economy can achieve the long-run steady state earlier. Macroeconomic policies therefore exert a noticeable impact on the adjustment of key macroeconomic variables during the short, medium and long run adjustment process, and therefore should be implemented with great care. The adoption of a one policy suits all philosophy of the IMF during the early stages of the financial crisis for the crisis afflicted economies of East Asia was therefore not at all appropriate, and instead contributed to financial and economic instability.

5.7 CONCLUSIONS

This chapter utilised a dynamic rational expectations macroeconomic model to analyse the adjustment processes arising from a variety of shocks emanating from the financial and economic crisis in Thailand that erupted in July 1997. A numerical simulation analysis that focused upon important aspects of the financial and economic crisis in Thailand was emphasised. Particular emphasis was given to analysing competing macroeconomic policy responses in the light of the crisis.

A major conclusion derived is that implementing the IMF approach, tightening monetary and fiscal policies, produces a stronger exchange rate in the short run but at the cost of a more protracted decline in output, private capital stock and aggregate demand. Overall, the IMF approach produces more favourable effects in terms of external developments. Adopting the RS approach in the short term appears to be better in dealing with the panic phase of the crisis in the initial stage. The RS approach could alleviate the adverse effects arising from the severe contraction in domestic demand and supply during the crisis period. However, the cost of adopting this approach is that the depreciation of the real exchange rate is larger than that for the IMF approach.

Increased risk premiums on holding domestic bonds and equities can lead to severe temporary economic disruptions. However, large contractions in domestic demand can be offset partly through an improvement in the trade balance. Hence sustaining export growth is crucial for offsetting the collapse in domestic demand.

A major improvement in the performance in the Thai financial system is obviously required; in particular, improving systems of accountability so that more accurate evaluations of risk can be formulated. Restructuring of the financial sector is important but needs a more comprehensive and well-thought-out financial restructuring plan, otherwise it may lead to a collapse of aggregate supply brought about through financial and corporate sector insolvencies and bankruptcies which can exacerbate the extent of the crisis on the domestic economy as well as hinder the recovery of it.

NOTES

1 Krugman later changed his point of view on the causes of the crisis. A more recent analysis (Krugman 1999) argues that such weaknesses within the Asian economies, such as corruption and moral hazard, cannot explain the depth and severity of the crisis. It should, instead, be blamed on financial panic and overly liberalised international and domestic financial systems.

2 A fuller discussion of the underlying theoretical assumptions upon which the model is built can be found in Auepiyachut (2000).

3 Aggregate supply rather than aggregate demand is used, as it is a better measure of domestic income generated.

4   See Auepiyachut (2000) for a fuller discussion.
5   For example, through immediate bank closures, and a quick restoration of minimum capital adequacy standards for those banks that remained.
6   The numerical simulation procedure utilised to identify the steady state and adjustment process of the macroeconomic variables is known as 'Saddlepoint', devised for solving linear rational expectations models with constant coefficients. It is the continuous time analogue of the linear difference model with rational expectations studied in Blanchard and Kahn (1980).
7   Indicative of developments in the market valuation of Thai companies.
8   The simulation results presented were restricted to thirty time periods only and assumed that four time periods equal one year. In Figure 5.1, 0–0' represents the impact period, 0'–8 represents the short run period, 8–16 represents the medium run period and 16-onwards represents the long run period. In most cases steady state equilibrium was achieved quickly for most of the variables, but in other cases it took more than thirty time periods to achieve steady state.
9   Private consumption expenditure is not shown in Figure 5.1.

REFERENCES

Aschauer, D.A. (1989), 'Is Public Expenditure Productive?' *Journal of Monetary Economics*, **23**, 177–200.
Auepiyachut, W. (2000), 'Financial Liberalisation and Economic Crisis: Macromodelling the Thai Economy', unpublished PhD dissertation, University of Wollongong.
Austin, H.W. and W.H. Buiter (1982), 'Saddlepoint: a Program for Solving Continuous Time Linear Rational Expectations Models', London School of Economics, Discussion Paper: A37, November.
Bank of Thailand, *Annual Economic Report*, various issues.
Blanchard, O.J. and C.M. Kahn (1980), 'The Solution of Linear Difference Models under Rational Expectations', *Econometrics*, **48** (5), 1305–11.
Corsetti, G., P. Pesenti and N. Roubini (1998), 'What Caused the Asian Currency and Financial Crisis?', unpublished manuscript, available at <http://www.stern.nyu.edu/globalmacro/>.
Dornbusch, R. (1976), 'Expectations and Exchange Rate Dynamics', *Journal of Political Economy*, **84**, 1161–76.
Dornbusch, R. (1998), 'Asian Crisis Themes', mimeo, MIT-Massachusetts Institute of Technology.
Fischer, S. (1997), 'Capital Account Liberalisation and the Role of the IMF', 19 September, available at <www.imf.org/external/np/apd/asia/FISCHER.html>.
Fischer, S. (1998), 'The Asian Crisis: a View from the IMF', available at <www.imf.org/external/np/apd/asia/FISCHER.html>.

Harvie, C. (1993), 'The Macroeconomic Effects of Oil Shocks under Fixed and Flexible Exchange Rates – a Comparison', *OPEC Review*, Autumn.

Harvie, C. and L. Gower (1993), 'Resource Shocks and Macroeconomic adjustment in the Short Run and Long Run', *The Middle East Business and Economic Review*, **5** (1), 1–14.

Harvie, C. and C. Kearney (1994), 'Public Infrastructure Capital and Private Investment', *Proceedings*, Midsouth Academy of Economics and Finance, February, Biloxi, USA, pp. 229–38.

Krugman, P. (1998a), 'Bubble, Boom, Crash: Theoretical Notes on Asia's Crisis', mimeo.

Krugman, P. (1998b), 'What Happened to Asia?', mimeo, MIT.

Krugman, P. (1998c), 'Fire Sale FDI', mimeo, MIT.

Krugman, P. (1999), 'The Return of Depression Economics', *Foreign Affairs*, **78** (1), (January/February), 56–74.

McKibbin, W.E.G. (1998), 'International Mobile Capital and the Global Economy', in R.H. McLeod and R. Garnaut (eds), *East Asia in Crisis: From Being a Miracle to Needing One*, London: Routledge.

Nananukool, S. (1998), 'Learning from the Asian Currency Crisis – an Insider View from Thailand', paper presented at the Carnegie Mellon University, Graduate School of Industrial Administration, 13 March, available at <www.stern.nyu.edu/globalmacro/>.

NEDSDB, *National Income for Thailand-Statistical Tables*, various issues, 1960–1996.

Radelet, S. and J. Sachs (1998a), 'The East Asian Financial Crisis: Diagnosis, Remedies, Prospects', *Brookings Papers on Economic Activity*, **1**, 1–74.

Radelet, S. and J. Sachs (1998b), 'The Onset of the East Asian Financial Crisis', mimeo, Harvard Institute for International Development.

Radelet, S. and J. Sachs (1999), 'What Have We Learned so far, from the Asian Financial Crisis?', unpublished manuscript, available at <http://www.stern.nyu.edu/globalmacro/>.

Sachs, J. (1997b), 'The Wrong Medicine for Asia', *New York Times*, 3 November, <www.stern.nyu.edu/globalmacro/>.

Warr, P.G. (1998), 'Thailand', in R.H. McLeod and R. Garnaut (eds), *East Asia in Crisis: From Being a Miracle to Needing One*, London: Routledge.

6 Financial Crisis Management in Korea: Processes and Consequences

Junggun Oh, Hyun-Hoon Lee and Charles Harvie

6.1   INTRODUCTION

In late November 1997, Korea turned to the International Monetary Fund (IMF), and other international financial organisations, for emergency support funds to deal with the currency and financial crises that had broken out earlier that month. The government negotiated an extension of the maturities of financial institutions' short-term external debts in January 1998, and issued foreign-currency-denominated government bonds in April that year. In order to restore Korea's international credibility it launched economic stabilisation policies, in particular a high interest rate policy, and mounted a wide-ranging drive for structural reform of the financial, corporate, labour and public sectors, which had a positive effect on the recovery of confidence. Such increased confidence, bolstered by a huge current account surplus, boosted capital inflows and stabilised the exchange rate.

With the recovery of stability in the foreign exchange market, the stance of monetary policy then turned to achieve a lower interest rate so as to reverse the decline in domestic consumption and investment demand. As a result, a remarkable recovery began in the second half of 1998 that gathered momentum in 1999. Such a quick and strong V-shaped economic recovery from the crisis was mainly thanks to supportive monetary and fiscal policies, and progress in structural reforms. However, since the second half of 2000 the Korean economy has again begun to show some instability due to a slow-down of GDP growth and a bearish movement of the stock market. These, it can be argued, have mainly arisen from a too rapid V-shape recovery without a sufficient restructuring of the financial and corporate sectors (KDI 2000).

This chapter aims at reviewing and assessing the macroeconomic management and restructuring process to cope with the unprecedented financial crisis in the Korean economy. Section 6.2 discusses the macroeconomic management stance adopted by the Korean monetary authority in an effort to stabilise the currency, and to recover and maintain macroeconomic stability. This is followed in Section 6.3 by a discussion of the structural reform process pursued by the Korean government in an effort to address more fundamental weaknesses in the Korean economy. Section 6.4 will then identify external and internal challenges that Korea has to overcome in order to obtain a full recovery from the crisis and maintain sustainable growth. Finally, Section 6.5 presents some concluding remarks.

6.2   MACROECONOMIC POLICIES

6.2.1   Monetary and Exchange Rate Policies

After the crises had broken out, the Bank of Korea at first conducted monetary policy flexibly to assist the government's policy initiatives for economic stabilisation, focusing upon that of the financial markets, and structural reform. It also supported the government's financing of financial restructuring. After the financial markets regained their stability and the economy began to revive, the Bank placed the focus of its monetary policy on the building of a firm basis for price stability.

Foreign exchange market stabilisation
When the crises erupted the Bank judged that the most urgent task was to stabilise the foreign exchange and financial markets, and, consequently, its policies were directed toward this goal. To help stabilise the foreign exchange market the Bank pushed its market intervention rate up, dramatically, to 35 per cent per annum. This high interest rate policy was seen as the only viable option to engineer a rapid stabilisation of the foreign exchange rate and to curb capital outflows. The foreign exchange market subsequently settled down rapidly from early in the second quarter of 1998. This reflected the government's success in negotiating a prolongation of financial institutions' short-term external debts, the issuing of foreign-currency-denominated government bonds, and the continued monthly surplus on the current account from January 1998.

However, results from empirical studies on the effects of the high interest rate policy on the stabilisation of the foreign exchange market during the crisis in Korea, produce conflicting conclusions. Goldfajn and Baig (1998) and Park and Choi (1999) show that the increase in the interest rate did not significantly affect the devaluation of the exchange rate, while according to Cho and West (1999) and Basurto and Ghosh (2000) the increase in the interest rate did significantly affect the extent of the devaluation of the exchange rate. In another study Oh (2000c) shows that the positive correlation between the interest rate and the exchange rate obtained for Korea, which is contrary to the traditional theory of the interest rate parity condition, is mainly due to the fact that the stock market is more developed and active than the bond market.

This is contrary to the basis of the theory behind the interest rate parity condition. Lee (1999), however, argues that the IMF's emergency operation was built on a wrong diagnosis and prognosis, which intensified the financial crisis and caused the economic contraction to be a full-fledged one.

In fact, there were a number of pernicious side-effects accompanying the high interest rate policy. It accelerated the slow-down in real economic activities through its contraction of consumption and investment, and it greatly increased the incidence of corporate failure and the accumulation of bad loans by financial institutions. In response, in order to prevent too deep a contraction of the real economy, from the second quarter of 1998 the Bank shifted its policy focus from stabilising the foreign exchange market to preventing the economy from contracting too deeply. The Bank steadily lowered its market intervention rate from the second quarter, when foreign exchange market conditions had improved considerably, thanks to the sustained current account surplus, the arrival of support funds from the international financial institutions, and renewed inflows of foreign investment capital. The scale and pace of the reduction of interest rates was cautiously conducted, taking into consideration developments in the real economy and the foreign exchange market, since the external environment was still unsettled with international financial markets in turmoil. Call rates consequently dropped to 8.5 per cent by the end of August 1998. As the Bank steadily brought down its market intervention rate, the call-market rate eased to 6.5 per cent by the end of December. In addition, in September 1998, the Bank lowered the interest rate on the 'aggregate credit' it supplies to banks from 5 per cent to 3 per cent, thus inducing them to reduce their lending rates. This effectively brought about a steady decline both in market interest rates and in the lending rates of financial institutions (see Figure 6.1).

During the first half of 1999 the financial and foreign exchange markets attained a fair degree of stability. In contrast, over the second half of the year, financial markets experienced increased uncertainties, and their re-stabilisation became a primary consideration for policy-makers. In particular, the difficulties of the troubled Daewoo Group and investment trust companies' overhang of potential beneficiary certificates redemptions, led to a renewed focus on financial market stability in the framing of interest rate policy from August onwards. The Bank regarded the stabilisation of the financial markets as the most pressing issue and thus reduced the call rate step by step, finally bringing it to the level of 4.75 per cent in May 1999 where it was maintained until January 2000.

Rapid economic recovery

From the fourth quarter of 1998 the economic restructuring efforts began to achieve very gratifying results. Real GDP growth which had registered a deeply negative figure in 1998, bounced back to 10.3 per cent in 1999 led by the revival of domestic demand and by the expansion of exports (see Figure 6.2). The unemployment rate, which had peaked at 8.6 per cent in February 1999, then started to ease and stood at 4.8 per cent in December 1999. The current account meanwhile achieved a sizeable

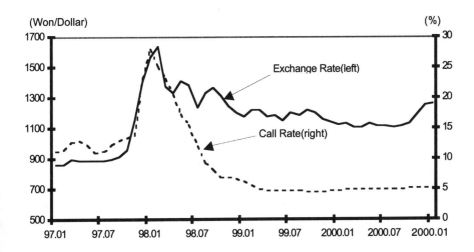

Note: Monthly average
Source: The Bank of Korea

Figure 6.1   Exchange Rate and Interest Rate Movements

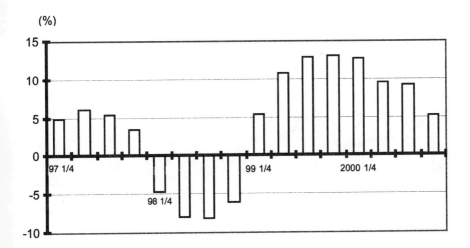

Note: Quarterly.
Source: The Bank of Korea

Figure 6.2   GDP Growth Rate (%)

surplus of US$24 billion in 1999 following a surplus of US$40 billion in 1998. The rapid recovery of the domestic economy continued until mid-2000, and the current account also remained in surplus to the tune of US$10 billion in 2000.

With the help of the low interest rate policy the real economy accelerated its upward trend, with a GDP growth rate of 10.3 per cent achieved in 1999. With such a rapid V-shape recovery the economy was estimated to have returned back to its potential production level around the beginning of 2000, and, indeed, to have shown some excess demand during 2000. As a consequence long-term interest rates had been rising in response to the rapid expansion of the real economy and fears of financial market instability, thus widening the spread between long-term and short-term rates. Taking these points into consideration, the Bank of Korea decided to raise its target for the overnight call rate from 4.75 per cent to 5.00 per cent in February 2001.

From the beginning of 1998 inflation maintained a downward trend, and remained low throughout 1999. However, inflationary pressures began to re-emerge during 2000. Consumer prices showed a sharply rising trend after June 2000, mainly due to the surge in international oil prices, increases in public service charges, and in the price of farm–livestock–fisheries products (see Figure 6.3). However, inflation remained well below its pre crisis rate.

Financial markets, on the other hand, showed large fluctuations at one stage due to a combination of factors including: a rapid rise in international oil prices; the drop

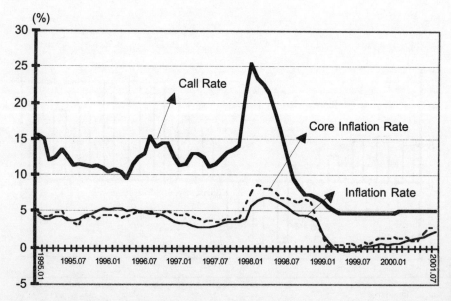

Source: Bank of Korea

Figure 6.3   Call Rate and Inflation Rates

in semiconductor prices; and the breakdown of the planned deal for Daewoo Motor Company. Market apprehensions, however, have subsided somewhat following the blunting of the surge in international oil prices and the publication of the government's plan for further corporate and financial restructuring. Taking price movements and the situation of the financial markets into consideration, the Bank of Korea decided to raise its target for the overnight call rate from 5.00 per cent to 5.25 per cent in October 2000.

However, since the second half of 2000, the Korean economy has again begun to show some instability due to the slow-down of growth and the bearish movement of the stock market. Some argue that this was mainly the result of a too rapid V-shape recovery without the necessary restructuring of the financial and corporate sectors (KDI 2000). In particular, the unveiling of the unhealthy financial structures of some subsidiaries of the Hyundai group in mid-2000 again increased uncertainty in financial markets, and this seemed to represent a turning point in terms of changing the recovering trend to one of a slow-down of the economy. In response to the newly changed situation the Bank of Korea decreased the call rate from 5.25 per cent to 5.0 per cent in February 2001, reversing the upward shift in the previous October.

Stock prices exhibited a sharp increase over a short period of time, from mid-1998 to early 2000, raising apprehensions over an asset price bubble. With the help of a boom in the stock market, stocks worth 35 trillion Korean won, equivalent to 14 per cent of total market capitalisation, were newly issued in 2000. As a result, an excess supply phenomenon began to appear in the stock market. Consequently, stock prices began to ease from the second quarter of 2000 (see Figure 6.4). On the other hand, a boom in the stock market, encouraged by the low interest rate policy, induced an inflow of capital into the Korean stock market, which led to an appreciation of the Korean won. As a result, the surplus on the current account began to narrow (see Figure 6.5). In view of this it seems difficult for a small open economy, such as Korea's, to carry out monetary policy focusing only on price stability without taking into consideration the current account position and financial market stability, even if it adopts inflation targeting. In other words, it faces the problem of attaining 'the impossible holy trinity'.[1]

6.2.2   The Adoption of the Inflation Targeting System

The monetary policy framework was also fundamentally changed after the crisis. An inflation targeting system was introduced in Korea under the provisions of the fully-revised Bank of Korea Act of 1997.[2] The Act is concerned with establishing the neutrality[3] and autonomy[4] of monetary policy, with price stability being declared the sole objective of the Bank of Korea. Under its provisions the Bank of Korea is required to set an inflation target every year and do its best to achieve it. The Bank of Korea has set an annual target since 1998 in accordance with the related provisions of the Act.

The Bank of Korea adopted the Consumer Price Index (CPI) in 1998 as its

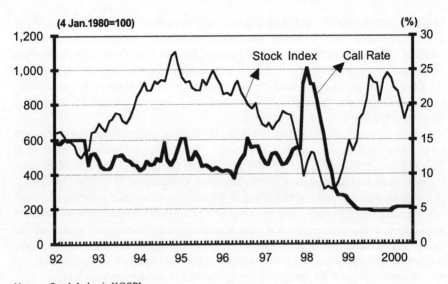

(4 Jan.1980=100)

Note: Stock Index is KOSPI
Source: The Bank of Korea

Figure 6.4   Call Rate and the Stock Price Index

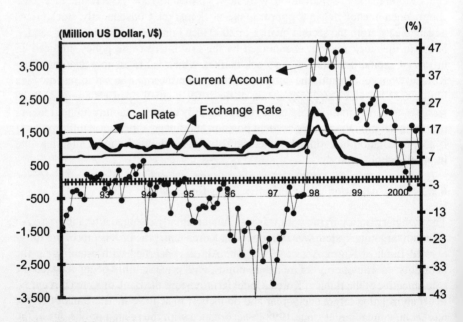

Source: Bank of Korea

Figure 6.5   Call Rate, Exchange Rate and the Current Account

benchmark indicator when the inflation targeting system was first implemented. The CPI is, however, seriously affected by temporary or transitory shocks such as natural disasters or sharp fluctuations of international oil prices. Accordingly, the Bank decided that monetary policy should be formulated and implemented on the basis of the underlying trend of prices since 2000. There are various methods of adjusting the CPI to find the underlying trend of prices, such as the method of adjustment by exclusion and the trimmed mean method. Among these options the Bank of Korea judged the method of 'adjustment by exclusion' best suited for the adjustment of the CPI in Korea,[5] and then decided to employ, from 2000 onwards, the underlying inflation rate which strips out from the CPI index the price changes of petroleum-related products and agricultural products except cereals.

The Bank of Korea used a short-term inflation target with a one-year time horizon when it established the inflation targets for 1998 and 1999. There is, however, a time lag in the monetary transmission mechanism. The Bank of Korea therefore resolved to set, in addition to an annual inflation target for the coming year, a mid-term inflation target from 2001 onwards, so as to maintain the consistency of monetary policy over the medium term.[6] For the year 2001 onwards, the Bank set the mid-term inflation target of 2.5 per cent on an annual average basis each year. In addition, the Bank of Korea also introduced various measures to enhance the transparency, credibility and accountability of monetary policy[7] (see Figure 6.6).

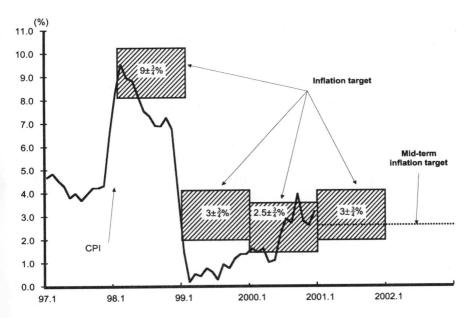

Figure 6.6   Inflation Targets and Inflation Rates

In Korea, three years have passed since the inflation targeting system was introduced. Accordingly it seems too early to assess the performance of the new system. Nevertheless, a few observations can be made in regard to Korea's experiences.

First, the average rate of inflation since the adoption of the inflation targeting system is much lower than that before it was introduced. In 1998 and 1999 the actual inflation rates even remained far below the inflation targets, with the help of strong deflationary factors: the reduced costs of imports due to the continuing appreciation of the Korean won; the reduced burden of financial costs borne by business firms owing to improved financial structures and the easing of interest rates; a decline in manpower costs reflecting improved labour productivity and labour market flexibility; and price competition between retailers having become intense in the fight to secure customers in the severe economic depression after the crisis.

In 2000 the economy seemed to have returned to a normal situation. In particular, the effects of a sharp rebound of the Korean won after its depreciation during the crisis, which had contributed to making the inflation rates remain below the lower bound of the inflation target in 1998 and 1999, had been almost fully absorbed. Nevertheless, the inflation rate in 2000 remained within the band of the inflation target.

Second, Korea has been carrying out ongoing financial and corporate sector restructuring and reform. Accordingly, although inflation targeting has been adopted, the Bank of Korea should take into account financial stability as well as price stability in implementing monetary policies. Upon the outbreak of the currency crisis the Bank, in consultation with the IMF, had dramatically raised its market intervention rate to 35 per cent, in order to engineer a rapid stabilisation of the exchange rate. Thus, major market interest rates had increased to between 30–40 per cent at the end of 1997, and they remained at around the 20-per-cent level until March 1998. On the other hand, since 2000, inflationary pressure had been increasing, but the Bank increased the call rate step by step, by 0.25 of a percentage point each time, taking into account the ongoing instability of the financial market.

6.2.3   Fiscal policy

Expansionary fiscal policy, along with the easing of monetary policy, contributed to economic recovery. Increased outlays, focused on assisting the unemployed and small and medium-sized enterprises, boosted Korean government spending. According to the fiscal impulse indicator, expansionary fiscal policy had continued consecutively from 1997 to 1998 (see Table 6.1). Support for financial sector restructuring and increased spending to combat unemployment resulted in a large fiscal deficit of just over 4 per cent of GDP in 1998 (see Table 6.2). In response, in order to reduce the large fiscal deficit, the government turned the stance of fiscal policy from an expansionary one to a tight one from the second half of 1999, when the economy showed a sharp recovery. A tight policy stance continued into 2000. In 2000, an unexpectedly high increase in tax revenue and a decrease in the expenditure on the

Table 6.1
Fiscal Impulse Indicator (%)

1995	1996	1997	1998	1999	2000
0.2	0.0	1.7	0.7	−0.3	−3.1

Note: A positive value denotes an expansionary fiscal policy while a minus value indicates a tightening of fiscal policy.
Source: Oh, Kim and Bae (2001)

Table 6.2
Consolidated Government Budget Balance (Trillion Won, %)

	1996	1997	1998	1999	2000
Consolidated Budget Balance	1.1	−7.0	−18.8	−13.1	5.6
(Ratio to GDP (%))	0.3	−1.5	−4.2	−2.7	1.1

Source: Ministry of Finance and Economy, Korea

unemployed due to economic recovery, along with the tight fiscal policy itself, resulted in a budget surplus of 1.1 per cent of GDP.

The issue of government bonds was expanded substantially to finance the budget deficits during the worst of the crisis in 1997–98. Accordingly, government debt substantially increased. The gross debt of the general government, including the central and local government, increased from 14.4 per cent of GDP in 1997 to 23.1 per cent in 2000 (see Table 6.3), although this was still well below the OECD average of about 70 per cent of GDP. However, government-guaranteed debt also increased rapidly from 3 per cent of GDP in 1997 to 14 per cent in 2000. As a consequence, the overall debt ratio reached nearly 38 per cent of GDP at the end of 2000. The impact of expanding government indebtedness on the budget is reflected in the sharp increase in interest payments. Limiting the rise in government debt is important, therefore, given the pressure for increased social welfare spending and the need for further resources to be devoted to financial restructuring.

The Bank of Korea urged that government and public bonds be issued at market rates, thus paving the way for a dramatic development of the domestic bond market. Prior to the crisis, large-scale issues of government bonds had previously been unusual and they had been absorbed either by the Bank of Korea or by financial institutions at a predetermined price. Thus, their pricing had failed to incorporate market interest rates and market liquidity conditions. From 1998, after consultations with the Bank of Korea, government and public bonds have been issued through competitive bidding

Table 6.3
Government Debt (Trillion Won, %)

	1997	1998	1999	2000
Central Government Debt	50.5	71.4	89.7	100.9
(Ratio to GDP (%))	11.1	15.9	18.6	19.5
General Government* Debt	65.6	87.6	107.7	119.7
(Ratio to GDP (%))	14.4	19.5	22.3	23.1
Including Government-				
guaranteed Debt	78.6	159.6	189.2	194.2
(Ratio to GDP (%))	17.3	35.5	39.2	37.5

* Central government and local government
Source: Ministry of Finance and Economy, Korea

among financial institutions. Following the improvement of the system of issuing government bonds the interest rate on Treasury bonds now plays a major role as a benchmark for investment decisions in the domestic bond market, which also facilitates efficient monetary policy implementation.

6.3   STRUCTURAL REFORMS

Because the Korean crisis had its roots in the weakened fundamentals of the economy, attempting to stabilise only the financial market, without an emphasis on structural reforms, would be like treating the symptoms without addressing the cause.[8] Accordingly, since the onset of the financial crisis in 1997, the Korean government has pursued structural reforms in almost all areas of the economy. The discussion in the remainder of this section focuses upon reforms, and progress made, in five key sectors: the financial sector; the corporate sector; the labour market; the public sector; as well as in the capital and foreign exchange markets.

6.3.1   Financial Sector Restructuring

Before the financial crisis the Korean government was actively involved in the industrialisation of the economy. This government-led economic development policy was considered to have led the nation to its remarkable economic successes in the 1960s–1980s. However, after the crisis, the IMF, and others, criticised the government-led economic policies as they had resulted not only in corruption but also moral hazard among enterprises and banks. They also criticised the Korean government's imprudent liberalisation of financial markets during the early 1990s; since appropriate supervision and prudential regulation had not accompanied the rapid liberalisation of these markets.

Without an appropriate regulatory and supervisory framework, financial liberalisation encouraged Korean financial institutions, commercial banks as well as non-bank financial institutions, to borrow from overseas. This, increasingly, took the form of short-term borrowing in foreign currency at lower interest rates, encouraged by the liberalisation of borrowing in this form from 1993. These funds were then lent in the form of domestic long-term loans at higher interest rates. These developments led to a serious mismatch in maturities between borrowing and lending, and to over exposed risk without proper hedging, and to making financial institutions vulnerable to financial shocks. This was compounded by moral hazard problems[9] whereby these financial institutions held the belief that the government would not allow them to fail.[10] Korea's total external liability at the end of November 1997 amounted to US$161.8 billion. Of this, nearly 60 per cent was short term debt with a maturity of less than one year. At the end of 1996, this figure was as high as 64.4 per cent. On the lending side, nearly 83.7 per cent of total outstanding loans had a maturity of more than one year. This maturity imbalance between short run borrowing and long run lending was particularly pertinent with regard to the merchant banks. The build up of short term unhedged debt and the term structure imbalance, exposed Korea to a sudden deterioration of international lenders and investors' confidence in the economy (Sakong 2000). This fragile debt structure played a crucial role in triggering the financial crisis. The onset of the financial crisis further exposed the many weaknesses of the financial sector, such as its unsound lending practices, unhedged foreign borrowing, weak liquidity positions, and its ineffective supervisory system.

The financial sector was, therefore, the most urgent one in need of reform, among other reasons because of its importance for reform in other sectors. In the short run financial sector reform and restructuring was aimed at stabilising the financial system by eradicating the problem of non performing assets, and restructuring, or closing, insolvent financial institutions and rehabilitating viable ones. In the long run the focus would be on attaining international standards in the governance, soundness and efficiency of financial institutions, as well as for the regulatory and supervisory institutions. In order to enhance financial supervision, two financial supervisory authorities, the powerful Financial Supervisory Commission (FSC) and Financial Supervisory Service (FSS), were newly created in early 1998. In addition, in order to facilitate financial sector reform, the Korea Asset Management Corporation (KAMCO)[11] and the Korea Deposit Insurance Corporation (KDIC) were reorganised.

In the wake of the financial crisis the authorities closed or suspended the operations of a number of non-viable financial institutions, including, most notably, the operations of a number of merchant banks. The merchant banks are wholesale financial institutions engaged in underwriting primary capital market issues, leasing and short term unsecured lending. A key component of their funding activities is borrowing in foreign markets. At the end of 1996, there were 30 merchant banks operating in Korea. They often competed directly with commercial banks but were subject to less stringent regulatory regimes. They were not subject to the same ownership limitations as commercial banks, and many were in fact owned by large industrial groups to whom they provided finance. They were permitted to assume much higher interest rates and currency risk than the commercial banks. Merchant banks usually lent without collateral and therefore had less protection in the case of default. Korea's merchant banks had become very aggressive lenders before the crisis relying heavily on foreign currency funding, and hence their currency mismatches were larger than those of the commercial banks. Internationally, the merchant banks also developed considerable loan exposure to southeast Asia and other emerging markets which were badly affected by the 1997 crisis. In addition to the merchant banks, other non bank financial institutions including securities companies and investment trust companies all had significant exposure in currency, bond and equity markets.

In November and December 1997 KAMCO bought 3 trillion won in impaired loans from the merchant banks and reimbursed depositors for 5 trillion won. Also in December the operations of fourteen merchant banks were suspended, and all thirty were ordered to submit restructuring plans by 31 December. These plans had to specify how these banks would reach BIS capitalisation ratios of 4 per cent by March 1998, 6 per cent by June 1998, and 8 per cent by June 1999. If the rehabilitation plan was accepted banks would be obliged to sign a managerial contract with the government, which would include an explicit commitment to meet these deadlines as well as to achieve other performance indicators. If their plans did not meet approval then their licences would be revoked. The rehabilitation process was applied in a stringent way, with the government demonstrating a clear intent to close insolvent institutions. In the event, fourteen merchant banks were closed when their plans were judged to be unacceptable. If the remaining banks did not meet the performance criteria in their agreements, stronger corrective measures would be applied including closure of the bank. Due to a continual decline in the financial strength of the merchant banks, it was inevitable that further fatalities would occur. Indeed, by the end of 2000 the number of merchant banks fell to 10 from a pre crisis total of 30.

As for the commercial banks, at the end of 1997 14 out of the 33 (including Korea First Bank and Seoul Bank) had less than the 8 per cent minimum capital asset ratio. Korea First Bank's capital was in fact negative, while Seoul Bank's capital ratio was less than 1 per cent. Thus, a sizeable portion of the banking system was clearly under capitalised. In January 1998 two of Korea's largest banks, Korea First Bank and Seoul Bank, were recapitalised with public funds and effectively nationalised.[12] Korea First Bank was subsequently sold to a foreign consortium. The remaining 12 banks whose capital adequacy ratios had fallen short of 8 per cent at the end of December 1997, were required to prepare a rehabilitation plan by 15 April 1998 demonstrating how they would achieve the required ratio of 8 per cent within two years. These banks were also required to sign contracts with internationally recognised accounting firms to conduct diagnostic reviews and provide an assessment of the recapitalisation plans. They would also be used as part of the FSC's assessment of the bank. On 29 June 1998 the FSC announced that five insolvent, or 'disapproved', commercial banks would be closed and absorbed by purchases and acquisitions in July 1998 by healthier banks. The seven 'conditionally approved' banks took corrective actions imposed by the FSC to further improve their soundness, and would be monitored closely thereafter. The FSC also signalled that a review of all banks would take place. They would be required to engage in similar diagnostic reviews by internationally recognised accounting firms. If a bank's capital adequacy ratio fell below 8 per cent in the future, that bank would be obliged to submit to restructuring procedures already enforced on the original 12 undercapitalised banks.

Since 1997 the number of financial institutions has noticeably declined, as shown in Table 6.4. The number of commercial banks decreased to 22 at the end of 2000 from 33 at the end of November 1997. Of the 30 merchant banks operating in 1997, 21 have been either closed or merged, respectively, and as a result only 10 were in business at the end of 2000. The number of other non-bank financial institutions has also been reduced over the period, except for securities companies whose number increased from 36 to 43.

The public sector contribution to the restructuring of the financial sector has been substantial. At the beginning of the crisis the government had allocated 64 trillion won (US$53.3 billion) in public funds to support financial sector restructuring. By the end of 1999 the government had used the entire allocation of funds to purchase 20.5 trillion won (US$17.1 billion) in NPLs from banks and secondary financial institutions through KAMCO. It also provided 43.5 trillion won (US$36.2 billion) in recapitalisation and deposit repayment support through KDIC. In 2000, an additional 35 trillion won (US$29.2 billion) was injected. From November 1997 to December 2000, the government has injected 127 trillion won in public funds (US$105.8 billion) into the financial sector (see Table 6.5). However, this is not the end. In December 2000, the government decided that it would need to raise a further 40 trillion won (US$33.3 billion).

Thanks to the injection of public funds and massive rights offerings, the BIS ratios of domestic banks continued to rise. At the end of 1999 the average BIS ratio of 17 commercial banks was 10.8 per cent, which was well above the BIS recommended level of 8 per cent. At the same time the total amount of domestic financial institutions' NPLs has rapidly decreased from 112 trillion won (March 1998) to 66.7 trillion (December 1998) and to 50.2 trillion won (December 1999).

In addition, measures to improve the governance structures of remaining banks, securities companies, investment trust companies, and merchant banking corporations have also been put in place. An outside director system and an audit committee system were introduced through amendment of the legislation concerning these financial institutions. Outside directors must be appointed to make up over half (with at least 3 persons) of the total board membership and an audit committee must be set up with outside directors forming at least two-thirds of the membership. Criteria for internal

Table 6.4

Number of Financial Institutions[a] in Korea (1997–2000)

	End of 1997 no. of financial institutions	1998			1999			2000			End of 2000 no. of financial institutions
		Closed	Merged[b]	Newly installed	Closed	Merged[b]	Newly installed	Closed	Merged[b]	Newly installed	
Commercial Banks	33	5	3	–	–	2	–	–	1	–	22
Merchant Banks	30	16	–	–	1	3	–	1	–	1	10
Securities Companies	36	6	–	1	–	–	1	–	1	12	43
Investment Trust Companies	31	6	–	–	–	1	–	–	–	3	27
Insurance Companies	45	4	1	–	–	–	–	1	5	–	34
Others[c]	1 897	91	16	13	126	55	6	111	55	2	1 464
Total	2 072	128	20	14	127	61	7	113	62	18	1 600

Notes: a Branches of foreign companies are excluded.
         b Number of companies reduced, due to M&As
         c Others include mutual savings and finance companies, and credit unions.

Source: The Bank of Korea, 'The Major Results of Financial Restructuring in 2000', *Josatongye Wolbo (Monthly Economic Bulletin)*, February 2001 (in Korean).

126

Table 6.5

The Contribution of Public Funds to the Financial Sector Restructuring (November 1997 – December 2000) Unit: Trillion Won

	KDIC	Re-capital-isation	Purchase of NPLs	Purchase of acquired asset	Deposit reim-burse-ment	KAMCO	Gov't Budget	Bank of Korea	Total
Commercial Banks	39.7	20.9	10.5	8.3	–	21.0	18.0	0.9	79.6
Merchant Banks	11.6	1.5	–	–	10.2	1.8	–	–	13.4
Securities Companies	4.9	4.9	–	–	0.01	0.1	–	–	5.0
Investment Trust Companies	–	–	–	–	–	8.2	0.90	–	9.1
Insurance Companies	10.8	8.8	1.6	0.3	–	1.7	–	–	12.5
Others[a]	5.2	0.0	0.0	–	5.2	2.1	–	–	7.3
Total	72.3	36.1	12.2	8.6	15.4	34.9	18.9	0.9	126.9

Note: a Others include mutual savings and finance companies, and credit unions.

Source: The Bank of Korea, 'The Major Results of Financial Restructuring in 2000', *Josatongye Wolbo (Monthly Economic Bulletin),* February 2001 (in Korean).

controls and a system for compliance were introduced to strengthen the soundness of financial institutions. The legal rights of minority shareholders have been strengthened by lowering the holding thresholds for certain rights.

Thus far the restructuring of the financial sector has primarily focused on the clearance of depressed assets under government supervision. However, the increasing presence of foreign financial companies in Korea is likely to further drive market-oriented reforms. Capital market liberalisation and the promotion of FDI are, therefore, also important aspects of the restructuring process. Various measures were taken by the Korean government to liberalise the capital market and to promote FDI. The ceiling on foreign investment in Korean equities was raised from 26 per cent to 55 per cent in December 1997, and was completely abolished in May 1998. Thus, foreign financial institutions have been allowed to establish subsidiary banks and security companies, and to set up joint-venture banks. Virtually all restrictions on foreign investors' access to the bond markets had been lifted by 1 January 1998. With new players in the market, competition among financial companies will become stiffer. Moreover, as major international banks become larger and more diversified, strategic alliances and M&As among financial companies in Korea will increase. Easing rules governing ownership was seen as one means of strengthening governance, permitting both foreign and domestic interests to acquire strategic stakes in Korean institutions. Foreign ownership of up to 100 per cent was allowed as of April 1998. However, as foreigners reach the thresholds of 10 per cent, 25 per cent, and 33 per cent of total equity, they are subject to increasingly strong review by the FSC. Similar rules were also imposed on domestic investors seeking strategic positions in banks.

Up until recently financial sector restructuring has primarily focused on the commercial and merchant banks. However, attention is now increasingly turning to the restructuring of other non-bank financial institutions. In particular, many of the investment trust companies (ITCs), which had expanded their exposure to the corporate sector in 1998 and 1999, are undercapitalised, and remain vulnerable to turmoil in the corporate sector. The restructuring of ITCs has been postponed several times. For example, the government had already declared Korea Investment Trust and Daehan Investment Trust to be insolvent financial institutions, and had agreed to inject 8 trillion won into the two largest investment-trust firms. Yet, only 3 trillion won in public funds had been injected into these by early 2000. Confidence in the trust companies has ebbed quickly and their investors have withdrawn, thereby putting the squeeze on the huge family-controlled conglomerates, or *chaebols*, the trust companies' biggest borrowers. The Korean government has decided to provide an additional 4.9 trillion won in public funds to the two troubled investment trust companies. However, the public funds are unlikely to cover the total amount of the two investment companies' liabilities.

6.3.2   Corporate Sector Reform

The very high leverage and over investment of Korean firms played another crucial role in causing the financial crisis. In particular, the *chaebols* in Korea tended to borrow excessively through cross payment guarantees among inter-linked subsidiaries.[13] By the end of 1997 the top 30 *chaebols* had deb–equity ratios of 519 per cent, in sharp contrast with the 154 per cent in the United States and 193 per cent in Japan. Poor corporate practices and governance also contributed to the 1997 crisis in the form of inaccurate company financial information, non transparent corporate decision making, no credible exit threat, insufficient financial institution monitoring, and few legal rights and forms of protection for minority shareholders (Joh, 1999). Hence, the priority in corporate sector reform has been to focus on achieving a major reduction in corporate indebtedness, bringing corporate governance practices into line with international standards, and in attaining corporate international competitiveness.

Korea has taken a three pronged approach to reforming the corporate sector. First, the five largest *chaebols*, known as the Big Five, were to be reformed and restructured through specific plans to improve their capital structure. The parameters within which corporate reform of the Big Five has proceeded are contained in an agreement on the five major principles made in January 1998 between the then President-elect Kim Dae-jung and the leaders of the five largest *chaebols*. The five principles are: (1) heightening of the transparency of corporate management, (2) prohibition of cross-guarantees between affiliates, (3) improvement of corporate financial structure, (4) business concentration on core competence, and (5) responsibility reinforcement of governing shareholders and management. Under these five principles, the top five *chaebols* and their creditors reached an agreement on debt reduction and other restructuring measures in early 1998. The agreement included: (1) adoption of consolidated financial statements from fiscal year 1999; (2) compliance with international standards of accounting; (3) strengthening of voting rights of minority shareholders; (4) compulsory appointment of at least one outsider director from 1998; (5) establishment of an external auditors' committee; (6) prohibition of cross-subsidiary debt guarantees from April 1998; and (7) resolution of all existing cross-debt guarantees by March 2000.

The Korean government also required the top five *chaebols* to reduce their debt–equity ratios to 200 per cent by the end of 1999 and improve their financial structure by asset sales, recapitalisation, and foreign capital inducement. They had to remove existing cross guarantees between subsidiaries in different lines of business, and consolidate businesses by exchanging non-core businesses with other *chaebols*. The latter process became known as 'Big Deals', and had the objective of enhancing the competitiveness of the largest *chaebols*. The 'Big Deals' were pursued with the objective of streamlining over-investment and enhancing efficiency in such key industries as semiconductors, petrochemicals, aerospace, railway vehicles, oil refining, power plant facilities, and vessel engines. The plan involved 17 subsidiaries of the five *chaebols*. In December 1998 the top five *chaebols* reached agreement on many of the deals. Tax incentives were provided to these companies to reach such an agreement. The Big Deals, for the semiconductors, oil refining, aerospace and railway vehicles industries, were completed. However, the Big Deals for the other industries eventually failed or were delayed.

Second, the mid-ranking *chaebols* and other large corporations, the 6th to 64th largest *chaebols*, were subject to restructuring through out of court workout programmes with their designated lead creditor bank based on the London Approach. Financial institutions signed the Corporate Restructuring Agreement, which provided informal debt-workouts as an alternative to the formal procedures of the insolvency law regime. These workout programmes involved term extensions, deferred payments and/or the reduction of principal and interest. As of February 2000, 77 corporations of the 6th to 64th *chaebols* were under work-out programmes.

Under these work-out programmes, creditor banks are required to oversee the management of work-out firms as well as the rescheduling of their debts. Many of these creditor banks, however, lacked management expertise and their role was limited to external supervision, leaving management responsibilities in the hands of company officials. To promote more efficient management of insolvent firms under work-out programmes, the Korean government recently established Corporate Restructuring Vehicles (CRVs). A CRV is an independent agency specialised in corporate restructuring. In place of creditor banks, it assumes the authority to manage debt work-out firms.

Third, the restructuring of small and medium-size enterprises (SMEs) has been left to the creditor banks and has been largely postponed. To prevent insolvency and preserve employment, these firms were allowed easy access to working capital. In Korea, compared with other crisis countries, SMEs account for a relatively small fraction of outstanding bank loans. While this justifies the delay in restructuring SMEs, a comprehensive programme to work out these debts is still urgently needed.

Despite the corporate reform efforts, however, there have been mixed results regarding the success in restructuring the Big Five, and in the out of court work-outs of other large corporations. The positive developments are discussed first.

The number of affiliates of the top thirty *chaebols* decreased from 804 in April 1998 to 567 by January 2001. The average debt-equity ratio of the top four *chaebols*, excluding the dismantled Daewoo Group, fell to below 200 per cent by the end of 1999, down from 352 per cent in 1998 and from over 500 per cent in 1997.[14] The average debt–equity ratio of the top 30 *chaebols* fell to 219 per cent by the end of 1999, from 380 per cent in 1998 and from 520 per cent in 1997. All of the cross debt guarantees were resolved by March 2000, as planned, and *chaebols* are required to publish consolidated financial statements. Legal proceedings for corporate rehabilitation and bankruptcy filing have been simplified to facilitate market exit for non viable firms, and to ensure better representation of creditor banks in the resolution process. Various measures for enhancing the corporate governance structure were also introduced. The legal rights of minority shareholders have been strengthened by lowering the holding threshold of certain rights.[15] Appointment of outside directors and auditors has been made compulsory. For corporations, outside directors must be appointed to form one quarter of the total board membership, and an audit committee must be set up with outside directors forming at least two-thirds of its membership. In addition, owners who play an active role in the management of corporations should be registered as their directors. These have the objective of making corporate decision-making more transparent.

However, there are still a number of shortcomings associated with corporate restructuring. For example, the concentration of economic power in the hands of the top five *chaebols* has deepened. According to the Fair Trade Commission, the total amount of the top five *chaebols'* assets increased by 13.8 per cent in 1998. Furthermore, the total debts of the top five *chaebols* increased to W 234 trillion in 1998, up from W 221 trillion in 1997. Nonetheless the debt–equity ratios of the top five *chaebols* decreased due to the fact that the *chaebols'* mode of financing has changed drastically in favour of direct financing through the stock market. Some *chaebols* attracted liquidity through trusts and mutual funds. Nevertheless, the will of the founding families of *chaebols*, rather than the market and shareholders, still wields absolute power through cross shareholding among affiliates. In addition, the board of directors often fails to assume the role as an actual decision-making body.

Since the restructuring of the Big Five and out of court work-outs of other large corporations have had mixed results, the lead banks have been accused of including firms that should have been immediately liquidated. Given their financial fragility, the banks have been reluctant to absorb losses, and are trying to keep many troubled firms on their balance sheets that are in fact unlikely to survive. The lead banks have also been unable to devise a comprehensive set of work-out criteria involving debt–equity swaps, debt write-downs, and debt rescheduling. The absence of comprehensive criteria has raised concerns about the fairness and effectiveness of using differential measures to support different firms in various industries. Disagreements over loan loss provisioning, disputes over asset valuation, and managers' resistance to losing control all have further complicated the process. Consequently, many firms are likely to fail to meet their obligations to their lead banks.

The restructuring impact of the Big Deals is also mixed. Whether or not the excess capacity problems that plagued Korea's *chaebols* have been solved is not clear. Evidence is also mixed on whether the Big Four have fulfilled their commitments to improve corporate governance and slim down to a few core businesses. The effectiveness of the Big Deals remains unclear. The new firms made by the Big Deal remain in financial distress due to unimproved finances because there has been no debt reduction or injection of new capital. Without lay-offs and plant closures, excess capacity problems also remain and reducing the number of firms is likely to reduce competition and facilitate collusive behaviour. As for the workout programmes, some critics argue that preferential financial treatment for the indebted firms might unnecessarily prolong the lives of failing firms, eat away at banks' assets and exacerbate the credit crunch on other firms.

The commercial banks have faced major losses from the debt work-out. For instance, the restructuring of Daewoo, Korea's second largest *chaebol* until domestic creditors decided on a debt-rescheduling programme for its subsidiaries, caused bank losses estimated at US10.4 billion. The requirement that the Big Five reduce their debt to equity ratios to less than 200 per cent by the end of 1999 also led to debt write-downs and debt–equity swaps that cut the earnings of major commercial banks. These costs made it difficult for Korean banks to build the capital and loan-loss provisioning needed to absorb the losses from further corporate restructuring.

The Korean government has repeatedly announced that the structural reforms have been and will be driven by market forces. However, it is fair to say that the structural reform efforts have been driven by government initiative. The government deeply intervened in the pace and methods of the restructuring process. For example, the government supported the Big Deals for the *chaebol* subsidiaries, informally selected the bankrupt firms for work-out programmes, set a uniform reduction of the debt–equity ratio regardless of the characteristics of the business, and implicitly placed a limit on *chaebols'* entry into new business. (Samsung Economic Research Institute 2000). Thus, the Korean government needs to reduce its level of corporate intervention and institutionalise a basic corporate governance system, and the direction of corporate sector reforms should be more concentrated on profit maximisation, or cost minimisation, rather than just fitting the standard itself.

6.3.3   Labour Market Reform

The rigidity of the labour market was a key factor that contributed to the weakening of the international competitiveness of Korean firms, and thereby contributed to the onset of the financial crisis. According to Fitch ICBA (1999), with the advent of democratisation in 1987 and the subsequent liberalisation of trade unions, nominal wages increased 15 per cent per annum up until 1996, exceeding productivity, which rose by 11 per cent. However, tight labour market conditions and strong trade union power ensured that labour market reform went untouched. The labour market was plagued with rigidities. An excessive degree of job protection prevented lay-offs and encouraged over-manning, inflexible working hours and few limits on strike action. Therefore, a major goal of the reform programme is to ensure flexibility in the labour market.

The Tripartite Commission, composed of representatives from labour, management and government, was established in January 1998, and the Tripartite Social Accord was signed in February 1998. The Accord covers not only labour-related, but also a wide range of socioeconomic matters. It includes issues such as the promotion of freedom of association, management transparency, business restructuring, labour market policy, reform of the social security system, wage stabilisation, the improvement of labour–management cooperation, and the enhancement of labour market flexibility.

In February 1998, greater labour market flexibility was instituted with the revision of the Labour Standards Act (LSA), which legalised lay-offs for 'managerial reasons' and the recruitment of temporary workers. Specifically, lay-offs became possible if four preconditions could be met. First, there must be an urgent managerial need; second, all efforts to avoid lay-offs should have been exhausted; third, workers to be laid off should be selected by a reasonable and fair standard; and fourth, agreement should be reached with labour union representatives. In spite of its very demanding preconditions, the new LSA facilitated necessary lay-offs in the process of financial and corporate sector reforms. In addition to the new LSA, legislation allowing the establishment of manpower dispatching businesses took effect in July 1998. Manpower dispatching businesses provide employment-outsourcing services for 26 work types and 118 job classifications, including computer professionals, interpreters, secretaries and tour guides. This measure is also expected to further enhance labour market flexibility.

On the other hand, the basic rights of workers have been strengthened. Teachers have been allowed to organise labour unions. The coverage of both unemployment insurance and industrial accident compensation insurance has been widened. Indeed, many policies and programmes were designed to assist the unemployed. However, they have been able to provide support for only a fraction of those who have lost their jobs due to the financial crisis (Lee and Lee 2000). Social safety nets have been reinforced and expanded with the implementation of the National Basic Livelihood Security Law, which will increase the number of recipients of subsistence benefits from 0.5 million in 1999 to 1.5 million in 2001.

6.3.4   Public Sector Reform

Poor productivity and rampant inefficiency in the public sector have been notorious in Korea. In the wake of the financial crisis the Korean government declared it would launch its own reforms aiming at remodelling the government's role, and improving the efficiency and transparency of public administration. The downsizing of the government has been an important feature of the public sector reform. The Korean government has pursued streamlining of its organisational structure. In February 1998 the first reshuffling of the central government structure was implemented, and 11 chambers, 42 bureaux and 53 departments were scrapped. As a result the number of government employees was to be reduced by 11 per cent by the end of the year 2000. In addition, another downsizing plan has been put in place to reduce as many as 16 per cent of total employees by the year 2001. Local governments have also streamlined their organisations; by October 1998, 12 per cent of total jobs had been eliminated. Additionally, the quasi-government sector, including public institutions and various associations, has also been streamlined.

State-owned enterprises (SOEs) have also been subject to drastic overhaul by means of privatisation or management reform. In August 1998 a plan for the privatisation of SOEs was announced. Among the 108 SOEs, 38 would be immediately privatised, 34 gradually privatised, 9 would be merged into others or liquidated, and 21 would go through restructuring. The 89 subsidiaries of the 30 parent SOEs are also subject to privatisation or management reform. Out of 24 non-financial SOEs (parent companies), 5 SOEs were to be privatised by 1999, 6 SOEs will be gradually privatised by 2002, while the remaining SOEs are targeted for managerial reform and consolidation.

Elimination of excessive regulation has been another important task in the process of public sector reform. The Regulation Reform Committee (RRC) announced that in 1998 it abolished approximately 49 per cent of the total 11,125 government regulations pertaining to the private sector. It is fair to say, however, that many of the public sector reform tasks, and their actual implementation, have hardly been satisfactory. Many critics argue that the government, in particular, which has led the structural reform in other sectors, has not followed through with its own public sector restructuring. In addition, there has been considerable antagonism towards the privatisation of SOEs among their workers and labour unions more generally.

6.3.5   Capital Market Liberalisation and Foreign Exchange Liberalisation

Financial liberalisation and market opening have been accelerated to induce long-term and stable foreign capital inflows, and to enhance external credibility. The markets for government and corporate bonds (December 1997), and short-term money market instruments such as Commercial Papers (CPs) (May 1998), were opened up earlier than planned, and ceilings on foreigners' stock market investment (May 1998) have been completely abolished.[16] Hostile take-overs by foreigners is allowed and the scope of business areas opened to them widened (May 1998). Controls related to foreigners' acquisition of real estate, such as its use, size and other qualifications, were eased or abolished in July 1998.

In June 1998 the government announced a plan to liberalise all foreign exchange transactions in two stages, for the purpose of establishing a new foreign exchange system under which emphasis is placed on ex post facto management through reports and prudential supervision rather than on prior regulation. The first stage of liberalisation, which took effect on 1 April 1999 with the replacement of the old 'Foreign Exchange Control Act' with the new 'Foreign Exchange Transactions Act', included deregulation of most foreign exchange transactions related to the operations of enterprises and financial institutions. In terms of liberalisation of current account transactions, except for a few types of international current account transactions, all current account transactions by business firms and banks other than individuals were fully liberalised on 1 April 1999.

In terms of the liberalisation of capital account transactions, the legal regulatory framework was changed from a Positive List System to a Negative List System. In order to enhance transparency, all capital account transactions were basically liberalised unless otherwise specifically prohibited on the negative list. In addition, to reduce inefficiencies stemming from the selective licensing of foreign exchange banks, all financial institutions fulfilling the conditions required to maintain effective ex-post transactions management systems were allowed to participate in foreign exchange businesses.[17]

In the second stage of liberalisation, which took effect on 1 January 2001, restrictions on foreign exchange transactions including current account payments by individuals and domestic deposits by non-residents were lifted. In regard to foreign exchange transactions, the following measures have been implemented: liberalisation of residents' foreign exchange transactions, such as the elimination of ceilings on overseas travel expenses and foreign currency purchases as well as the abolition of restrictions on overseas deposits and trusts; liberalisation of non-residents' foreign exchange transactions, including the elimination of restrictions on non-residents' domestic deposits and trusts with maturities of less than one year; and streamlining the process of securities investment.

Considering the international capital movements and the domestic and international market environment, the government has retained the following restrictions on some capital transactions: limits on Korean won funding by non-residents; and restrictions on overseas short-term borrowings by financially unsound corporations.[18]

As a consequence of the further liberalisation of capital markets, along with the recovery of confidence in Korean financial markets, foreign portfolio investment has substantially increased. The net inflow of foreign portfolio investment was a mere US$1 billion in 1997 when the crisis broke out, but since then has considerably increased to US$5 billion in 1998, to US$5.5 billion in 1999, and then to a little under US$12 billion in 2000 (see Table 6.6). Accordingly, the ratio of foreign investment outstanding to market capitalisation has substantially increased. For the Korean Stock Exchange, it increased from 13 per cent in 1996 to 30 per cent in 2000. As a result, the movement of foreign portfolio investment now considerably influences the Korean stock market (see Table 6.7). In particular, the co-movement between the Korean market and the US market has substantially increased (see Figures 6.7 and 6.8).

Table 6.6
Foreign Portfolio Investment Trend (Billion US Dollars)

	1995	1996	1997	1998	1999	2000
Inflow	10.22	12.57	13.20	16.48	41.74	60.06
Outflow	7.77	8.00	12.12	11.70	36.25	48.45
Net Inflow	2.45	4.57	1.08	4.78	5.50	11.61
Total	17.99	20.57	25.32	28.18	77.99	108.51

Source: Bank of Korea

Table 6.7
Ratio of Foreign Investment Outstanding to Market Capitalisation (%)

	1996	1997	1998	1999	2000
Korea Stock Exchange	13.0	14.6	18.6	21.9	30.1
KOSDAQ	–	4.5	3.4	7.5	6.9
Bond Market	0.04	0.09	0.3	0.3	0.2

Note: As of the end of period.
Source: Bank of Korea

6.4   CHALLENGES AHEAD

Table 6.8 summarises developments in the major macroeconomic indicators for Korea since 1997. Korea's real GDP, which recorded a negative growth rate of 6.7 per cent in 1998, has shown positive high growth rates of 10.7 per cent and 8.8 per cent in 1999 and 2000, respectively. The inflation rate has remained very low, and the unemployment rate has decreased even though it still remains above the pre-crisis level. In terms of the country's public finances, a fiscal deficit was recorded in 1998 and 1999 equivalent to 4.3 per cent and 3.3 per cent of GDP respectively. However, in 2000 the budget had moved into a small surplus of 1 per cent of GDP. The current account has continuously recorded a sizeable surplus every year since 1998. Total external liabilities have decreased to US$136.3 billion in 2000 from US$159.2 billion in 1997. Indeed, Korea has become a net external creditor since 1999. As of the end of 2000 Korea's usable foreign exchange reserves reached US$96.2 billion from only US$8.8 billion in 1997, and represented a remarkable transformation. The exchange rate and interest rates have remained at levels below where they stood before the crisis erupted. Even though these indicators tended to become more volatile in early 2001, it seems that the Korean economy has overcome the worst of the crisis and the possibility of a repetition of 1997's external liquidity crisis has been significantly reduced.

However, unstable elements and conditions are increasingly appearing both inside and outside the nation. Among the destabilising factors inside Korea is the staggering structural reform process underway, and foreign investors' loss of confidence in the prospects for the Korean economy. Even if the Korean government had pledged to conclude most structural reforms in the four major sectors, identified previously, by the end of February 2001, it is fair to say that the structural reform process still has a long way to go. Remembering that the 1997 financial crisis erupted while the country had a lame duck government, arising from the presidential elections at this time, under President Kim Young-sam, some Korea watchers inside and outside the nation

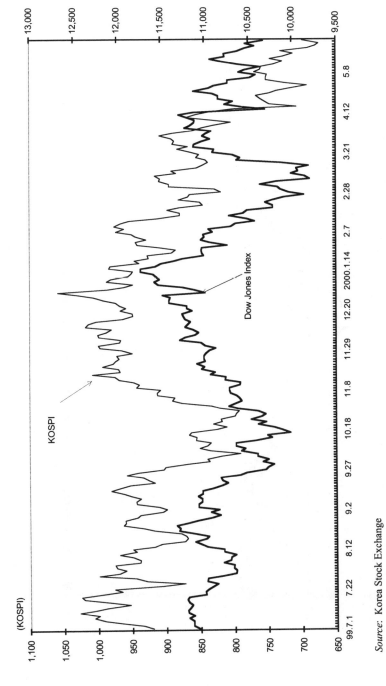

Source: Korea Stock Exchange

Figure 6.7   Movements of KOSPI and Dow Jones Indices

137

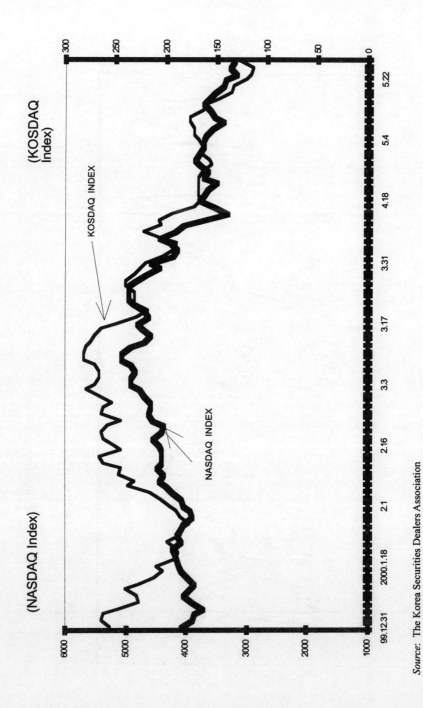

Source: The Korea Securities Dealers Association

Figure 6.8   Movements of KOSDAQ and NASDAQ Indices

Table 6.8
Major Economic Indicators

	1997	1998	1999	2000
Real Economy				
– Real GDP growth rate (%)	5.0	−6.7	10.7	8.8
– Inflation rate of CPI (%, year average)	4.4	7.5	0.8	2.3
– Core inflation (%, year average)	3.4	5.9	0.3	1.8
– Unemployment rate (%, year average)	2.6	6.8	6.3	4.0
Public finances (% of GDP)				
– Consolidated central government revenues	20.6	21.8	22.3	26.4
– Consolidated central government expenditures	22.3	26.0	25.6	25.4
– Balance[a]	−1.7	−4.3	−3.3	1.0
Balance of payments				
– Current account (US$ billion)	−8.2	40.6	25.0	10.5
– Current account (% of GDP)	−1.7	12.8	6.1	2.2
– Total External liabilities (US$ billion, end yr)	159.2	148.7	137.1	136.3
– Long-term Liabilities (US$ billion, end of yr)	95.7	118.0	97.8	92.1
– Short-term Liabilities (US$ billion, end of yr)	63.6	30.7	39.2	44.2
– Short-term Debt/Total Debt (%, end of year)	39.9	20.6	28.6	32.4
– Total External Credit (US$ billion, end of yr)	105.2	128.5	145.4	166.9
– Net External Credit (US$ billion, end of yr)	−54.1	−20.2	8.3	30.6
– Foreign Exchange Reserves (US$ billion, end of year)	8.8	48.5	74.1	96.2
– Short-term Debt/FX Reserves (%, end of yr)	714.6	63.3	53.0	45.9
Money and Credit				
– M3 growth rate (% change, end of yr)	13.8	12.5	8.0	6.0
– Overnight call rate (%)	17.8	7.0	4.8	5.4
– 3-year corporate bond rate (%)	24.3	8.3	9.9	9.6
Exchange Rate				
– Won–US$ nominal exchange rate (year average)	951.3	1401.8	1188.8	1131.1
– Nominal effective exchange rate (1995=100)	92.4	64.5	73.1	78.4
– Real effective exchange rate (1995=100)	97.3	72.3	82.1	88.8

Note: a Data prior to 2000 exclude the civil service pension fund; in equivalent terms, the balance in 1999 was −3.8 per cent.

Sources: The Bank of Korea; Centre for Economic Information, Korea Development Institute (http://epic.kdi.re.kr/home/english/index.html).

worry that the incumbent Kim Dae-jung government is losing momentum for the reform efforts as there will be a Presidential election in December 2002.

In addition, the prospects for the global economy in 2001, at the time of writing, are not encouraging, as the United States is experiencing a severe economic downturn and the Japanese economy also remains weak. As the US and Japan are the two largest markets for the products of East Asian countries, including Korea, the 1997 crisis-hit countries in East Asia may experience further economic and financial turmoil. During the first quarter of 2001 these countries, including Korea, were experiencing financial instability with falling stock prices and their currencies were losing value against the US dollar.

The large current-account surpluses in 1998, 1999, and 2000 have helped the commercial banks and the *chaebols* to repay, or refinance, some of their short-term foreign debts, and for the government to have amassed huge foreign-exchange reserves as previously mentioned. With the growth of the US economy steadily declining since late 2000, Korea's exports to this country have been experiencing difficulties and, consequently, the current-account surpluses are shrinking rapidly. In view of these uncertainties there is an even greater need to ensure that the necessary structural reforms are pursued in an even more rigorous manner.

The social consequences of the financial crisis, and subsequent structural reforms, also warrant closer inspection. There have been tumultuous and painful side effects for most Koreans in all segments of Korean society. In particular, the crisis and Korea's structural reform process have had significant and adverse effects on equitable growth in Korea. Specifically, low-income households and marginal workers, such as women, young workers, the less educated, wage workers, and first-time job-seekers, were the hardest hit. The existing social protection systems have been unable to adequately cope with the social consequences of the crisis, and, as a result, income distribution in Korea has deteriorated (Lee and Lee 2000). Therefore, special efforts to strengthen social protection systems are greatly needed.

There remain many internal and external obstacles to the full recovery of the Korean economy. If any of the obstacles are not adequately overcome, the crisis could turn out to be an even more enduring pain for the Korean people. On the other hand, if positive preconditions are met and the structural reforms are accomplished smoothly, the crisis could turn out to be a blessing in disguise that will pave the way for another economic miracle and sustainable growth for Korea in the 21st century (Lee 1999a). Therefore, there is a strong need for continued strenuous efforts to safeguard macroeconomic stability, implement structural reforms, and attain sustained growth through increases in efficiency and productivity. In line with this Korea has to establish a true market economy – an economy led by the private sector and the basic principles of transparency, accountability and fair competition, but guided by prudential supervision (Lee, Lee and Yang (forthcoming)).

6.5   SUMMARY AND CONCLUSIONS

The financial and economic crisis that afflicted Korea in 1997 and 1998 took many by surprise. The country's traditionally strong economic fundamentals, including high economic growth, rapid export growth, low unemployment, and sustainable current account deficits, masked fundamental and growing weaknesses in the country's corporate and financial sectors that were to combine in 1997 to unravel both domestic and international confidence in the economy. Since this time the new government, under the Presidency of Kim Dae-jung, has taken concerted action to put the economy once again on the path to high and sustainable economic growth. This has involved the use of both monetary and fiscal policy to bring about stability in financial markets by restoring investor confidence in the case of the former, and to restructure the Achilles heels of the economy, its financial and corporate sectors, as well as maintain domestic demand using the latter. While both of these are essential for the attainment of stability in the short term, this will prove to be fruitless unless fundamental structural reforms of the economy are implemented. Focus has been given in this chapter to reform in five key areas: the financial sector, the corporate sector; the labour market; the public sector; and further liberalisation of the capital and foreign exchange markets. While much progress can be identified in each of these areas, much still needs to be done. It remains essential for the authorities to maintain the reform momentum.

Korea's recovery from the depths of the economic crisis in 1998 has been truly remarkable, with a rapid V-shaped recovery in economic growth apparent. However, there is no room for complacency. Since the second half of 2000 the growth of the economy has slowed and confidence in the economy has retreated. Internal and external factors indicate that the economy faces a bumpy ride in the imminent future. However, maintaining macroeconomic stability and the reform momentum must remain the centrepiece of government policy, if sustainable economic growth is to be achieved over the medium to long term.

NOTES

1   The three elements of the holy trinity are exchange rate stability, monetary policy independence and perfect capital mobility. These are argued to be mutually incompatible.

2   Oh (2000b) reviews the Korean inflation targeting system.

3   This means that the Bank of Korea neutrally establishes monetary policy not for the government or the benefit of a certain group, but for the benefit of the whole people of Korea.

4   This means that the Bank of Korea autonomously implements the monetary policy neutrally established, based on its own judgement, with its own

accountability and without any interventions or pressures from the government or any group.

5   Oh (1999) estimates two underlying inflation rates using the method of 'adjustment by exclusion' and another using the 'trimmed mean' method. He then examines their stability and usefulness for monetary policy to find which would be the most suitable for inflation targeting in Korea. Among the two types of underlying inflation rates produced by the method of adjustment by exclusion, one strips out the prices of agricultural and marine products and of energy from the components of the Consumer Price Index and the other additionally excludes the prices of public utilities. On the other hand, a trim of 15 per cent off both tails of the frequency distribution was adopted to estimate the trimmed mean inflation rate. The results of his empirical analysis show that the underlying inflation rate under the first approach produces a relatively better performance in terms of stability and usefulness for monetary policy. Thus it can be considered a better alternative than the other available variables as the target variable for inflation targeting.

6   The mid-term inflation target was set at the same level as, or lower than, the short-term inflation target for the year in order to inspire confidence that the Bank would keep inflation low and stable in the long run. The mid-term target was quoted as a point target without a toleration band, because it was judged more important to demonstrate the strong commitment of the central bank to prevent the spread of inflationary expectations among the public than to take economic uncertainties into account.

7   First, the Bank of Korea sets a price stability target for the following year in consultation with the Government before the end of each year, and formulates and promulgates an operational plan for monetary and credit policies including this price stability target within fifteen days after the setting of the price stability target. Second, every month the Bank of Korea officially announces the monthly direction of monetary policy immediately after the Monetary Policy Committee of the Bank has decided it, and the Governor explains its details in a press briefing. Third, the Bank of Korea regularly publishes the minutes of Monetary Policy Committee meetings three months after each meeting. Fourth, the Bank of Korea submits a Monetary and Credit Policy Report to the National Assembly twice a year, normally in March and October, and the Governor is required to answer the questions of members of the National Assembly on the report.

8   Drawing upon the analogy between a financial crisis and a human stroke, Lee (1999b) shows how numerous factors, such as fundamental weaknesses, an unfriendly environment, policy mistakes and exogenous shocks, were systematically intertwined in causing the financial crisis.

9   See for example Krugman (1998).

10   Until 1997, the authorities had never allowed any financial institution to fail.

11   The objective of KAMCO is to purchase impaired assets and to liquidate them as efficiently as possible. To this end, in November 1997, the Non Performing

Loans Liquidation Fund was formed to purchase and dispose of the bad loans
of commercial and merchant banks. The funds initially made available to
KAMCO came from the Bank of Korea, the Korea Development Bank and
other financial institutions, with the remainder to come from bond issuance.

12   The government invested 750 billion won in each institution and the KDIC also
     invested the same amount in each bank.

13   For more discussion of the *chaebols*, see Lee and Lee (2000).

14   Sakong (2000) suggests that the debt to equity ratio of the top five *chaebols* fell
     to 150 per cent in 2000, although the absolute amount of the *chaebols*' debt
     remained about the same as in 1997.

15   Initiating derivative suits: from 1.0 per cent to 0.01 per cent of total issued
     shares. Requesting dismissal of directors: from 3.0 per cent to 0.5 per cent of
     total issued shares. Right to inspect the books and records: from 3.0 per cent to
     1.0 per cent of total issued shares. Shareholders' right to make a proposal: from
     3.0 per cent to 1.0 per cent of total issued shares.

16   Except for public enterprises, for example, the Korea Electric Power Corporation.
     The aggregate foreign ownership ceiling is 30 per cent, while the individual
     ownership ceiling is 3 per cent.

17   Along with the above liberalisation, some countermeasures were also introduced
     to avoid unnecessary instability of the foreign exchange market. First, cross-
     border capital movements have been closely monitored by a newly established
     comprehensive foreign exchange monitoring network, and individual foreign
     exchange transactions are being automatically recorded in the computer system
     of the Foreign Exchange Information Brokerage Centre. Information collected
     in the centre is shared by the relevant supervisory authorities. Second, the Korea
     Centre for International Finance (KCIF) was established in April 1999 to collect
     and analyse information on foreign exchange and international financial market
     trends. Third, a legal framework was introduced to allow the Korean government
     to take emergency safeguard measures when necessary. However, the terms
     and conditions for invoking the measures will be very stringent and conform to
     international standards, such as the BOP safeguard provisions of the OECD or
     IMF. Examples of such measures are Variable Deposit Requirements,
     Concentration of foreign exchange, Permission requirements for capital account
     transactions.

18   Meanwhile, in order to cope with possible capital flight following the
     deterioration of internal and external economic environments and the increase
     of illegal transactions such as money laundering and tax evasion, the government
     has strengthened procedural aspects of its monitoring efforts through such means
     as the following: strengthening the requirements for reporting some foreign
     exchange transactions to the National Tax Service and to the National Customs
     Service; maintaining the existing system that requires capital account transactions
     to be processed through foreign exchange business institutions; introducing a

system for reporting large external payments to the Bank of Korea; and, introducing a system that requires annually reporting balances of overseas deposits and trust assets exceeding certain amounts to the Bank of Korea.

REFERENCES

Basurto and Ghosh, (2000), 'The Interest Rate-Exchange Rate Nexus in the Asian Crisis Countries', IMF *Working Paper,* WP/00/19, February.

Bank of Korea (2001), 'The Major Results of Financial Restructuring in 2000', *Josatonggye Wolbo (Monthly Economic Bulletin)*, February (in Korean).

Cho, Dongchul and Kenneth D. West, (1999), 'The Effect of Monetary Policy in Exchange Rate Stabilisation in Post-Crisis Korea', paper presented at the Conference of the Korean Econometric Society, November (in Korean).

Fitch ICBA, (1999) *Rating Report: Republic of Korea*.

Goldfajn, Ilan and Taimur Baig (1998), 'Monetary Policy in the Aftermath of Currency Crisis: The Cases of Asia', IMF *Working Paper,* WP/98/170, December.

Joh, Sung Wook, (1999), 'The Korean Corporate Sector: Crisis and Reform', KDI Working Paper No.9912.

Korea Development Institute (KDI) (2000), 'Macroeconomic Management after the Crisis' (in Korean), Seoul: KDI.

Krugman, P. (1998), 'What happened to Asia', unpublished paper, MIT, January.

Lee, Hyun-Hoon (1999a), 'Korea's 1997 Financial Crisis: Causes, Consequences and Prospects', *Agenda* (Australian National University), **6**: 353–65.

Lee, Hyun-Hoon (1999b), 'A "Stroke" Hypothesis of Korea's 1997 Financial Crisis: Causes, Consequences and Prospects', *University of Melbourne Research Paper* No. 696. [Available at <http://www.ecom.unimelb.edu.au/ecowww/research/696.pdf>]

Lee, Jong Won, Hyun-Hoon Lee and Doo Yong Yang (forthcoming), 'Structural Reform in Korea: its Process and Consequences', in Tran Van Hoa (ed.), *The Asia Recovery: Issues and Aspects of Growth, Development, Trade, and Investment*, Cheltenham, UK: Edward Elgar.

Lee, Young-Youn and Hyun-Hoon Lee (2000), 'Financial Crisis, Structural Reform and Social Consequences in Korea', in Tran Van Hoa (ed.), *Social Impact of the Asian Financial Crisis*, London: Macmillan, pp. 57–84.

Oh, Junggun (1999), 'How Useful Is an Underlying Inflation Rate for Inflation Targeting?', *Economic Papers,* **2** (2), December, pp. 29–63.

Oh, Junggun (2000a), *The Financial Crisis and Financial and Monetary Policies,* (in Korean), Seoul: Dasanbooks.

Oh, Junggun (2000b), 'Inflation Targeting: A New Monetary Policy Framework in Korea', paper presented at the International Symposium on Inflation Targeting, The Bank of Thailand, Bangkok, October.

Oh, Junggun (2000c), 'Dynamic Correlations between Interest Rates, Stock Prices, the Exchange Rate and the Current Account in an Open Economy in which the Stock Market Is More Active than the Bond Market', *Working Paper*, No. 104, Economic Research Office, The Bank of Korea, May (in Korean).

Oh, Junggun (2001), 'Governance Reinvented: The Progress, Constraints and Remaining Agenda in Bank and Corporate Restructuring in Korea', paper presented at the ESCAP/Korea University International Conference, Korea University, Seoul, May.

Oh, Junggun, J. Kim and B. Bae (2001), *Effectiveness of Economic Policies,* Seoul: The Bank of Korea (in Korean).

Park, D and I. Choi (1999), 'Was High Interest Rate Policy Effective to Stabilise Exchange Rate?', paper presented at the Seminar, The Bank of Korea, November (in Korean).

Sakong, I. (2000), 'Korean Economic Restructuring: Current Status and Prospects', keynote address at the conference 'Has Economic Reform in Korea Stalled? Assessing Progress in Restructuring the Korean Economy', Korean Society, New York USA, 11 December.

Samsung Economic Research Institute (2000), 'Two Years after the IMF Bailout: A Review of the Korean Economy's Transformation', mimeo, March.

7 Vietnam: Economic and Financial Management

Tran Van Hoa and CIEM

7.1 INTRODUCTION

Vietnam and China are two major transition developing economies in Asia and two potentially huge markets for the rest of the world. In their economic development and growth programmes, both have instituted reforms with far-reaching economic and political impact, not only on their economies but also on their old (such as Russia) and new (such as the European Union, the US and the Association for Southeast Asia Nations (ASEAN)) trading partners in and outside Asia. Within the spirit of these reforms, both Vietnam and China have developed and implemented numerous significant policies to attract foreign investment and promote open trade and business in recent years. Unlike other major Asian countries in the region or Russia (a major Western transition economy) outside it, however, Vietnam and China seem to have escaped the serious political and social effects (experienced elsewhere in some major countries in the region) of the damaging contagion of the Asia economic and financial crisis of 1997. The economic and trade impact of the crisis on China and Vietnam has nevertheless not been negligible. And, nearly four years on since the emergence of this crisis, the impact still has had important implications for development, growth and the living standard of the people in the two countries and their trade and cooperation with the rest of the world. An understanding of the economic management and its issues and problems, if any, for China and Vietnam, is beneficial not only for the two countries' future direction of development and international cooperation but also of mutual interest to other developing and developed economies in the region and beyond.

This chapter will focus particularly on Vietnam's economic management in the past few years and covers both the pre- and post-crisis periods. It first surveys economic activities and performance of Vietnam in recent years from a macroeconomic perspective. It then focuses on issues and problems in economic management that Vietnam has had to face and resolve since its introduction of Doi Moi (renovation) and through the initial stages of development in the late 1980s, the Asia crisis in the

146

late 1990s, and then the post-crisis period in 2000 and 2001. General comments and an assessment of the perspective by international organisations (for example, the Asian Development Bank (ADB), the World Bank (WB) and the United Nations Development Program) on Vietnam's economic management are given in the final section.

7.2   VIETNAM'S FISCAL AND MONETARY POLICIES

7.2.1   State Budget Revenue and Expenditure

Monetary and fiscal policy of Vietnam since the Asia crisis can be discussed and assessed for the period 1997–2000, or principally for 1997–1999, as official statistics and data for 2000 were not yet available at the time of writing (early in 2001). A summary of Vietnam's major economic activities during the period 1995–1999 is given in Table 7.1.

From this table, we note the impact of the crisis on Vietnam's trade balance, total consumption and gross capital formation. While its gross domestic product (GDP) was only slightly affected by the contagion from such crisis countries as Indonesia, Korea, Malaysia and Thailand, Vietnam's trade balance fell from 20.530 trillion Vietnamese dong (VND) in 1998 to 9.225 trillion VND in 1999. Total consumption

Table 7.1
National Accounts: Principal Sources and Uses
(1994 prices in billion VND)

	1995	1996	1997	1998	1999
				revised	revised
Sources	213 444	234 016	249 016	265 126	265 494
GDP	195 567	213 833	231 264	244 676	256 269
Trade Balance	17 877	20 183	17 752	20 530	9 225
Uses	213 444	234 016	249 016	265 126	265 494
Total Consumption	158 893	173 072	182 975	190 923	194 350
Gross Capital Formation	53 249	60 826	66 529	74 931	72 678
Statistical Discrepancy	1 302	118	–488	–728	–1 534

Sources: General Statistical Office, *Statistical Yearbooks 1975–2000*, and World Bank (2001c)

was seen to be stagnant at 265.126 trillion VND in 1998 and 265.494 trillion VND in 1999. Gross capital formation was at 74.931 trillion VND in 1998, but declined to 72.678 trillion VND in 1999. Coupled with a savage reduction in foreign direct investment during 1997–1999 (from 29 per cent of GDP in 1997 to 19 per cent – or US$600 million – in 1999) largely from East Asia and Japan, Vietnam was clearly in a difficult time for its planned development and growth targets (World Bank, 2001a).

State budget revenue

The total 1999 state budget revenue was 74.5 trillion VND which was equal to 18.7 per cent of GDP, of which the revenue from taxes and fees was 66.5 trillion VND and accounted for 89.2 per cent of the total state budget revenue. The state budget revenue percentage to GDP has continued a declining tendency since 1995, after it reached the record level of 23.3 per cent of GDP (Table 7.2). In particular it can be seen that the revenue from taxes and fees as the share of GDP decreased from 22.6 per cent in 1995 to 16.7 per cent in 1999.

The main reason for the decrease in recent years of the budget revenue ratio to GDP was the reduction of economic growth, reflecting an unattractive domestic investment environment and the impact of the regional financial crisis and slow-down in production and business activities. The year 1999 was also the first year that the Law on VAT (value added tax) came into effect. Because of the poor preparation and the inappropriateness of application timeframe of the Law on VAT, there were a

Table 7.2
State Budget Revenue, 1995–1999

	1995	1996	1997	1998	1999
(Bil. VND)					
Total revenues	53 374	62 387	64 264	68 770	74 500
Total expenditures	62 679	70 539	76 831	80 000	94 000
Budget deficits	9 305	8 152	12 567	11 230	19 500
(GDP per cent)					
Taxes	19.2	19.0	16.7	15.8	na
(Taxes and fees)	22.6	22.4	20.0	18.5	16.7
Total revenues	23.3	22.9	20.5	19.0	18.7
Total expenditure	27.4	25.9	24.5	22.1	23.6
Budget deficits	4.1	3.0	4.0	3.1	4.9

Note: 1999 figures are estimates at time of writing
Sources: General Statistical Office and CIEM estimates

lot of problems in VAT operation and implementation, such as the high rates of VAT inappropriate for some commodity items, the availability of 'asking and giving' mechanisms, which all generated a negative impact on many enterprises.

During this difficult economic situation, the proposal to impose income taxes on high income farmers and on income earners from activities such as passenger motorbikes, lottery sales, and others, caused many complaints from the public, and it had to be adjusted. The performance of imports and price changes in the international markets also had both positive and negative impacts on the state budget revenue. The increase in crude oil revenue and the introduction of VAT on imported goods partly reduced the state budget revenue.

State budget expenditure

The state budget expenditure, especially capital expenditure, reflects the government's 'demand stimulus' efforts. Total budget expenditure in 1999 was estimated at 94 thousand billion VND, or an increase of 17.5 per cent, versus 4.1 per cent in 1998, 8.9 per cent in 1997, and 12.5 per cent in 1996. As a share of GDP, total budget expenditure in 1999 was 23.6 per cent, which was higher than 22.1 per cent in 1998. The 23.6 per cent figure was lower than the share of total budget expenditure to GDP in the years 1995 to 1997. However, the state budget deficit in 1999 was the highest during this period, and was equal to 5 per cent of GDP.

The increase in investment from the state budget (including state credit) was an important source of revenue altering the decreasing resources from foreign direct investment inflows. Capital expenditure from the state budget was estimated at 26.5 thousand billion VND, approximately 6.7 per cent of GDP, which was much higher than 5.3 per cent in 1998, and was the highest ratio for the previous five years. The investment structure by the resources from the state budget had been adjusted by focusing more on key programmes and projects that helped to increase economic efficiency. The government also instructed local authorities to review investment projects under their management to improve resource allocation. A large part of the state budget expenditure for development investment was used for rural and agricultural development programmes and projects such as rural transport, rural and social infrastructure as well as poverty reduction programmes and projects. In 1999, the percentage of state budget expenditure for development investment allocated for rural and agricultural development doubled that in 1998.

However, the 'demand stimulus' measures through increasing expenditure on development investment from the state budget were far from efficient. In fact, capital expenditure started to increase only in the second quarter of 1999, after the National Assembly approved the proposal for additional capital expenditure allocation. Investment projects were implemented slowly because of various obstacles in the approval of projects, procurement and disbursement policies and procedures. These problems together can explain why the resources were available and 'waiting for' appropriate investment projects. On the other hand, the increase of capital expenditure from the state budget by increased borrowings from the public could crowd out non-state sector investment, which suffered large shortages of financial resources. The poor performance of bond issuance by the government in 1999 showed that people were not confident of a better economic perspective in the coming years. At the same time, many enterprises, especially the state owned enterprises (SOEs) could take this as a good opportunity to 'invest', because the government would pay a higher interest rate than the rate of returns from their business activities.[1]

In 1999, the state budget current expenditure was estimated at 14.1 per cent of GDP, which was not much higher than 13.9 per cent in 1998. However, by 15 November 1999, the budget allowed for many current expenditure items was already exhausted. The additional resources were allocated to current expenditure items for food emergency in the central provinces of the country. However, the state budget deficit was controlled within a level less than 5 per cent of GDP, as approved by the National Assembly.

7.2.2   Foreign Debt Management

Until now, the burden of foreign debt and debt payment liabilities has been kept within the controlled limits. However, the situation will be worse in the near future without proper foreign debt management solutions. The total foreign debt already reached US$ 10.8 billion at the end of 1998 and accounted for 42 per cent of GDP, two thirds of which were foreign debts claimed on the State or guaranteed by the State. About one half consisted of the concessional loans, and the remainder comprised commercial loans, largely through foreign investment.

Although the current account surplus occurred for the first time for Vietnam in 1999, high demand for imports of a developing country like Vietnam (while the high growth rate of exports was not sustainable), the increase in foreign debt burden, and the decrease in foreign direct investment inflows altogether may create pressure on Vietnam's balance of payments, especially in the near future. Therefore, Vietnam should be more cautious with external borrowings by enhancing its debt management. More importantly, Vietnam should increase the efficiency of the use of external loans.

7.2.3   Money Supply and Monetary Policies

In 1999, Vietnam's total money supply (M2) was estimated to increase by 23 per cent compared with the level on 31 December 1998. Total deposits for the previous 11 months increased by 22 per cent compared with the level on 31 December 1998, of which domestic deposits increased by 19.5 per cent and foreign deposits increased by 27.4 per cent. Although the interest rate on savings was continuously falling, domestic saving deposits increased by 40.3 per cent while foreign deposits increased only by 32.6 per cent.

Under the conditions of economic crisis and recession where the consumer price index was continuously decreasing and the investment resource absorptive capacity of the economy was low, Vietnam's State Bank decided to implement an expansionary monetary and credit policy by adjusting financial instruments to stimulate demand in the economy.

The reserve requirement ratio for credit institutions was adjusted from 7 per cent to 5 per cent of total balance of less than 12 month time-deposits. For rural joint stock commercial banks, central people credit funds, and regional people credit funds, the reserve requirement ratio was set at one per cent. The Rural and Agricultural Development Bank was allowed to reduce the reserve requirement ratio below 3 per cent, so that they could expand credit services to rural borrowers.

In a period of more than 5 months, since the end of May 1999, the State Bank adjusted the interest rate on refinancing capital four times and the interest rates on mobilised domestic deposits were reduced from 1.1 per cent per month to 0.5 per cent per month. In 1999, the State Bank adjusted the ceiling of lending interest rates five times, from 1.2–1.5 per cent in January to 0.85 per cent in October (see Table 7.3). Since August 1999, the ceiling of the lending interest rates on the long-, medium, and short-term loans was unified into a single level. The interest rate on mobilised foreign deposits of legal entities was reduced from 3–3.5 per cent to 2.5–3 per cent per year to curtail the returns from deposits. At the same time, the lending interest rates were also reduced to encourage enterprises to expand investment in production, and the ceilings of the domestic interest rates were reduced to prevent the transfer from VND to US dollars.

The adjustment of interest rates in 1999 was different from that in 1998. The latter was aimed at controlling the pressure of accelerating inflation, the former was to expand credit service. By the end of November 1999 however, credit supply increased by 11 per cent from the level in 1998, and was one half of the deposit growth rate (22 per cent). The estimates on credit supply and deposit growth rates in 1999 were 12 per cent and 24.5 per cent respectively.

The reason for this situation was the economic slow-down and the low investment

Table 7.3
The Credit Institutions' Ceilings on Lending Interest Rates

Types of loans	1/2	1/6	1/8	1/9	22/10
Medium- and long-term loans in urban areas	1.15	1.15	1.05	0.95	0.85
Short-term loans in urban areas	1.10	1.15	1.05	0.95	0.85
Rural joint stock commercial banks	1.25	1.15	1.15	1.05	1.00

Source: CIEM (2000)

absorptive capacity of the country. Many enterprises, especially the state-owned enterprises (SOEs), were unprofitable and fell into debt. Facing business risks, commercial banks were unable and did not dare to expand credit services because clients and enterprises were not able to pay back or did not dare to borrow. Commercial banks themselves were under a restructuring process to improve their balance sheets. Some of the problems facing these banks were attributed to the State Bank governance. The expansionary monetary policy measures were implemented in the second half of 1999. In the context of a depressed economy, the reduction of the interest rate ceiling was not necessary, especially when investment resource absorptive capacity of enterprises was low and commercial banks were not able to expand credit services.

The fundamental feature of the implementation of the government's demand-driven measures was the increase in State investment, relaxing monetary policy and expanding credit which posed a conflict between the need to maintain the high economic growth rate in the short term and the need to restructure the economy (including the economic sectors, ownership, and aggregate demand expenditure). The structural reforms could not be isolated from the increase of the autonomy and responsibility of the agencies directly implementing the policies, or from the improvement of the fiscal and monetary instruments.

7.2.4   Exchange Rate and Foreign Exchange Control

According to Decision 64/1999/QD-NHNN issued on 25 February 1999 by the State Bank, the exchange rate management mechanism has changed. Instead of announcing the daily VND/US$ official exchange rates, the State Bank will announce the average inter-bank transaction exchange rates during the previous working day. Although the new mechanism is more 'market-oriented', the State Bank is prudent towards exchange rate governance (the exchange rate is allowed to change within a band not exceeding 0.1 per cent of the announced exchange rates).

The State Bank has also applied prudential measures aimed at gradually liberalising the transactions through the current account, while the capital flows were strictly controlled. On 19 August 1999, the government issued Decision 170/1999/QD-TTg to encourage a monetary remittance to Vietnam by overseas Vietnamese so that Vietnam could attract more foreign exchange. Decision 173/QD-TTg (see CIEM 1999) was replaced by Decision 180/1999/QD-TTg issued on the 30 August 1999. According to this new Decision, the ratio of foreign exchange surrender reduced from 80 per cent to 50 per cent and, as a result, enterprises would have more autonomy in foreign exchange use.

In spite of these developments, confidence in domestic currency as well as in the perspective of the Vietnamese economy has not been established or strengthened. Moreover, domestic currency depreciation was expected in the future. In the case of deflation and low lending interest rates on US dollar deposits, the level of foreign deposits was high and the foreign exchange holdings by the public had been popular.

Table 7.4
Aggregate Monetary Balance ('000 VND)

	12/96	12/97	12/98	06/99	09/99
Net foreign assets	14.2	21.0	31.4	43.0	49.8
Foreign assets	31.2	37.9	47.9	56.4	62.5
Foreign liabilities	17.0	16.9	16.5	13.5	12.9
Net domestic assets	50.4	60.6	69.7	73.5	71.2
Net domestic credit	55.3	66.8	79.3	86.4	83.3
Net credit to government	4.4	4.4	6.7	4.7	4.2
Net credit to SOEs	26.8	31.0	38.0	na	na
Net credit to other sectors	24.1	31.4	34.7	na	na
Net other items	−4.9	−6.2	−9.6	12.9	na
Total liquidity	64.7	81.6	101.1	116.5	121.0
Total dong liquidity	51.5	62.9	76.2	85.0	88.7
Currency	22.6	25.1	27.0	25.7	27.0
Demand deposits	10.8	14.9	18.2	20.4	22.8
Time deposits and savings	18.1	22.9	20.1	28.3	28.6
Bonds			10.9	10.6	10.3
Total foreign deposit	13.2	18.7	24.9	31.5	32.3

Source: CIEM (2000)

7.3   SOME KEY POLICY REFORMS IN 1999

7.3.1   Measures Dealing the Asia Crisis

In 1999, the regional financial crisis's effect on the Vietnamese economy became clearer and more widespread. At the same time, the structural weaknesses of the economy reflected deeply and widely the seriousness of this effect, and became burdened by additional difficulties. Deflation and the decrease in aggregate demand became more obvious.

The focus of government policies was to prevent the economic recession and to gradually recover the high economic growth rate of the pre-crisis period. In 1999, the government continued to implement policy measures that became effective in the previous years. At the same time, the government had to issue new policies to overcome new problems and difficulties arising from the crisis. In the medium and long term, these two groups of measures may not be effective in confronting and overcoming the 1999 economic difficulties.

7.3.2   Law on Value Added Tax (VAT)

In 1999, the Law on VAT was put into effect without a good deal of preparation and at an inappropriate and difficult time when the economy had suffered low growth rates. The implementation was carried out regardless of proposals to postpone it. As a result, in the early days of implementation, a series of irrationalities and difficulties (as expected) became evident. These are:

1   decrease in enterprise profits and the population's purchasing power;
2   increase in tax avoidance;
3   use of the domestic factor inputs was discouraged;
4   increases in production costs and lack of capital became more widespread among enterprises;
5   enterprises and tax authorities spent a lot of time on tax refunding and the 'asking–giving' practice became abnormally popular (see Saigon Economic Times, 1999). It took the government time and effort to adjust and deal with the problems arising from the implementation of the VAT regulations. The adjustments in the VAT implementation might have 'distorted' the Law on VAT and made the Law's objectives difficult to achieve. Because of these problems, the implementation of the VAT Law did not help with overcoming the social and economic problems Vietnam suffered in 1999.

7.3.3   State Enterprise Reforms

Along with the economic decline in Vietnam, the growth rate of state owned enterprises (SOEs) had also been decreasing since 1996. In 1999, the growth rate of SOEs was one quarter of that of the foreign invested enterprises. SOEs now have an important role in providing the majority of pubic goods and services, infrastructure such as transportation, ports, electricity, water supply, telecommunications, and socioeconomic development services to remote mountainous and inland areas. But goods and services by SOEs were not cost effective. A few of the SOEs had spent great efforts to fight against smuggling and trade fraud, some even were involved in illegal activities themselves. Corruption and lack of transparency were common with many SOEs. According to an assessment made by the Enterprise Renovation Bureau, more than 50 per cent of SOEs had suffered a rate of return to their total assets being lower than the normal saving interest rate. Labour redundancy rate increased from 15 per cent in 1995 to 25 per cent in 1998, and this will probably continue into the future.

The objective of the establishment of the State General Corporations (SGC) was to form powerful economic conglomerations as economic frameworks that would operate with high efficiency and competitiveness. Currently, the State General Corporations' member enterprises shared 25 per cent of the total number, 66 per cent of the capital, 68 per cent of the revenue, and 55 per cent of the employees in the SOE sector. By being in this position, some SGCs were able to increase their competitiveness in bidding for contracts and to provide credit guarantees to member enterprises. They also assisted member enterprises to overcome other operational difficulties. However, the weaknesses of SGCs were a lack of financial and technological linkages between enterprise members and the SGC and, as a result, members do not feel any real need to join the SGC. In addition, there was no regulation to distinguish the entities and the assets of the SGC and the enterprise members.

Despite the merger of enterprises into SGCs or big companies, the number of SOEs has remained high and with a small scale of operation in terms of legal capital as given below:

25 per cent of SOEs	below 1 billion VND;
36 per cent of SOEs	between 1 to 5 billion VND;
16 per cent of SOEs	between 5 to 10 billion VND;
23 per cent of SOEs	above 10 billion VND.

According to the government's criteria of small and medium-size enterprises (SMEs), the number of SME-SOEs currently accounted for 60 per cent of the total number of SOEs. Most of them were inefficient, and with backward technologies and low competitiveness. The Ministry of Finance estimated that up to 50 per cent of SOEs were not profitable, 20 per cent were profitable, and the remainder were breaking even. However, the enterprises making profits, especially telecommunications, electricity and airline enterprises, have benefited from their monopoly position or the protection policy for them introduced by the government.

After the IVth Central Party Committee Resolution was put into effect in December 1997, the government has followed the SOE reforms more closely. The measures to restructure and to reorganise the SOEs became more diversified and feasible. However, these measures were still far from being synchronous, systematic or comprehensive. There was inconsistency in policy as well as in its enforcement. Therefore, the reform performance was not as expected, that is, to create an impetus for the next stage in economic development.

The measures for the SOE *equitisation* (privatisation) that were specified in Decree 44/1999/ND-CP have been widely implemented throughout Vietnam. This Decree was followed by Decision 145/1999/QD-TTg issued by the Prime Minister on 28 June 1999, specifying the regulation on the sale of securities to foreign investors. Under the Decision, 11 economic activities have been specified for foreign investors to be eligible to buy shares, but with the limit of not exceeding 30 per cent of their registered capital. The list of these economic activities comprised textiles and garments, footwear, leather processing, agriculture, forestry, fishery processing industries, consumer goods production, construction materials production, road, river, cargo and container transportation, production of educational equipment and instruments, the toy industry, trade, services, hotels, and mechanical industry.

Due to the equitisation measures listed above and the committed and consistent leadership of the government instructions, the number of equitised enterprises in 1999 exceeded the accumulative number of equitised enterprises in the previous years. In 1999 more than 250 enterprises were equitised and registered as shareholding companies, raising the accumulated number of equitised enterprises to 370. Thus, the equitisation performance in 1999 was much better than in the previous years. However, this number was still much lower than the planned figure of 400 equitised enterprises for the year 1999.

Many ministries, regional departments, and provincial localities did not have a concrete plan for equitisation and showed little interest in it. Some enterprises felt embarrassed by the equitisation planning so they deliberately delayed the submission of financial, accounting and auditing reports, and this had resulted in further delays. Although equitisation proposals at lower capital value than 20 billion VND were approved, equitisation in some enterprises remained slow. Notably, the number of equitised enterprises with a registered capital above 10 billion VND accounted for only 13.3 per cent of all equitised enterprises. The remainder had a registered capital below 10 billion VND. According to the government regulation, the maximal value of shares that one legal entity can buy is 20 per cent, for individuals 10 per cent, and for foreign investors 30 per cent of the registered capital of an enterprise. It may pose great obstacles to the equitisation process. This implies that the government was cautious about selling shares to outside investors.

Enterprise property valuation under equitisationi has also created many difficulties, because of its complexity. It requires valuation not only of tangible assets, but also of intangible assets, such as enterprise reputation, the professional qualification of staff, and others. However, until now, no specific implementation guideline has been given. In addition, debt issues, including the non-performing debts, have created restrictions on the equitisation process itself.

Decree 103/1999/ND-CP issued on 10 September 1999 on the outright divestiture, transfer, sale, and lease of SOEs, was an important step in the SOE reform process. According to this Decree, the divestiture, transfer, sale, and lease are applied in order to restructure and reorganise small SOEs.

However, the criteria for divestiture, transfer, sale, and lease of SOEs stipulated in the Decree has not been clear or specific. For enterprises in group (a) (see Box), there is a need to 'wait' for detailed instructions about the concept of 'running a long lasting unprofitable business' and the concept that 'the government does not need to hold shares'. Surprisingly, the SOEs running the consultative, designing, and control services are usually a small-capital-sized enterprise and their operation may not have any impact on the state sector. These enterprises, however, are excluded from the list of enterprises in group (b) eligible for the regulations of the Decree. For group (c) enterprises, the criteria and the required conditions of the eligible enterprises are also neither clear nor specific. In addition, the enterprises in the second group have to wait for a decision by the Prime Minister. Other complex problems such as land-use rights, employment, and debts, are causing delays in the implementation of the Decree on the divestiture, transfer, sale, and lease of SOEs. For these reasons, it is very difficult to implement the equitisation of the SOEs, especially if their state-owned property

---

The enterprises eligible for divestiture, transfer, sale and lease under Decree 103/1999/ND-CP are:

(a) The independent enterprises and the enterprise members of the State General Corporations which are:

- With the state-owned property value recorded in the accounting books below one billion VND; and

- The enterprises posting losses running a long and lasting unprofitable business or

- Those in which the government does not need to hold shares.

(b) The state-run agricultural and forestry farms, the enterprises running the consultative, designing and control services are not eligible under the regulations of Decree 103/199/ND-CP.

(c) The independent enterprises and the enterprise members of the State General Corporations are evaluated by the government on an individual basis if:

- Their state-owned property value recorded in the accounting books falls between one to five billion VND; and

- The enterprise is posting losses running a long and lasting unprofitable business but not in the position of going into bankruptcy, which cannot improve after various solutions with the support of the government.

---

value recorded in the accounting book is above one billion VND. The procedures on the equitisation of the SOEs are administrative rather than market-oriented. Nevertheless, Decree 103/1999/ND-CP has contributed positively to the diversification of the stage of the reform and it affirms the government's efforts to reform and increase the efficiency of the SOE sector.

7.3.4 'Demand Stimulus' Measures

In the second half of 1999, the focus of the government's demand stimulus measures was to prevent economic decline as well as to recover economic growth by 2000 and in the future. These measures were stipulated in Resolution 08/1999/NQ-CP issued on 9 July 1999. The seven groups of measures stipulated in this Resolution are as follows:

1   Stimulating the demand on consumption and investment in order to activate the internal resources, and so encouraging the development of production and business activities;
2   Encouraging export activities;
3   Monetary and financial measures;
4   The measures for stabilising the investment, production, and business environment and further measures for restructuring SOEs;
5   The measures for poverty reduction and the assistance to extremely difficult communes;
6   The social measures;
7   The management and governance measures.

Despite these efforts, the achievement was lower than the expectations. Demand stimulus measures were applied to expand the state investment expenditures for a small number of industrial enterprises and these measures mostly benefited large SOEs. The mobilisation of four trillion VND from government bonds issuance for increased state budget capital expenditures would be justified if the resources were used for feasible economic development projects and programmes. However, it reduced the consumption level of domestic residents and had negative impact on the country's economic growth rate as a whole. The funds disbursement procedures were not in consistency with the 'demand stimulus' policy while these measures were subject to continuous changes in the regulatory framework relating to investment management, project appraisal and procurement All this made the 'demand stimulus' policy less effective in promoting economic growth.

7.3.5   The Enterprise Law

The Enterprise Law, approved by the National Assembly on 12 June 1999, marked a turning point in the transition process of Vietnam's economy into a market-oriented economy. This Law encompasses many new features, some of which are:

- The legalisation of freedom to run business activities by citizens in pursuance of the 1992 Constitution; citizens do not have to 'ask' for and the government does not have to 'give' the right to run a business;

- The freedom to establish, manage, and operate business activities by citizens was appreciated and secured;

- An important legal framework was created to follow one negative list of businesses (enterprises are allowed to do what is not prohibited by laws. In contrast, in the past, enterprises were only allowed to do what was permitted by law or by state authorities).

The Enterprise Law clearly and simply stipulated the rules for business establishment and registration. As specified in the Law, the regulations on the establishment and the business registration of enterprises can restrict arbitrary implementation because of the arrogance, and the bureaucracy of some government officials or authorised agencies. The Enterprise Law abolished a significant number of unnecessary certificates, licences, permissions, and approvals, which, in fact, created administrative and bureaucratic obstacles to the expansion and the diversification of business activities. Enterprises can freely choose, register, expand, and diversify the business activities that are not prohibited or restricted by law. With these new features, the Law is likely to have positive effects on the business environment in Vietnam in the following ways:

- The unanticipated risks derived from the arbitrary implementation of laws by state officials and agencies can be reduced. The transaction costs would be reduced considerably and, as a result, the efficiency and the competitiveness of enterprises would increase, and business activities would become more active and dynamic.

- The market mechanism would operate more efficiently and be more flexible; and the competition in markets would increase.

- Markets would be expanded and be more unified.

- The transparency of the business environment would increase and, as a result, the rent-seeking behaviours would decrease. The relationship between 'enterprises and state' would become more sound. Party and state policies and measures would be implemented faster and more efficiently.

- The improvement in the investment environment, as mentioned above, would certainly raise the confidence of investors and would encourage them to invest more. As a result, the economy would have a new impetus for future growth and development.

7.3.6   Banking Reforms

Banking reforms have also been carefully implemented. In 1999, the economy continuously revealed weaknesses and complexities and the banking system was confronted with many difficulties. Monetary policies and financial instruments were complex.

The financial status of the commercial banks was not clear or was questionable during recent years. The percentage of overdue and non-performing loans exceeded the allowed limit and, as estimated, was ranging from 13 per cent to 15 per cent of the total outstanding loans. The overdue and non-performing loans of state commercial banks accounted for 82.3 per cent of the total overdue and non-performing loans, and joint stock commercial banks accounted for 15.2 per cent (see Figure 7.1).

One of the main reasons for the large amount of overdue and non-performing loans in the commercial banks in the last two years was that credits to SOEs rapidly

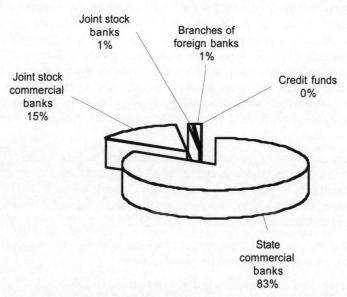

Sources: Vietnam State Bank and CIEM 2000 estimates

Note.   The actual proportions were: state commercial banks 82.33 per cent, joint stock commercial banks 15.23 per cent, joint stock banks 1.22 per cent, branches of foreign banks 0.83 per cent, and credit funds 0.40 per cent.

Figure 7.1   Overdue and Non-performing Loans in Vietnam Banking System (30 April 1999)

increased from 15 per cent between 1995–1997 to 22 per cent in 1998. Commercial banks were allowed to reduce the reserve requirement ratio in short-term deposits from 10 per cent in 1998 to 5 per cent in 1999. A large part of the increased credits to SOEs was given by the government nomination and as medium- and long-term loans for infrastructure projects whose profitability was low and with a long period of operation before returns were attained. Some enterprises also used the credits for production activities to prevent workers' lay-offs during economic recession. A large part of these loans was given without collateral so the risks were high.

Because of poor monitoring over the loan utilisation, unreliable financial reports of borrowing enterprises, and lack of debt collection regulations, many joint stock commercial banks, the shareholders of which are SOEs and private economic organisations, could not collect back money for bad loans. Furthermore, many joint stock commercial banks, which were established with low equity or with inadequate registered capital, would be easily exposed to the danger of bankruptcy. Because of competition in the banking system, and the continued decrease in the lending interest rate in order to expand credits for the 'demand stimulus' measures, the profit rate of commercial banks also decreased. The majority of joint stock commercial banks were disadvantaged when they had to compete with the state commercial banks. This was because the state commercial banks dominated the credit markets with 80 per cent of the total customers. Thus, in order for the joint stock commercial banks to increase their competitiveness, they had to reduce lending interest rates to a lower rate than the lending interest rate of the state commercial banks and, in turn, the profits of these joint stock commercial banks would diminish and they would fall into further difficulties.

The commercial banks could survive with an increasingly large amount of overdue and non-performing loans because their business capital consisted mainly of foreign loans, state credits borrowed at a low interest rate and their own assets. Despite rearrangements and reorganisations made within the system of joint stock commercial banks, the business governance in this system has been still very weak.

Following the government policies on banking reforms, the State Bank intensified the supervision and investigation of credit institutions to restructure them and to improves the situation of overdue and non-performing loans. The four main principles of the banking reforms are as follows:.

1   Restructuring state commercial banks and joint stock commercial banks;
2   Improving regulatory, institutional and legal frameworks;
3   Create an equal playing field for all banks; and
4   Human capacity building to the banking system.

The State Bank has asked the government to increase the registered capital for state commercial banks and to improve gradually the performance of those banks by freezing or solving their overdue and non-performing loans. By June 1999, 586.753 trillion VND and US$1.575 million of the overdue and non-performing loans of state commercial banks were written off, 574.212 trillion VND and US$36.810 million were frozen, and 308.004 trillion VND and US$23.688 million were extended. These measures should be considered however as 'subsidies' given by the state to the state commercial banks and were not effective in improving their efficiency.

It should be noted that, as part of the country's banking reform, the State Bank paid its special attention to restructuring joint stock commercial banks (JSCB). Several of these banks were placed under strict control and special measures were applied to prevent uncertainty in the whole banking system. The State Bank allowed some JSCBs to merge or to be taken over. For example, the Dai Nam JSCB was merged with the Phuong Nam JSCB; the East Asia JSCB took over the Long Xuyen Quadrangle JSCB; and Sai Gon Trade JSCB took over the Orient JSCB. In addition, the plans for partially restructuring each JSCB have also been prepared. These plans have focused mainly on the debt solutions and recapitalisation, including the increase in limit to foreign ownership of 50 per cent. The government also allocated a certain amount of capital from the state budget to refinance several banks. At the same time, the partial deposit insurance measures were applied to the small depositors in order to gain the public's confidence in keeping their deposits in the banks.

The government also intended to establish a company for property management to deal with the bad loans that had been pledged with collateral. This company will be granted by the government with a large amount of funds for registered capital and can get involved in purchasing and selling the bank loans which were with collateral but banks cannot be put up for sale because of the nature of the property used as collateral, the lack of necessary documents, and other reasons.

Despite the weaknesses in the banking system in the country, the government measures for banking reforms by restructuring the banking system have been deemed very appropriate and have helped the banking system to operate more efficiently and more suitably in accordance with the international financial standards and practice.

7.4   ISSUES IN VIETNAM'S ECONOMIC MANAGEMENT IN 2001 AND BEYOND

Issues for Vietnam in 2000 and its planned economic attainment for 2010 were focused early in 2001 on the three aspects of economic management: SOE reform and equitisation, banking reform and small and medium-size enterprises (SMEs) promotion and private sector development (World Bank 2001b).

In its Socioeconomic Development Strategy (2001–2010) draft, Vietnam envisages developing an efficient, competitive and financially healthy and growing SOE sector. This covers not only utilities but also manufacturing and trading enterprises. SOE reform and equitisation are necessary as Vietnam has agreed to open up trade and investment under the ASEAN free trade arrangement (AFTA) and the US bilateral trade agreement (USBTA) that are to be implemented in the next five to ten years.

SOEs account for 30 per cent of GDP, 25 per cent of all investment, 15 per cent of non-agricultural employment and about 50 per cent of outstanding domestic bank credit. SOEs were also an important employment-generating sector. In 2001, there were 5300 SOEs (500 of which had been equitised in the past year) employing around 1.6 million people. However in 1997, there were 5800 SOEs and about 60 per cent of them were not profitable and the debt–asset ratio of most of them was excessive (World Bank 2001b).

It has to be recognised that the government's plan for SOE reform and equitisation focuses on urgent and important issues (such as diversification of SOE ownership, liquidation of non-viable SOEs, restructuring SOEs still under the government's control, and establishing a social safety net for SOE workers, and has its merits. From our discussion of various problems with the implementation of SOE reform above, however, we must conclude that the target of this reform may be elusive and may take a much longer time to achieve.

Related to SOE reform is banking reform which also is part of the Socioeconomic Development Strategy (2001–2010) draft of the government. There were plans to extend reforms beyond the banking sector to cover the financial-sector issues. The vision of Vietnam's banking reform, a priority objective, is to develop a sound and stable banking system that can mobilise domestic savings effectively and channel them to efficient investments. The final outcomes of such a reform are rapid growth achievement and significant poverty reduction.

Under this reform, banking services are to be diversified, and the banking system will be made solvent and competitive within five years. To achieve these objectives, a number of obstacles and challenges have to be resolved to some significant extent. These include: poor accounting practices, inappropriate regulatory and supervisory systems, limited tradition of commercial (as compared to privately arranged) lending, non-performing loans, and low profitability. The planned actions by the government to achieve the vision above involve: restructuring JSCBs, state commercial banks, improving the legal, regulatory and supervisory framework, and levelling the playing field for all banks, state and non-state (World Bank 2001b).

Issues of SME promotion and private sector development of the Socioeconomic Development Strategy draft (2001–2010) have to be looked at from a long-term perspective in which accelerating industrialisation in the 'socialist orientation' and creating a foundation for Vietnam to become an industrialised country by 2020 are the government's vision.

The key steps needed to achieve this vision include an enhancement of a legal environment for SMEs through: the promulgation of a decree on SME promotion policies structure (simplifying the tax system, streamlining administrative procedures, reducing red tape and corruption); the introduction of the New Enterprise Law in January 2000; improving land use rights; levelling the playing field for SOEs and private enterprises (World Bank 2001b).

7.5   CONCLUSIONS

The above discussions and assessment of Vietnam's economic management in the years immediately before and after the Asia crisis of July 1997 appear to focus on a number of points.

First, in spite of the fact that Vietnam has not yet had a stock market and a fully convertible currency (the VND) – the two transmission mechanisms of regional and international crises – its economy was still affected to some extent by the negative impact from the contagion of the Asia turmoil (see also ADB 2001). While this impact was not as serious politically and socially as that in Indonesia, Korea, Malaysia and Thailand, it has nevertheless had a significant effect on the government's economic management and the speed of reform and development. This impact also had all the characteristics of a medium or long term nature (see Tran Van Hoa 2001).

Second, while Vietnam has attained the status of an APEC member, it still has to become a member of the World Trade Organization to take advantage of available opportunities to support its policy of open trade and investment with the rest of the world. The process of globalisation is slow but pervasive in all countries, big or small, market-oriented or centrally planned or autocratically controlled, around the world. Vietnam's economic management has to take all these developments on the internationally scene into account.

Third, while Vietnam's objectives in policy planning and implementation are consistently economic development and growth, poverty reduction and international cooperation or integration, the country still is burdened with a structure of an administration and framework of a war-ravaged, developing and transition economy in Asia. This may pose real internal challenges for a fast and efficient implementation of government restructuring and reforms in the public, economic, financial and banking, SME and SOE sectors.

The external factors likely to affect Vietnam's socioeconomic development strategies are numerous. These factors are real and emerging in spite of previous more positive forecasts on developed and developing countries by the international organisations such as the International Monetary Fund (IMF) and the WB and the ADB (see Tables 7.5 and 7.6). The most notable factors include, during 2001, a slow-down in the world economy, especially the US (with a slower growth rate) and the European Union (with the occurrence of BSE and then foot and mouth diseases), the impact of higher crude oil prices from the Middle East to developed economies, and the inability of the Japanese government to resolve its long-lasting and serious

Table 7.5
Economic Growth Rates and International Trade (%, 1998–2000)

	WB (December 1999)			IMF (September 1999)		
	1998	1999	2000	1998	1999	2000
GDP						
World	1.9	2.6	2.9	2.5	3.0	3.5
Developed countries	2.0	2.6	2.5	2.2	2.8	2.7
Developing countries	1.6	2.7	4.2	3.2	3.5	4.8
International trade	4.2	5.0	6.4	3.6	3.7	6.2

Note: Estimated data for 1999 and forecast data for 2000
Sources: WB, 1999, *Global Economic Prospects 2000*, December; IMF, 1999, *World Economic Outlook*, September; ADB, 1999, *Asian Development Outlook 1999*, August. The growth rate of the world economy in 2000 was expected to be 3.5 per cent (in 1998: 2.5 per cent and in 1999 more than 2.5 per cent) and the growth rate of international trade in 2000 was expected to be 6 per cent (in 1998: 3.3 per cent and in 1999: 4 per cent).

Table 7.6
The GDP Growth Rates of the East Asian Countries

	IMF (September 1999)				ADB (August 1999)			
	1997	1998	1999	2000	1997	1998	1999	2000
South Korea	5.0	−5.8	6.5	5.5	5.5	−5.8	8.0	6.0
Indonesia	4.7	−13.7	−0.8	2.6	4.9	−13.2	2.0	4.0
Malaysia	7.7	−6.7	2.4	6.5	7.7	−7.5	2.0	3.9
Philippines	5.2	−0.5	2.2	3.5	5.2	−0.5	3.0	4.5
Singapore	9.0	0.3	4.5	5.0	7.8	1.5	5.0	6.0
Thailand	−1.3	−9.4	4.0	4.0	−1.3	−9.4	3.0	5.0
China	8.8	7.8	6.6	6.0	8.8	7.8	6.8	6.0

Note: Estimated data for 1999 and forecasted data for 2000
Sources: See Table 7.5

economic management problems and to restore its economy to an active and high growth economy.

These international developments will surely pose additional challenges for economic management and reforms in Vietnam.

NOTE

1 Up to 80 per cent of the bonds issued by the government were bought by enterprises (including the financial and insurance institutions), and especially by SOEs. In Ho Chi Minh City, where the average income per capita was highest in the country, the percentage of bonds bought by the public was very low.

REFERENCES

Asian Development Bank (2001), Economic outlook data taken from <www.adb.org>.
CIEM (Central Institute for Economic Management) (1999), 1998 *Vietnamese Economy Review*, Hanoi: Education Publishing House.
CIEM (2000), *Vietnam's Economy in 1999*, Hanoi: Statistical Publishing House.
Saigon Economic Times, Nos. 28–29, 8 July 1999.
Tran Van Hoa (2001), *The Asia Recovery*, Cheltanham, UK and Northampton, MA: Edward Elgar.

World Bank (2001a), Development in Vietnam/Macroeconomic Update, <www.worldbank.org.vn/econdev/mac001.html>, March.

World Bank (2001b), Vietnam 2010: Entering the 21st Century – Partnerships for Development, <www.worldbank.org.vn/rep22/c2–01.htm>, March.

World Bank (2001c), Vietnam 2010: Entering the 21st Century – Pillars of Development, <www.worldbank.org.vn/econdev/appet24.htm>, March.

8 The Philippines: Crises and Economic Crisis Management

Tran Van Hoa

8.1   INTRODUCTION

The Republic of the Philippines (named after King Philip II of Spain) has been a member of the Association of the Southeast Asian Nations (ASEAN) since its foundation in the mid-1960s. Strategically, it lies along an important sea route, rich in oil and other mineral reserves, linking the Middle East, the subcontinent and northeast Asia. Geographically, it is bounded by the Philippine Sea to the east, the Celebes Sea to the south, and the South China Sea to the west and north. In spite of its location, the country's demography, history, economy and recent political and social developments set it apart from the rest of the ASEAN. These characteristics of the Philippines would, especially in recent years, make any standard or conventional analysis of its economy and economic management more difficult, not only in an Asian context but also in the context of orthodox fiscal and monetary policy often practised in the Western economies since World War Two.

The Philippines is an archipelago of some 7100 islands and islets lying about 800km off the coast. It has a total land area of 300 000 square kilometers with its capital, Manila, being located on the biggest island, Luzon. After being ruled by Spain for 333 years since the 16th century, the country came under the US tutelage for another 48 years before gaining its independence in 1946. This kind of more or less involuntary association has made the Philippines more closely related to Western culture than with an Asian outlook. It is, for example, the fourth most populous country in the world in which English is an official language and spoken by almost half of the population (even though a version of the native language Tagalog, namely Pilipino, has been promoted with some success by the government since 1939 as a second language) including nearly all professionals, academics, and government workers. The Philippines is the only predominantly Roman Catholic country in Southeast Asia with about 90 per cent of its people being Christian and in which Buddhism and Islam have never had great impact and influence. Its peoples, originally of Malay and

Indonesian stock and, more recently, of Chinese and Indian mixture, are however Asian in consciousness and in aspiration and also by origin from various parts of the adjoining Asian landmass. In many ways, Filipino society has been regarded as being composed of paradoxes with the great extremes of wealth and poverty in the nation (*Britannica* 2001).

Since the end of World War Two, the Philippine economy has had a mixed history of growth and development. Over the years, the country has gone from being one of the richest countries in Asia (after Japan) to being one of the poorest. Important sectors of the economy include agriculture (accounting for one fifth of economic production) and industry (particularly food processing, textiles and garments, electronics and automotive parts). Most industries are concentrated in the urban areas around metropolitan Manila. Mining is also important and the country possesses significant reserves of chromite, nickel and copper. Recent natural gas finds off the islands of Palawan also add to the country's substantial geothermal, hydro and coal energy reserves. Philippine agriculture produces sugar, coconut products, rice, corn, pineapples, bananas, aquaculture, mangoes, pork and eggs (*Britannica* 2001).

Relevant Filipino history can be divided into four periods: the pre-Spanish period (before 1521), the Spanish period (1521–1898), the American period (1898–1946) and the post-independence period (1946–present). Of interest to our study in this chapter is the take-off stage of major Asian economies (including particularly the Philippines) in the region since the 1960s and the Asia crisis of 1997 and its impact and management issues after this period. In Section 8.2, we give a brief description and analysis of the growth and trends of major economic activities in the Philippines in recent years. Section 8.3 deals with important issues of crisis and economic crisis management arising from the Asia meltdown in 1997 and its contagion on the Philippine economy. Critical comments and an assessment of the country's prospects are finally given in Section 8.4.

8.2   RECENT GROWTH AND TRENDS IN THE PHILIPPINE ECONOMY

8.2.1   The Philippines and the Asia Economic Crisis

In a number of previous studies (see, for example, Tran Van Hoa 2000a and 2000b), we have reported on the growth path and development trends of major 'miracle' economies in Asia over a period of over 30 years. These studies have provided a critical analysis of the causes of the Asia crisis that started in Thailand in July 1997 and its impact on these economies. They have also discussed the subsequent prescriptions recommended by international organisations and adopted by crisis countries in the region and evaluated their outcomes. The countries that have been identified as having initially suffered most, in terms of a decline in their GDP growth and as a result of this crisis, were found to be the so-called Asia–4: Indonesia, Korea, Malaysia and Thailand. The Philippines and two major transition economies in Asia, namely China and Vietnam, were found to be less affected by the turmoil and its contagion.

Evidence from more recent official economic and trade statistics appears to support the previous findings from these studies that the Asia crisis and its contagion had impacted not only on developing and transition economies alike in Asia but also on the newly industrialised economies (NIEs) or countries (NICs) (such as Hong Kong, Korea, Singapore and Taiwan) in the region. The level of impact was, however, different for different groups of countries. Unfortunately, the impact has also been found to be not of a short-term nature with only temporary effects on growth and development and trade and investment of crisis economies. Rather, it appears to be of a long-term nature with lingering damaging results on a large number of economic activities and international relations. Appropriate and effective cures and policies for this long-term problem have not been found.

Some of the more recent evidence on growth and development of crisis economies is reported in Figures 8.1 and 8.2. Figure 8.1 depicts the annual movements of gross domestic product (GDP) at market prices for four Asian developing economies (Indonesia, Malaysia, the Philippines and Thailand) and two transition economies (China and Vietnam) for the period 1979–98. The data trace the trends over two decades of economic achievement in these countries and the immediate aftermath of the 1997 Asia crisis. Figure 8.2 contains the quarterly growth rates of Japan and four Asian NIEs (Hong Kong, Korea, Singapore and Taiwan) for the period December 1995 to September 2000. The data are quarterly and therefore capable of depicting the short-term fluctuations of GDP in more detail. The data for Figure 8.1 were collected from the 2000 World Bank World Tables, and those for Figure 8.2 from the 2001 Australian Bureau of Statistics time-series databases. For consistency in comparison, the selected period in the two figures only covers the years or quarters when data for all countries under study (except Vietnam) are available.

From Figure 8.1, we note that all six Asian developing and transition economies had posted remarkable achievements in GDP growth since 1979. These achievements were uneven for these countries, however, and also for the different sub-periods in our sample timeframe. For example, China appears to be the country with a highest GDP growth generally (reaching 15.2 per cent in 1985), but in the two consecutive years 1989–1990 of internal turmoil where its growth rates were merely 4.1 and 4.0 per cent respectively, it was overtaken by all other listed Asian economies. During the two years 1989–1990, Thailand's growth reached its second highest level in Figure 8.1 with 12.2 and 11.2 per cent respectively, followed by Malaysia (9.2 and 9.6 per cent) and then Indonesia (9.1 and 9.0 per cent).

The Philippines seems to stand out as an odd case in the group. During the period 1979–98, its growth rate seems to be the lowest of all six countries under study and reaching its highest level at 6.6 and 6.2 per cent only in 1989 and 1990. During the internal political 'people power or Marcos' crisis of the mid-1980s, its growth rate

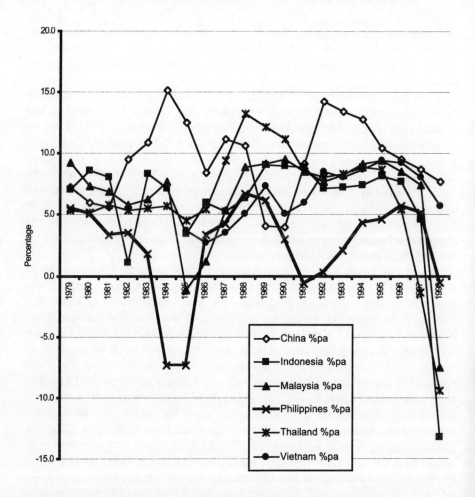

Figure 8.1   Growth in Major Developing Economies (1979–1998)

plummeted to –7.3 for two consecutive years, 1984 and 1985, and then again to –0.6
and 0.3 per cent in 1992 and 1993. Malaysia also had its crisis over the period 1979–
1998 especially during 1985–86 when its growth was –1.1 and 1.2 respectively, but
its growth trend was generally good at over 6 per cent per year on average.

Figures 8.1 and 8.2 show that all 11 Asian countries under study (developed,
developing and transition alike) had been affected by the 1997 Asia economic and
financial crisis. When we compare the growth rates in 1997 and 1998 to that achieved
in 1996 (the immediate pre-crisis year), the worst affected country is Indonesia (4.7
and –13.2 per cent against 7.8 per cent respectively), followed by Thailand (–1.5 and
–9.4 per cent against 5.5 per cent), Malaysia (7.5 and –7.5 per cent against 8.6 per

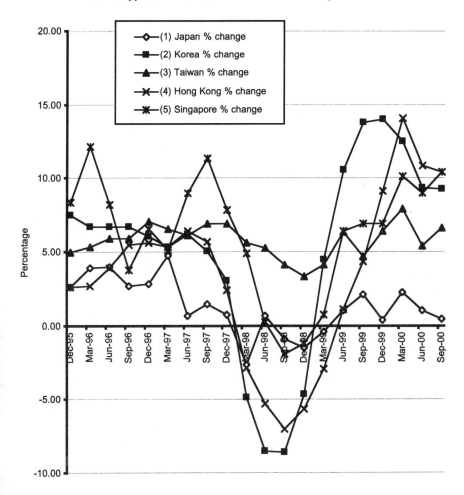

Figure 8.2   Growth in Japan and Major Asian NIEs (1995–2000)

cent), and the Philippines (5.2 and –0.5 per cent against 5.8 per cent). The two major transition economies in Asia, China and Vietnam, were also affected by the Asia crisis and its contagion but the impact was only slight with a declining growth rate of 8.8 and 7.8 per cent for 1997 and 1998 against 9.6 per cent in 1996 for China, and 8.1 and 5.8 per cent against 9.3 per cent for Vietnam.

Figure 8.2 shows that Japan and the four Asian NIEs (Hong Kong, Korea, Singapore and Taiwan) were also affected by the 1997 Asia crisis. Japan, which had experienced serious economic and financial woes resulting in low and even declining economic growth over a decade or so, recorded a growth rate of –2.60 per cent in March 1998 and three consecutive negative rates of –0.86, –1.42 and –0.38 per cent in September and December 1998 and March 1999 respectively. The four Asian NIEs posted, in September 1998, their negative growth rates as low as –8.57 per cent for Korea, –6.99 per cent for Hong Kong, and –1.85 per cent for Singapore. Taiwan also suffered declining growth as a result of the Asia crisis but managed to obtain 3.38 per cent in September 1998 compared to 6.96, 5.63, 5.27 and 4.14 per cent for the four previous quarters (December 1997–September 1998).

The above discussion seems to indicate that the Philippines, like most other Asian economies, was affected by the Asia crisis and its contagion. However, by its historical and social make-up and its own way of association and development in recent times, the impact can be seen in two quite different perspectives. First the impact was much milder than that experienced by other fast-growing Asian developing economies such as Indonesia, Thailand and Malaysia or other Asian NIEs such as Korea. Second, while it did escape the serious burden of the Asia crisis, it suffered more damage than transition and developing economies in the neighbouring region (such as China and Vietnam). Economic management in the Philippines in recent years has reflected these kinds of features in its economy.

8.2.2   Trends in Philippine Trade

The relative so-called lacklustre economic achievement of the Philippines and, probably because of it, the more resilient resistance of it toward the contagion and impact of the Asia crisis can be further seen through the country's pattern and composition of international trade over the past three decades or so and given in Figures 8.3–8.8. Figures 8.3–8.6 depict the Philippines' total imports (in US$ and in percentage) and total exports (also in US$ and in percentage) with nine major trading blocs in the world. These nine trading blocs cover nearly all of Philippine world trade and consist of: the US, Japan, Australia and New Zealand, India, China, four Asian NIEs (Hong Kong, Korea, Singapore and Taiwan), OPEC (Organization of Petroleum Exporting Countries) Africa, the former USSR, and the European Union (EU).

From Figures 8.3–8.4, the Philippines' most important trading bloc in terms of its imports is Japan, followed by the US, four Asian NIEs (Hong Kong, Singapore, Korea and Taiwan), OPEC and, very recently, China. In 1998 (the last year of available data in the 2000 CHELEM-CEPII databases), Japan's exports to the Philippines (which were declining from the 1996 and 1997 levels) was still valued at US$7371.3 million (or 28.1 per cent of all of the Philippines' imports), followed by the US with US$6629.5 million (25.2 per cent), four Asian NIEs with US$6282.5 million (23.9 per cent), and the EU with US$3459.7 million (13.2 per cent).

From Figures 8.5–8.6, we note that most of the Philippines' exports went to the US, followed by the EU, Japan and four Asian NIEs. In 1998, the US imported goods were valued at US$11238 million from the Philippines and accounted for 45.9 per cent of all of Philippine exports, followed by the EU at US$4471.6 million (18.2 per cent), Japan at US$4182.9 million (17.1 per cent), and four Asian NIEs at US$3856.8 million (15.7 per cent).

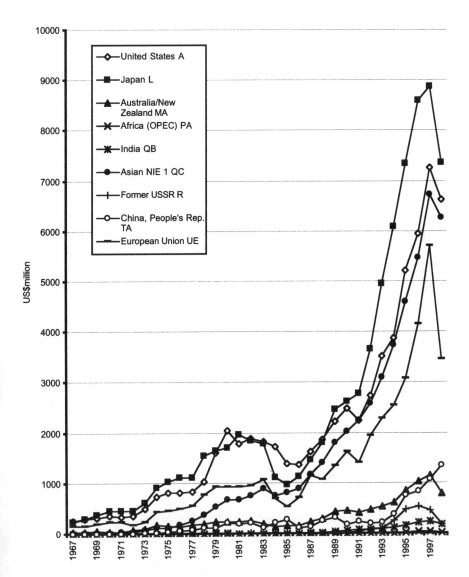

Figure 8.3   Phillipines' Imports from the World

The Philippines' exports to the world can also be broken down into more detailed tradable commodities. The patterns and trends of these commodities over a period of more than 30 years (1967–98) are given in Figures 8.7 and 8.8.

Among the 10 groups of tradable commodities classified by CHELEM-CEPII (construction products, basic metals, textiles, wood paper, metal products, chemicals,

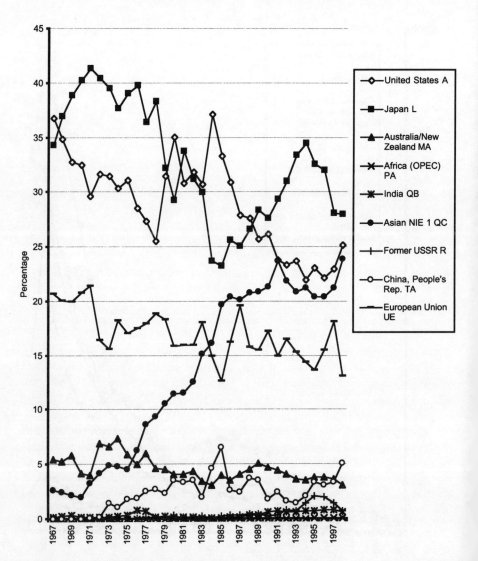

Figure 8.4   Phillipines' Imports from the World (%)

mining, energy, agriculture and food products), the largest group of exports from the Philippines was metal products (including electronics and automotive parts), followed a long way down by textiles and food products. In 1998, metal product exports were valued at US19643.3 million and accounted for 71.5 per cent of all exports from the Philippines. This was followed by textiles at US$2966.3 million (10.8 per cent) and food products at US$1648.8 million (6 per cent). In fact, in the recent years, metal product exports were the only growing commodity group both in terms of its value and percentage in the Philippine economy. During 1995–1997 for example, these exports had increased from US$8646.5 million or 51.4 per cent of all exports in 1995 to US$13111.4 million (61.7 per cent) and US$17999.4 million (69 per cent) in 1996 and 1997 respectively.

8.3   THE PHILIPPINES' POLITICAL AND ECONOMIC CRISES

For the Philippines, crises had been many and varied since its independence from the US in 1946. Throughout these many and varied crises, two clear developments have merged, that is, first, the country has lagged behind most of its Asian neighbouring economies in terms of growth and economic development and, second, it has inherited some of the worst political and social problems in its history. It is true that the country under its long succession of presidential leaderships from Marcos, to Aquino, Ramos, Estrada and Macapagal-Arroyo, has tried, by adopting numerous policies and reforms with the assistance from international organisation, banks and agencies, to redirect the country's path towards more and sustainable economic growth and development and meaningful social condition improvement. All these efforts seem to have produced less than expected or planned. Added to the country's woes were alleged corruption at the highest level, the growing Muslim separatist movement, and sometimes the effect of unpredictable climatic changes. An example of the latter is the El Niño effect in 1998 that severely affected the country's agricultural production resulting in the sector's growth of –1.1 per cent that year.

The outcomes are that, in 1960, the Philippines enjoyed an income per capita of US$711 (at the 1995 US prices) and was ranked second (after Malaysia with a per capita income of US$997) in the group Asia–5 (China, Indonesia, Malaysia, the Philippines and Thailand). This income was almost three times that of Indonesia (at US$249) and 52.2 per cent more than that of Thailand (at US$467) at the time. However in 1998, Philippine per capita income was only US$1050 and ranked almost equal to that of Indonesia (at US$972) and at about 40 per cent of Thailand (at US$2593). In 1998, Malaysia's income per head was US$4251, or more than four times that of the Philippines.

Official statistics issued by such organisations as the Asian Development Bank (which has its headquarters in Manila) have painted an equally gloomy picture for the Philippines early in 2001. These data were gathered late in 2000 and seemingly have not taken into account the slow-down early in 2001 in the US and Japan, two of the most important markets for the Philippines (and other major Asian economies) in the past 50 years or so. According to these statistics, the Philippine industrial production index was stable in 1999 and 2000 at about 144, the unemployment rate was increasing from 9.7 per cent in 1999 to 11.1 per cent in 2000, real wage growth declined from

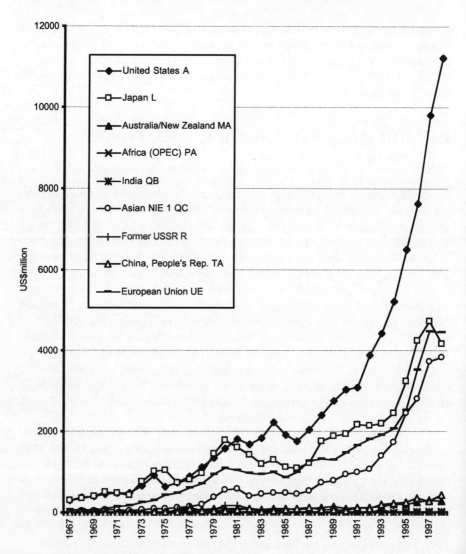

Figure 8.5   Phillipines' Exports to the World

1.4 per cent in 1999 to –0.2 in 2000, and the government budget deficit was slightly reduced from –3.7 in 1999 to –3.3 in 2000. In addition, foreign direct investment continued to fall, from US$1.7 billion in 1998 to US$1.1 billion in 1999 and US$1.0 billion in 2000, total external debts stood at US$46.3 billion (or 0.7 per cent of GDP) in 1998 and US$52.2 billion (0.7 per cent) in 1999.

Alarmingly, the debt service ratio continued to rise, from 11.7 per cent of all exports of goods and services in 1997 to 11.4 per cent in 1998 and 12.7 per cent in

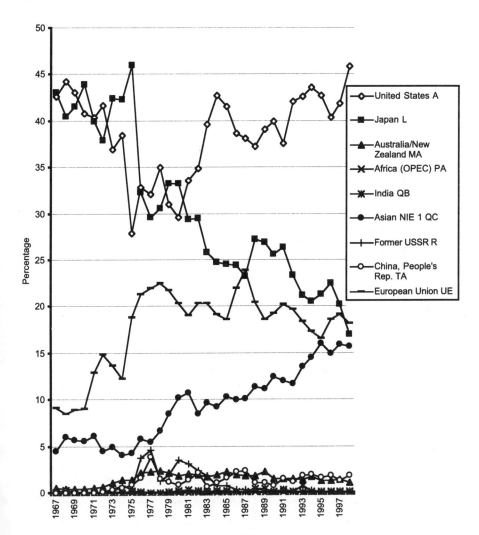

Figure 8.6   Phillipines' Exports to the World (%)

1999, and the stock market index (with December 1994=100) fell from 76.9 in 1999 to 59.2 in 2000 (Asian Development Bank 2001). The non-performing loan (NPL) ratio of the commercial banking system rose from 10.4 per cent in 1998 to 12.3 per cent in 1999 and 15.1 in 2000, and the exchange rate of the peso became weaker from 39.2 peso/US$ in 1998 to 40.3 peso/US$ in 1999 and 50.0 peso/US$ in 2000 (ARIC 2001). The only good news seems to be that the level of international reserves steadily increased from 10.7 per cent of imports of goods and services in 1998 to 15.0 per cent in 1999 and 15.1 per cent in 2000.

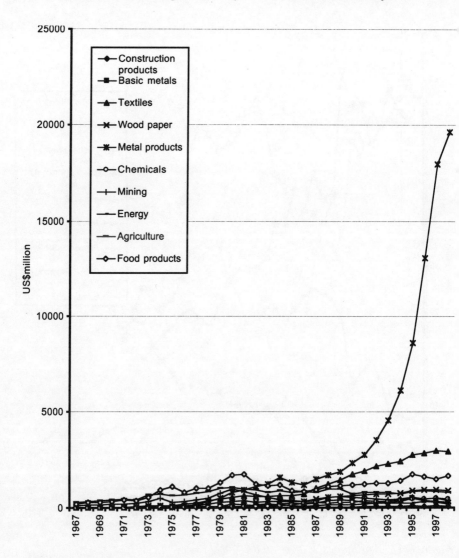

Figure 8.7   Phillipines' Exported Commodities

Faced with this kind of development in the country, the Philippine government has had to resort to drastic measures and policies to arrest further deterioration of the economy, reduce further political instability and cut back further worsening of the poverty level. These measures have been essentially centred around the fundamentals of monetary and fiscal policy that have been practised in similar economic crises in Latin America and elsewhere in the early 1990s.

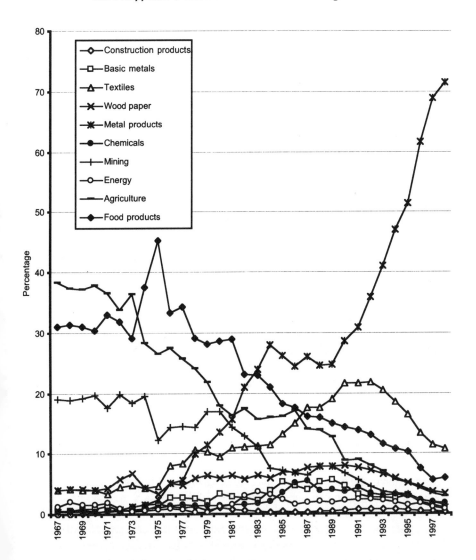

Figure 8.8   Phillipines' Exported Commodities (%)

Late in 1997, the Philippine government adopted the now well-known stance of the International Monetary Fund (IMF) to raise interest rates and to cut government spending to curtail the economic crisis and its damaging impact on the economy. As a result, interbank short-term call rates rose to 15.8 per cent in 1997, falling down to 13.8 per cent in 1998, and 10.8 per cent in 1999 and 2000. Subdued inflation was the argument used to justify the authorities' decision to reduce these rates early in 2000.

However, subsequently for most of 2000, monetary policy was tightened due to the subsequent deterioration (depreciation) of the Philippine peso, the rise in the US interest rates and emerging inflationary pressure. On 12 March 2001, the overnight borrowing rate was again cut to 10.5 per cent in an effort by the central bank to invigorate the economy. The easing of monetary policy had some effect on the financial sector in the sense that there was a turnaround in the real credit growth. However, banks, being burdened with high NPLs, remained reluctant lenders, and demand for credit from the private and corporate sector was weak (ARIC 2001).

During the economic crisis, the Philippine government had used its fiscal policy to stimulate the economy, even though initially a tight budget was the cure recommended by international organisations. A policy of more government expenditure has found favour with many governments in Asia due to its inherent regulated or control nature preferred by public service staff. This so-called Asian style of economic management has often been used and also advocated for adoption in other Asian economies by Japan. However, this policy of demand management has its downside. Early in 2001, official data indicated that the budget deficit seemed to have widened (to 4.1 per cent of GDP in 2000 from 3.7 per cent in 1999) due to shortfalls in revenue generation. Worse still for the country, the estimated budget deficit of 62.5 billion peso in 2000 was blown out to 136.1 billion peso. This shortfall was attributed to the failure of the government to meet its privatisation targets. The new administration of President Macapagal-Arroyo had announced in January 2001 that while it would not present the 2001 budget until after the May 2001 election, it had plans to limit the deficit to below 4 per cent of gross national product in 2001 and to balance the budget in a five- to six-year period.

8.4   ISSUES IN CRISIS MANAGEMENT AND PROSPECTS

The discussion in the preceding sections indicates that the Philippines, a major Asian developing economy and an important member of the ASEAN, has had its share of crises, be they economic, financial, political or ethnically and religiously motivated, since its independence from the US in 1946. Some of these crises, especially of the political kind, have had their resolutions (through a transfer of executive power) even though these resolutions had taken many months or years to achieve. Some of the crises (for example, the Muslim separatist movement in the south of the country) still await their resolutions. Some (for example, the great divide between the very rich and the very poor) may, because of the country's traditional age-old social construct, never find a resolution of mutual benefit or acceptable to all parties concerned.

In terms of its economic management, the Philippine government may have more flexibility and opportunities to promote growth and development (through, for example, raising standards of corporate and government governance and transparency and invigorating more forcefully the multi-sectoral – that is, power, banking, corporate

– structural reform agenda); to improve its people's living standard (including the Mindanao strategy and the status of displaced persons); and to enhance its international economic relations and cooperation. It is true that economic reform and restructuring would be more successful if the political climate were stable, society was more coherent and united in its purpose and objectives and the population were knowledgeable of a high order. The success (or failure) of policies adopted and implemented may also depend on external factors that are beyond the control of the government itself.

Official reports on the prospects for the Philippine economy in 2001 and beyond have not projected a rosy and promising picture in a number of aspects. These include the assets markets (with the low peso, falling equity prices and rentals), the real sector (low growth, slow-down or even faltering in most economic sectors, and languishing fixed investment), the fiscal and monetary developments (budget blowouts and rising inflation), the balance of payments (weakened current account and declining balance of payments), financial and corporate sector developments (high NPL ratio and the falling capital adequacy ratio (CAR)), and social sector developments (worsening unemployment).

The outcome of all these developments and their associated concerns for the Philippine economy would be that GDP growth for 2001 and beyond will fall well below the level achieved in 2000 due to a general slow-down in global and regional economic activity and that the inflation rate will be around 6.7 per cent in 2001 which is in line with government targets. Restoring fiscal credibility should be a high priority but the success of this policy depends crucially on the success of revenue generation or mobilisation.

The above analysis is based on the concept of short-term or ad hoc policies and seems to be the preference also by international organisations and agencies. It is rather ambitious or even unreasonable, however, to assume that short-term prescriptions can fix long-term problems. A permanent cure for a country's ills has to be based or integrated on more deep-rooted and long-term aspects and issues.

On a long-term basis, an examination of the country's fundamentals in societal, cultural and trade construct that may have profound impact on its economy and people and their relationships with the rest of an increasingly globalised world seems to be an important prerequisite. In this context, an evaluation and incorporation of the observed historical pattern and composition of the Philippines' international trade with its major trading partners in a national trade policy is a necessity. Within this historical framework, a policy to diversify tradable commodities and to widen trading partners may be more appropriate than a policy that restricts to one group of exportable commodities (for example, metal products) or to one or two trading blocs, even though they are currently important (for example, the US and Japan). The slowdown in the US and Japan early in 2001 shows that a trade policy of less reliance on these two economies, however major and important they may be, would be more appropriate for the Philippines in the long run.

On the more fundamental question of whether a monetary or fiscal policy as traditionally practised in the past 50 years by most (free market) governments through the use of the Phillips curve or other similar concepts would be more appropriate for crisis economies such as the Philippines in the past few years, one has to seriously ask whether a one-instrument policy is adequate or suitable to provide definitive resolutions for output generation (with subsequent poverty reduction) or unemployment arrest or decline as well as for releasing inflationary pressure. A more appropriate policy of macroeconomic mix in which both fiscal and monetary policy has to be used simultaneously to deal with two or more economic targets has been proposed in a number of studies in the past (see, for example, Perkins and Tran Van Hoa 2000) to deal specifically with this kind of question and to achieve its desired resolution.

REFERENCES

Asia Recovery Information Center, Asian Development Bank (ARIC) (2001), Data available at <www.adb.org>.

Asian Development Bank (2001), Data relating to the Philippines, March, at <www.adb.org>.

Australian Bureau of Statistics (2001), TSS Databases on DX, Canberra, 2001.

Britannica (2000), <www.britannica.com>.

CHELEM-CEPII (2000), CHELEM International Trade Databases, Paris: CEPII, 2000.

Perkins, J.O.N. and Tran Van Hoa (2000), 'Towards the Formulation and Testing of a More General Theory of Macroeconomic Policy (1987)', in J.O.N. Perkins (ed.), *The Reform of Macroeconomic Policy: From Stagflation to Low or Zero Inflation*, London: Macmillan.

Tran Van Hoa (2000a), *The Asia Crisis: The Cures, Their Effectiveness and the Prospects After*, London: Macmillan.

Tran Van Hoa (2000b), *The Social Impact of the Asia Crisis,* London: Macmillan.

World Bank (2001), World economic outlook data, March, available at <www.worldbank.org>.

9 Indonesia: Managing Economic and Social Collapse

Charles Harvie

9.1 INTRODUCTION

Before the onset of the Asian financial and economic crisis of 1997–98, Indonesia's economic performance ranked among the best in the developing world, with real gross domestic product (GDP) growth since 1970 averaging about 7 per cent annually. The structure of the economy had become more diversified with dependency on the oil sector declining as an export-oriented manufacturing base developed. Key to this economic success was the adoption of prudent macroeconomic policies, high investment and savings rates, and market-oriented trade and exchange rate regimes. Macroeconomic balance was maintained: the budget was balanced; inflation was contained at relatively low levels; current account deficits remained moderate; and international reserves were maintained at comfortable levels. In addition, broad-based labour-intensive growth in line with the country's comparative advantage, together with sustained improvements in basic education and health services, produced a dramatic reduction in the incidence of poverty – from 58 per cent in 1972 to 11 per cent by 1997. This reflected a strong commitment of the New Order regime, under the Presidency of Suharto, to bring about broad gains from economic development and to reduce the incidence of poverty.

The onset of the Asia currency contagion in 1997 and resulting regional financial and economic crisis, however, resulted in an unprecedented reversal of economic and social fortune for the country, such that by May 1998 the economy was near collapse. A major crisis of confidence afflicted the country that was reflected in a collapse of the currency and equity prices, and unprecedented corporate and banking sector insolvency. From mid-1997 to mid-1998 the cumulative depreciation of the rupiah reached over 80 per cent, with over half of this decline occurring from the end of November 1997. The fall in the Jakarta stock exchange index reached 50 per cent over this same period.

Despite corrective action by the government, from the outset the rupiah remained under pressure. For example, to discourage speculative attacks the exchange rate band was widened in July 1997 and in August 1997, in the face of continued pressure on the currency, the rupiah was allowed to float. This policy was backed by a significant tightening of liquidity conditions and a rise in interest rates and an announcement that the budget surplus would be preserved by postponing major infrastructure projects, cutting low priority development programmes, and extending the coverage of the luxury sales tax. At the same time, import tariffs on over 150 items, mainly raw materials and other intermediate goods, were reduced effective mid-September 1997, while the 49-per-cent limit on foreign holdings of listed shares was abolished. Further trade liberalisation measures, including removing monopoly restrictions on agricultural imports, were announced in November 1997. These actions, however, were not sufficient to restore confidence in the rupiah and the economy, which instead plunged even deeper.

By early 1998 there had been a dramatic change in the fortunes of the economy. Annual per capita income was down from around US$1200 to US$300; stock market capitalisation was down from US$118 billion to US$17 billion; only 22 of Indonesia's 286 publicly listed companies were considered to be solvent; and only four firms remained with a market capitalisation of US$500 million or more out of 49 from before the crisis. These adverse developments were further compounded by the social and economic upheavals in May 1998,[1] which left the country on the edge of economic and social collapse. The new government under President Habibie, recognising the severity of the crisis, committed itself to the rapid stabilisation of the economy, with the assistance of the International Monetary Fund (IMF), and to far reaching structural reforms. Changes in the macroeconomic framework as well as strengthening the social safety net to cushion the escalating effects of the crisis on the poor, were seen as priorities. In particular, the need to restructure the banking sector comprehensively became increasingly recognised as the top priority if the country was to recover from the crisis, let alone to achieve the rates of GDP growth attained before the crisis. A closely related issue was the need to also bring about major restructuring of the non-bank corporate sector.

In 1999 there were signs that the economic crisis in Indonesia had bottomed out after nearly two years of financial and economic turmoil. Democratic elections were conducted in June[2] and a new President, Abdurrahman Wahid, elected by Parliament in October. The new government's stated aims were to continue vigorously with the reform programme and to tackle corruption at the highest level and increase transparency in both the government and business sectors. Positive GDP growth was once again recorded and the crisis-induced surge in poverty also appeared to have peaked in early 1999. The recovery, initially underpinned by a rebound in agriculture, appeared to be gradually spreading to other sectors.

During the year 2000 GDP growth continued, driven by investment and export growth. Improving employment and real wages and a sharp decline in food prices, especially rice, resulted in a decline in poverty levels from the crisis period. However, there were signs that the economic recovery remained on shaky ground as exemplified by continuing weakness in the manufacturing and construction sectors, gradual increases in domestic interest rates, continuing susceptibility of the stock market to political events, and the re-emergence of inflationary pressures. There was also a slow-down in export growth during the fourth quarter of 2000 and first few months of 2001, mainly due to a deceleration in world trade. Lower projected oil prices were expected to compound this.[3]

Investor confidence remains weak due to political uncertainty, regional and ethnic strife, a deterioration in law and order, and a continued weak judicial system. The first quarter of 2001 saw a further increase in domestic uncertainties as ethnic violence escalated in the province of Central Kalimantan. Fighting also continued in Aceh, Irian Jaya, and Maluku (the Spice Islands). The IMF's review mission on progress in Indonesia's reforms that was scheduled for late December 2000 was delayed due to outstanding issues in four key areas: the Central Bank Law; fiscal decentralisation; the privatisation of Bank Niaga and Bank Central Asia (BCA); and corporate restructuring principles. The completion of such a review mission was seen as central to any moves in re-establishing investor confidence in the country.

The major objective of this chapter is to identify progress made by the authorities in tackling the crisis that has overwhelmed the country, focusing upon, in particular, progress made in regard to banking and corporate sector reform. In doing so it proceeds as follows. Section 9.2 identifies recent macroeconomic developments that have occurred in the wake of the crisis. Section 9.3 identifies the reform and policy framework operative after the crisis. Section 9.4 outlines the issues that remain to be tackled in the short and long terms if sustainable growth is to be re-established for the country. Finally, Section 9.5 presents a summary of the major conclusions from this chapter.

9.2   MACROECONOMIC DEVELOPMENTS SINCE THE CRISIS

Before the onset of the Asia currency crisis in July 1997 Indonesia's economic fundamentals appeared to be relatively strong. It had achieved: a sustained and high economic growth rate; relatively low inflation; low budget deficits; high domestic savings and investment; growth of exports which, despite the slow-down in 1996, compared well with its regional neighbours; a steady accumulation of foreign exchange reserves; a declining debt service ratio; an exchange rate float within a relatively wide band; and a rising but still favourable and manageable current account deficit. Of most concern was: the increase in the resource gap between saving and investment, reflected in the rising current account deficit; increasing reliance on foreign savings to fund this; and a fragile banking system. While FDI was an important source of foreign saving there was an increasing reliance on foreign borrowing. Gross external debt, consequently, was on the rise. About half of this in 1996–97 was private sector owed, primarily by the non bank corporate sector, and denominated in hard currency including US dollars and, of particular significance, Japanese yen. It was of an increasingly short run duration and considerably larger than the country's foreign exchange reserves. As a consequence the country became increasingly vulnerable to developments in the exchange rate, such as through a loss of confidence, and world interest rates, and this vulnerability was exposed by developments during the second half of 1997. By the end of 1997 and into early 1998 Indonesia became the most adversely affected crisis stricken economy in the region.

As indicated in Table 9.1 GDP growth in 1997 declined to 4.7 per cent although growth of industrial production remained strong at 13.2 per cent for the year. Gross domestic investment at around 32 per cent of GDP remained in excess of domestic national saving (29 per cent of GDP). The unemployment rate was 4.7 per cent, real wage growth at 4.1 per cent indicated rising living standards, and inflation was stable at a low 6.1 per cent. The government's fiscal balance suggested a small deficit and public sector debt was negligible. On the external front export growth remained strong and the trade balance remained in sizeable surplus. The current account deficit at 5 per cent of GDP remained problematic. Foreign direct investment was a healthy US$4.7 billion and total external debt of US$136.1 billion appeared not out of place in comparison to other regional economies. However, short-term debt was considerably in excess of available foreign exchange reserves and gold. Domestic credit growth was buoyant, the real effective exchange rate was relatively stable and the stock market also relatively stable. During 1998, however, the picture altered quite radically for many of these macroeconomic variables.

By the beginning of 1998, the financial crisis had developed into a full-blown economic crisis. The major factors behind this included: the increasingly desperate need to restructure sizeable, unhedged, private foreign borrowing arising from the collapse of the currency; the growing fragility of the financial system due to poor regulatory and legal foundations, compounded by insolvencies in the corporate sector; an apparent reluctance by the government to implement policies agreed with the IMF as part of a financial rescue package; an aging leader with no clear successor; spectacular wealth accumulation through 'KKN' (the Indonesian acronym for 'corruption, cronyism, and nepotism'); and the economic crisis beginning to develop into a social crisis with increasing social unrest. However, few could have predicted the speed or the scale of the crisis that was to afflict Indonesia during the remainder of 1998. This included a further collapse of the exchange rate to, at one point, around Rp 16 000 to the $US, representing one of the largest real exchange rate depreciations in the post World War Two era; a turnaround in economic growth of 18 percentage points (from positive 4.7 per cent GDP growth in 1997 to negative 13.1 per cent GDP growth in 1998), comparable only to that experienced by industrial economies during the Great Depression of the 1930s; a US$22 billion reversal of private capital flows, from inflows of US$10 billion in 1996/97 to outflows of US$12 billion in 1997/98, which was nearly as large as the total net private capital flows during the entire decade

Table 9.1
Indonesia's Macroeconomic Performance 1997–2000

Year	1997	1998	1999	2000
Key indicators:				
Output, employment and prices				
GDP (US$billion), based on end of period				
exchange rate	215.7	96.8	141.3	151.5
GDP (% change on previous year)	4.7	−13.1	0.8	4.8
Industrial production index (1993=100)	157.4	136.4	169.8	Na
(% change, previous year)	13.2	−13.3	24.5	Na
Gross domestic investment/GDP (%)	31.8	19.1	11.6	13.0
Gross national savings/GDP (%)	29.4	23.2	13.2	15.2
Unemployment rate (%)	4.7	5.5	6.4	5.9
Real wage growth (%)	4.1	−29.9	2.0	Na
CPI (% change, previous year)	6.1	58.5	20.5	3.7
Public sector				
Government balance (% GDP)	−0.6	−2.1	−1.5	−3.4
Domestic public sector debt (% GDP)	0.0	10.5	44.7	50.7
Foreign trade, balance of payments and external debt				
Trade balance (US$billion)	10.1	15.7	20.6	25.5
Exports of goods (US$billion)	56.3	50.4	51.2	62.5
(% change, previous year)	12.2	−10.5	1.7	22.0
Key export (% change, previous year)	−3.7	−36.7	38.2	50.8
Imports of goods (US$billion)	46.2	34.7	30.6	37.0
(% change, previous year)	4.5	−25.0	−11.8	21.1
Current account balance (US$billion)	−5.0	4.1	5.8	3.5
(% of GDP)	−2.3	4.2	4.1	2.3
Foreign direct investment (US$billion)	4.7	−0.4	−2.7	−4.6
Total external debt (US$billion)	136.1	150.9	148.1	140.6 [a]
(% of GDP)	63.1	155.9	104.8	93.1 [b]
Short term debt (US$billion)	35.1	23.7	19.0	Na
(% of GDP)	16.3	24.5	13.4	Na
Debt service/exports [c]	37.8	39.1	34.8	Na
Reserves, including gold (US$billion)	17.4	23.5	27.3	23.3
(months of imports of goods and services)	3.3	2.0	1.6	2.1
Financial markets				
Domestic credit (% change, previous year)	42.0	36.0	17.3	25.5
Short term interest rate (1 month deposit)	25.4	41.4	12.2	11.5
Exchange rate Rp/US$ (end of period)	2 909	9 875	7 855	8 520
Real effective exchange rate (1990=100)	96.6	47.3	68.1	Na
(% change, previous year)	−5.5	−51.0	43.9	Na
Stock market index (end period, Aug 88=100)	402	398	677	421

Notes: a At December 2000; b Third quarter 2000; c Fiscal year ending 31 March.
Sources: World Bank (2001), *East Asia Update – Indonesia*, p. 10, March; Central Bureau of Statistics, Bank Indonesia (various years), Ministry of Finance.

from 1985–95. The financial and economic crisis was accompanied by natural disasters, including a drought which reduced rice harvests and agricultural production generally and severe localised droughts that contributed to uncontrollable forest fires. In addition, the price of oil, Indonesia's key export commodity, fell to US$13 per barrel, its lowest level in real terms in 30 years, and enormous political developments took place including the standing down of President Suharto after 30 years in power. This historic combination of events created severe economic and social dislocation in the country. While Indonesia is justly proud of its rapid poverty reduction since the 1970s, the crisis resulted in large scale reversals of that progress.

The rapid depreciation of the rupiah, in conjunction with the country's worst drought in fifty years, resulted in a large increase in prices. The consumer price index (CPI) inflation rate increased from 6.1 per cent in 1997 to 58.5 per cent in 1998 (see Table 9.1). The official unemployment rate increased from 4.7 per cent in 1997 to 5.5 per cent in 1998. Real wage growth collapsed in the wake of rising prices and reduced domestic demand. Gross domestic investment, a traditionally important source of growth for the economy, collapsed in 1998. While saving, as a percentage of GDP, also declined, it was nowhere near as severe as that for investment. Consequently, the resource gap moved in favour of saving resulting in a turnaround of the current account from deficit in 1997 to surplus in 1998. The public sector position deteriorated, with the budget deficit moving into more sizeable deficit and public sector debt increasing substantially in the wake of the collapsing corporate and banking sectors. Exports declined by 10.5 per cent but this was swamped by a decline of almost 35 per cent in imports. This resulted in a boost to the trade account surplus and the surplus on current account. Foreign direct investment became negative for the year, external debt blew out to over 150 per cent of the collapsed GDP, short-term debt in absolute terms fell but increased as a proportion of GDP. Domestic credit growth slowed as credit from distressed banks dried up, and the domestic short-term interest rate increased rapidly to an average of over 41 per cent for the year. The nominal and effective exchange rate depreciated considerably, with the latter falling by over 50 per cent from its level in 1997. The stock market also showed a further decline from its already collapsed level in 1997.

The financial position of the domestic banking system dramatically deteriorated, and Bank Indonesia granted large scale liquidity support which contributed to additional pressure on the exchange rate and international reserves. In addition, foreign banks cut trade and other credit lines to Indonesian banks, resulting in domestic enterprises having difficulty in obtaining the imported inputs needed for production. After a number of false starts (see Harvie 2000a and 2000b), and against a background of rapid economic deterioration, the Indonesian government and the IMF reached agreement over a programme necessary for the recovery of the economy and for the advancement of further financial assistance. The Statement of Development Policy of 8 April 1998 identified the objectives of the reform programme as being the stabilisation and then recovery of the economy, while shielding the poor from the worst effects of the crisis.

Despite the agreed programme, and the likelihood of expanded international financial assistance, the economic situation and outlook worsened after April 1998. The country was shaken by social unrest in May which resulted in the resignation of President Suharto and the appointment of President Habibie. The social disturbances during this period and their political ramifications had a serious effect upon the economy, resulting in further disruptions to economic activity and a damaging decline in business confidence. The country was close to economic and social collapse, with expectations for a decline in GDP of between 10–15 per cent during 1998 and for inflation to increase to around 80 per cent being advanced by the authorities at this time. The exchange rate depreciated by 50 per cent from about Rp (Rupiah) 8000 at the beginning of May 1998 to Rp 16 000 by mid-June. In a thin market, the exchange rate was very volatile and dominated by sudden shifts in market confidence, and became particularly difficult to forecast. A conservative monetary policy kept interest rates near 60 per cent, imports fell by about 20 per cent in the first five months of 1998, and export growth also slowed. The macroeconomic framework remained subject to unusually large uncertainty. As a consequence of these adverse economic and social developments the agreed April programme was amended in June, although the basic framework remained.

The April programme provided the basis for the policy response to the economic difficulties facing the economy, and consisted of the following key components:

1   Maintaining macroeconomic stability with an emphasis on stabilising the rupiah at a level more in line with the underlying strengths of the economy, primarily through a tightening of monetary policy.
2   Reforming and strengthening the banking system.
3   Providing a framework for comprehensively addressing the debt problem of private corporations, emphasising the need for their restructuring.
4   Strengthening the implementation of structural reforms to create the foundations for a more efficient and competitive economy, and improved corporate governance.
5   Restoring trade finance to a normal basis, allowing domestic production and especially the export sector to recover.

The rapid deterioration of the economy after May 1998 led to an increased focus upon another key component:

6   Implementation of measures to protect the poor, sustain key human resource investments, and to maintain food security and the distribution system.

Each of these components was seen as being necessary for restoring stability, regaining the confidence of international investors, and resuming growth. The government anticipated that the programme would be reinforced by financial support from the international community, including trade financing and the provision of food and medical aid.

As indicated by Table 9.1 there were signs during 1999 that the economic crisis in

Indonesia had bottomed out after nearly two years of financial and economic turmoil. GDP recorded a 0.8 per cent increase and the crisis-induced surge in poverty also appeared to have peaked in early 1999. The recovery, initially underpinned by a rebound in agriculture, gradually spread to other sectors. However, strong growth of agricultural output in the first half of the year faded by the third quarter, and reached only 0.7 per cent for the year. The manufacturing sector expanded by 2.2 per cent because of a rebound in the export oriented oil and gas sector, while the construction sector grew by a modest 1.1 per cent. The service sector, however, declined by a further 1.5 per cent in 1999 because of a contraction in banking and financial services. On the aggregate demand side the recovery was initially aided by a rise in public spending, reflecting the government's fiscal stimulus to jump start the economy. Growth of private consumption then led the recovery. Private investment activity, however, continued to contract due to inadequate progress in corporate debt restructuring.

The fragile recovery did not prevent further employment problems. Unemployment increased from 5.5 per cent in 1998 to 6.4 per cent for 1999, and underemployment increased from 60 per cent in 1998 to 63 per cent in 1999. More significantly, although real wages went up in 1999 by a modest 2 per cent they remained some 20–25 per cent below the pre-crisis levels.

After averaging 58.5 per cent in 1998, consumer price inflation came down to 20.5 per cent in 1999. On a year on year basis it plummeted to 2 per cent at the end of December 1999, compared with 78 per cent a year previously. While falling food prices, especially of rice, was the primary cause of declining inflation, the restoration of food distribution channels, the appreciation of the rupiah, and a tight monetary stance also assisted. Despite volatility associated with political uncertainties, share prices in Indonesia rebounded because of considerably lower domestic inflation, greater exchange rate stability, and sharply reduced interest rates. Overall equity prices, as measured by the Jakarta Stock Market index, rose by 60 per cent in 1999. Market capitalisation climbed to US$58 billion at the end of 1999 from US$22 billion earlier in the year, still considerably below the pre-crisis level of US$90 billion. The strengthened equity market, however, improved the outlook for the government privatisation programme, and the Indonesian Bank Restructuring Agency's (IBRA) asset recovery effort that was now in full swing.

Although market anxiety over structural reforms and political uncertainties continued to influence fluctuations in the rupiah, it strengthened substantially in 1999 and traded around Rp 6800–9500 per dollar compared with Rp 7500–17 000 the previous year. The stronger rupiah was in large part attributable to a steady build-up of reserves, high interest rates early in the year, and a tight overall monetary stance. The rupiah ended the year at Rp 7855 per US dollar. Despite the appreciation of the nominal exchange rate the real exchange rate remained around 30 per cent below its pre-crisis level, giving Indonesian exporters a significant comparative advantage over its main regional competitors, Malaysia, the Philippines and Thailand.

The performance of the external sector, however, remained weak. Exports increased by only 1.7 per cent while import growth declined by a further 11.8 per cent, led by a decline in imports of capital goods due to declining domestic investment. Despite the large real appreciation of the rupiah and stronger oil export prices, exports remained depressed because of problems associated with high corporate indebtedness and access to credit. The current account surplus increased to US$5.8 billion in 1999, equivalent to 4.1 per cent of GDP, driven mainly by the aforementioned decline in imports as was the case in the previous year.

On the capital account, reduced inflows of net official finance were more than offset by lower net outflows of private capital due to loan rescheduling. As a result of the improved current account surplus and a smaller deficit in the capital account, reserves increased to US$27.3 billion (six months of import equivalent). At US$16 billion, net foreign assets were also well above Bank Indonesia's monetary programme floor of US$14 billion. The total external debt to GDP ratio fell to below 150 per cent, and the debt service ratio, after loan rescheduling, was about 35 per cent which was down from 39 per cent in 1998.

During the year 2000 GDP grew by 4.8 per cent. This was primarily driven by investment growth (17.9 per cent growth) and exports (which rose by 16 per cent), with the latter assisted by a depreciating rupiah and higher oil prices. Increasing real wages, improving employment and a sharp decline in food prices, especially rice, resulted in a further decline in poverty levels from that attained during the worst of the crisis period. Despite these encouraging developments there were indications that economic recovery was far from secure. Inventories continued to be drawn down sharply, but, contrary to the previous two years, gross fixed capital formation increased as well. In fact, investment growth overtook consumption and exports as the leading contributor to GDP growth. Despite this, gross domestic investment as a percentage of GDP in 2000 (13 per cent) remained well below its pre-crisis level. On the supply side, transport and communications, manufacturing, utilities and construction accounted for most of the GDP growth in 2000. According to the authorities capacity utilisation in the corporate sector reached 80 per cent in 2000 and was increasing. However, quarterly data suggested that growth in most sectors, other than agriculture, mining and quarrying, was slowing. The pace of recovery remained constrained by continuing liquidity problems and a massive overhang of corporate debt.

Inflation was on the rise with CPI inflation reaching 9.4 per cent (year on year) in December 2000, above Bank Indonesia's target of around 5–7 per cent which had been set at the beginning of the year. Inflation for the year 2000, however, only amounted to 3.7 per cent, down from over 20 per cent in 1999. Increases in administered prices, especially fuel, a rise in civil service wages, and the greater than expected depreciation of the rupiah all contributed to inflation.

As in previous years the fiscal deficit in FY (fiscal year) 2000 was again smaller than planned. This time around, though, the cause was almost exclusively on the revenue side. Higher oil prices, buoyant imports, and rising wages increased revenues by as much as Rp 55 trillion (or some 5 per cent of GDP) over what was budgeted. Although there was an offsetting increase in fuel and electricity subsidies, the deficit remained below 2 per cent which was less than half the planned 4.8 per cent. Government debt service payments accounted for about a third of government revenues in FY2000 and is estimated to be about 40 per cent of revenues in FY2001 (World Bank 2001). For the calendar year 2000 the government fiscal balance was over twice that for 1999. The domestic public sector debt was on average 50.7 per cent of GDP for 2000, increasing dramatically to 86.2 per cent of GDP at end 2000 (with just over half of it, US$68 billion, being owed to external creditors) (World Bank 2001).

For the year 2000, total exports were US$62.5 billion or 22 per cent higher than the previous year, and 11.1 per cent higher than 1997. Although this increase has been helped by high oil prices, non oil exports were 22.9 per cent higher than in 1999. Non-oil exports reached US$47.8 billion for the year 2000, while oil–gas exports reached US$14.2 billion. There has been some slow-down in export growth during the fourth quarter of 2000 and the first months of 2001, mainly due to a deceleration in world trade, especially to the US and Japan.

Total imports of goods and services recovered in 2000, growing by 21.1 per cent over 1999, but remained well below pre-crisis levels. The current account balance remained in surplus, equivalent to 3.5 per cent of GDP, and while private capital outflow continued, including that of foreign direct investment (FDI), Indonesia retained comfortable reserve levels at US$23.3 billion for the year.

The performance of the real sectors notwithstanding, financial indicators deteriorated in the last few months of 2000. The average rupiah exchange rate was Rp 8520 per US dollar in 2000, more than 20 per cent higher than the assumed Rp 7000 per dollar used by the authorities when defining their inflation target. While short-term interest rates for the year indicated a fall in comparison with that of 1999, upward pressure was becoming apparent towards the end of the year. With rising inflation the authorities were caught between pursuing a tight monetary policy to rein in inflationary pressures, and maintaining low domestic interest rates (to keep banks financially viable and the budget deficit manageable). The stock market weakened in 2000 arising from political uncertainties and an ongoing lack of investor confidence.

The fragility of the recovery in the economy was demonstrated on a number of fronts in 2000 and early 2001: quarterly growth in manufacturing and construction began to decelerate sharply; there was a gradual but continuing increase in domestic interest rates (with the 30 day SBI rate rising to 14.75 per cent in mid-February 2001, up from 14.5 per cent at the end of December 2000.); susceptibility of the stock market to political events with the Jakarta Stock Market (JSX) composite index at 432 down 36 per cent by end February from December 1999; the re-emergence of inflationary pressures; the exchange rate, which remained sluggish at around the Rp 9500/US$ mark in the last two quarters of 2000, slid to over Rp 10 000/US$ in March 2001; there was also some slow-down in export growth during the fourth quarter of 2000 and first few months of 2001, mainly due to a deceleration in world trade with lower oil prices compounding this; and in 2001 the fiscal situation is anticipated to deteriorate as a result of fiscal decentralisation, with windfalls in revenues being shared with the regions while the depreciating rupiah and rising interest rates are putting pressure on central government spending.

Political uncertainty, regional and ethnic strife, a deterioration in law and order, and a continued weak judicial system also combined to undermine investor confidence. The first quarter of 2001 saw domestic uncertainties increasing as ethnic violence escalated in the province of Central Kalimantan. Fighting also continues in Aceh, Irian Jaya, and Maluka (the Spice Islands). The IMF's review mission, scheduled for late December 2000, was delayed due to outstanding issues in four areas: the Central Bank Law; fiscal decentralisation; the privatisation of Bank Niaga and BCA; and corporate restructuring principles. Critical to restoring investor confidence in the short term will be a resumption of the programme with the IMF. The delay of the mission also severely contributed to the prevailing negative investor sentiment. These factors contributed to the rupiah exchange rate plummeting below the 10 000 Rp/US$ mark in March 2001. The weaker rupiah was putting increasing pressure on the fiscal situation of the government, including its ability to make timely debt service payments. On the other hand reserves remained comfortable at US$28.75 billion in mid-March 2001 (World Bank 2001).

9.3   STRUCTURAL REFORMS AND POLICY ISSUES

The reform momentum that developed under President Habibie was continued under the new administration of President Wahid from October 1999. The new government committed itself to maintaining the reform momentum and embarked on an ambitious program of time-bound structural reforms, recognising that the implementation of the ongoing reform programme would be crucial for the country's access to desperately needed foreign financing. The key areas of reform, and the related policy issues, are discussed at length in this section.

9.3.1   Macroeconomic Stability

Since late 1998, macroeconomic stability has been achieved with the recovery of economic growth, the easing of inflationary pressure, and a decline in interest rates from their crisis period level. Despite these achievements macroeconomic stability still remains fragile amid ongoing weaknesses in the banking and corporate sectors. The maintenance of prudent macroeconomic management at this crucial stage of the recovery remains pivotal in providing the basis for a sustained recovery of the economy.

The focus of monetary policy has been upon restraining inflation while permitting market forces to determine the exchange rate and interest rate. Reducing interest rates as quickly as possible to alleviate their painful effects on the finance and real sectors and to spur recovery remains highly desirable, however this must be weighed against concerns about the rekindling of inflation and the prospect of encouraging further capital flight. Although further declines in inflation allow room for more reductions in interest rates, they are unlikely to be substantial, given ongoing risk perceptions and banking sector weakness. Moreover, lower interest rates will not be sustainable unless they are in line with market expectations. However, the attainment and maintenance of monetary stability will be essential in keeping inflation down, strengthening the exchange rate, and ultimately reducing interest rates. Such an optimistic scenario would be particularly beneficial given the large corporate debt overhang. A stronger rupiah would be beneficial in the context of repayment of corporate foreign currency denominated debt, and a lower interest rate would also ease debt servicing costs on domestic currency denominated debt. However, the trade-off between a stronger rupiah to ease the corporate debt overhang and a more competitive exchange rate to boost corporate exports also needs to be carefully considered by the authorities. Hence the issues and policy options are not at all clear cut.

On the fiscal front, the period of the financial and economic crisis has seen a steady deterioration in the country's fiscal deficits, and a sharp increase in the size of public sector debt obligations. This has mainly arisen as a result of the extraordinary demand on public resources: to protect the poor; to recapitalise and restructure the insolvent financial and corporate sectors; to meet rapidly increasing interest payments on the outstanding debt itself; and to maintain an expansionary stance to counteract the economic contraction. The largest single public expenditure component now consists of interest payments on domestic debt. In FY2000 these amounted to 4.2 per cent of GDP, accounting for nearly one fifth of total expenditures (Asian Development Bank 2001).The budget deficit for the fiscal year ending 31 March 2000 was projected as a deficit of 6.8 per cent of GDP. In the event, because of delays in project implementation, the actual deficit was only 4 per cent of GDP, thereby nullifying to some extent the budget deficit's envisaged role of stimulating the economy. Hence the disbursement of programme assistance in particular needs to be accelerated. However, this must be balanced against the need to prevent corruption, collusion, and nepotism (KKN) practices in the implementation of projects and programmes.

In view of the severe impact of the crisis the need for expanded government expenditure will remain at least over the medium term, and the budget will therefore continue to be in deficit. The exact size of the deficit will, on the one hand, be influenced by the extent of government revenue generated, with this being dependent upon: the extent and sustainability of private sector activity; declining outlays on subsidies; and oil and gas revenues generated. Recent moves towards fiscal decentralisation could lead the fiscal position to deteriorate further, however, with windfalls in revenue being shared with the regions while the recently depreciating rupiah and rising interest rates put pressure on central government spending.[4] The overall fiscal challenge for the government will be to mobilise the required resources while keeping the deficit sustainable.

A major consequence of the crisis, as previously alluded to, has been a sharp increase in public debt. At the end of March 2000, total public sector debt increased to 95 per cent of GDP from only 23 per cent at the end of March 1998, representing a quadrupling in only two years. About 75 per cent of the rise in public debt resulted from domestic bond issues to recapitalise banks and repay Bank Indonesia's liquidity support to the banking system after the crisis.[5] Domestic public debt at this time totalled US$89 billion compared with US$63 billion in external public debt (ADB 2000). Outlays on domestic debt payments were projected to increase sharply to Rp 42 trillion for FY2001, more than twice the amount required to service public external debt, representing the interest on government recapitalisation bonds.

Together, domestic and external debt service expenditures make up 41 per cent of total current expenditures and 61 per cent of total tax revenues, and will therefore exert a severe drain on public resources for the foreseeable future. As the recovery becomes sustainable, the emphasis of public policy must shift from fiscal stimulus to fiscal consolidation, and then to fiscal sustainability. Given the high level of debt and a weak revenue base, achieving this will require more effective and transparent use of resources and reduced borrowing. The government therefore faces several urgent imperatives. First, vigorous efforts are needed to speed up domestic resource mobilisation through revenue raising measures, including assets sales through privatisation, and sales of assets acquired as a consequence of banking sector recapitalisation. Second, although outlay on the petroleum subsidy is projected to decline as the government increases electricity and fuel prices, other timely price adjustments are needed to reduce subsidies while the targeting of social subsidies to the poor need to be improved. Third, full transparency and accountability in the use of public resources are needed to ensure the greatest possible development effect and to eliminate leakage of funds. Fourth, careful programming of external assistance is required to prevent negative resource transfer.

9.3.2   Bank Restructuring

In the years preceding the crisis strong macroeconomic and social fundamentals, as reflected in high GDP growth accompanied by a sharp decline in poverty, masked growing weaknesses in the financial, and more specifically banking, sector. The banking sector became increasingly fragile and was characterised by lax regulation, high exposure to cyclical sectors such as real estate, short-term borrowings from abroad for long-term rupiah lending domestically, and connected and directed lending. The highly leveraged banking sector became exposed to credit risk at a level that could not be managed in a severe recession. When the financial crisis occurred in 1997, with the associated collapse of the rupiah, the resulting increase in the debt service burden on both the banking and the corporate sector was unsustainable. The corporate sector and already weak banking sector effectively became insolvent.

Of all the crisis economies, Indonesia's financial and corporate sector problems were the most acute (see Table 9.2). Non performing loans were initially variously estimated at between 60–85 per cent of all loans, and bank recapitalisation costs were estimated at a staggering Rp 643 trillion (about US$89 billion) or 58–60 per cent of

GDP. Even by the year 2000 the non-performing loans of State banks were estimated at 60 per cent and private banks at 40 per cent of total loans. During the crisis lending rates, although much higher than pre-crisis rates, could not keep pace with the sharp increase in deposit rates, resulting in negative intermediation margins for banks. The banking system was technically insolvent, with a negative net worth estimated at around a third of GDP. The negative intermediation spread continued to erode the capital base of banks on a daily basis. Such a financial environment was not sustainable in the long run.

The collapse of the banking sector paralysed the real sectors. Consequently, restructuring and revitalising banking became the most urgent priority for Indonesia, as economic recovery could not begin without a resumption of credit flows to the real sector. However, restructuring efforts got off to a slow start because of political constraints, and were conducted under expectations that it would take several years to restore the financial sector to health. The government's bank restructuring plan had four key components: (i) resolving the status of banks under the control of the Indonesian Bank Restructuring Agency (IBRA), and other banks, (ii) recovery of liquidity support, (iii) recapitalisation of potentially viable private banks, and (iv) implementing necessary legal and regulatory reforms.

The first step towards recapitalisation and structural reform of the financial sector occurred through the establishment of new institutions. The Indonesian Bank Restructuring Agency[6] (IBRA) was formed in January 1998 as an independent body to restructure troubled banks and their assets. Within this agency a specific Asset Management Unit was created in April 1998 to acquire non-performing loans (NPLs) from stricken banks. By the end of 1999 it held around two thirds of all NPLs and by the end of 2000 had begun to make some inroads into recovering these assets even though the legal, organisational and regulatory framework had been in place for much longer. By the end of 2000 it had probably become the single most powerful organisation in the country with assets equivalent in value to 57 per cent of the country's GDP, and had transferred NPLs worth 30 per cent of GDP.

The second major step towards the recapitalisation of private banks occurred on 29 September 1998, when the government announced a major recapitalisation scheme for private banks. To be eligible, banks had to have a capital adequacy ratio (CAR) of not less than –25 per cent of assets after full provisioning of impaired loans.[7] The banks had to inject new capital along with the government in the ratio of 1:4 to achieve a minimum CAR of 4 per cent under the scheme by March 1999. The government's contribution would be in the form of long-term bonds (both market-linked and indexed). The government would hold an equity position proportional to its capital injection in the form of ordinary preference shares. All private banks were to be classified into three categories: A (capital adequacy ratio above 4 per cent), B (capital adequacy ratio of less than 4 per cent but above minus 25 per cent), or C (capital adequacy ratio of less than minus 25 per cent) after the submission of their strategic business plans. After a review of their business plans all group C banks and

Table 9.2

Non-performing Loan Ratios, and Fiscal Costs of Recapitalisation, Crisis Countries (%), mid-October 1999

| Country | Share of non-performing loans to total loans | | | | Fiscal costs of restructuring as share of 1998 GDP | Funds disbursed | Expected additional costs |
| | Official estimate | | | Unofficial estimate peak level | | | |
	End 1997	End 1998	Sept. 1999				
Indonesia	na	na	na	60–85	58	10.6	47.7
Korea	na	7.6	6.6	20–30	16	12.5	3.6
Malaysia	na	18.9	17.8	20–30	10	4.2	5.8
Philippines	5.4	11.0	13.4	15–25	na	na	na
Thailand	19.8	45.0	44.7	50–70	32	23.9	8.0

na = Not available

Note: NPLs are measured on a three month basis, and the unofficial estimate includes assets carved out for sale by the asset management companies.

Sources: Central banks and supervisory agencies, World Bank (1999), Deutsche Bank (1999), J.P. Morgan (1999), Bank of America (1999), World Bank staff estimates.

non viable group B banks were closed in March 1999 (see Harvie 2000b).[8] In the period of one year 66 banks were closed and 12 taken over by the state.[9]

Restructuring of the State banks, on the other hand, only began later. The state banking system accounted for 75 per cent of the liabilities of Indonesia's banking system and 90 per cent of its negative net worth. Some estimates put around 80 per cent of the outstanding loans as non-performing. Consequently, despite the progress made in terms of private bank restructuring, most Indonesian financial institutions remained insolvent or under-capitalised, with lending operations still severely constrained.

The recapitalisation of the banking sector was financed by domestic bond issues, with the government and the recapitalised banks exchanging bonds for outstanding shares. The government planned to cover the interest cost of these bonds from the proceeds of privatisation and sale of assets transferred to IBRA, which included an estimated Rp 250 trillion in non performing loans transferred by the banking system in the restructuring process. In 1999 the total cost of recapitalisation was estimated at Rp 300 trillion ($40 billion) over three years.[10] The total interest cost over three years was estimated at about 100 trillion rupiah. The interest cost in FY2000 was Rp 34 trillion, of which Rp 16 trillion was accrued from asset sales by IBRA. The remaining Rp 18 trillion was charged to the budget. Realising Rp 16 trillion from sale of assets would prove to be difficult because of depressed asset prices. Another major complication has arisen from the estimate of the total recapitalisation cost. With the banks facing a continual negative intermediation spread, the capital base of the banks continued to erode by a large amount on a daily basis. The recapitalisation costs continued to increase and ultimately exceed the originally estimated Rp 300 trillion by a significant margin. This problem highlighted the need to complete the recapitalisation process expeditiously. However, public sensitivities concerning the moral hazard associated with the injection of public funds into private banks, and dealing with vested interests opposed to closures substantially delayed the process.

The dimensions of bank recapitalisation and restructuring were so large in Indonesia that it stretched to the maximum the financial and human resources of the country, and the momentum of reform slowed considerably in 1999. These two factors contributed to the initial stage of the private bank recapitalisation process only being completed in April 1999.

The bank recapitalisation programme, involving both private and state banks, was finally completed in October 2000, and was marked by the recapitalisation of three state banks (Bank Negara, Bank Rakyat Indonesia, and Bank Tabungan Negara) and a further three private banks (Bank Niaga, Bank Bali, and Bank Danamon). The total cost of bank restructuring including recapitalisation, closure, and liquidity support extended by Bank Indonesia was estimated to have reached Rp 670 trillion, equivalent to 55 per cent of GDP (ADB 2001).

With the completion of the bank recapitalisation programme the focus of financial sector reforms shifted to asset recovery and the resumption of bank lending to viable corporations. Targets for IBRA asset recovery were set. For example for FY2001 a target of Rp 27 trillion in cash and Rp 10 trillion in bond swaps was set, requiring the government to accelerate the pace of asset disposal and corporate debt restructuring. As of early 2001, IBRA reached resolution stage in the restructuring of Rp 77 trillion of debt, or 88 per cent, of its top 21 obligors' loan portfolio. IBRA, however, faces a complex task of selling its assets. Such sales are critical in reducing the public debt, but asset disposal has been very slow. By December 2000 IBRA had acquired 82.6 per cent of banking sector NPLs, paring the banking sector NPL down to 18.8 per cent, leaving the government owning 80 per cent of the banking systems total assets. Asset disposal has been slow because of: resistance from debtors; political influence; an ineffective bankruptcy system; and a lack of interested buyers. Foreign entities have been deterred from buying Indonesian banks due to concerns over: institutional weaknesses; insufficient transparency; and political uncertainties.

While IBRA continues to be preoccupied with the management of its asset portfolio, there is growing concern about the health of the recapitalised banks. With the rupiah depreciating and the interest rate continuing to rise in 2000 and early 2001 amidst a deterioration in market confidence, it is only a question of time before banks – particularly those recapitalised in large measure with fixed rate bonds – will once again suffer from negative interest margins. Even if interest rates were to stabilise, many banks will be ill-equipped to achieve the 8 per cent capital adequacy ratio requirement by the end of 2001.

One of the major reasons for the collapse of the banking system was the absence of an effective bank supervision system. Realising this weakness, Indonesia's authorities have taken steps to improve prudential regulations, bank supervision, and enforcement capabilities. Despite this, bank supervision remains limited because of weak enforcement capacity and a lack of trained staff. Significant progress has, however, been achieved in strengthening the legal and regulatory framework of the banking system. In December 1998, Bank Indonesia issued new prudential regulations concerning loan classification, loan loss provisioning, treatment of debt restructuring operations, liquidity management, foreign currency exposure, connected lending, the CAR, and publication of financial statements. A draft Central Bank law providing autonomy for Bank Indonesia from the government was enacted in March 1999. The amendments to the banking law approved by Parliament have come into force and aimed to empower IBRA. These provide for major improvements in bank licensing, ownership, openness to foreign direct investment, bank secrecy, and resolution of assets taken over by IBRA. However, the government must remain committed to implementing the legal and regulatory framework in the finance sector.

It is interesting and relevant to compare the enormity of the bank restructuring task facing Indonesia with that of its regional neighbours in terms of: approaches adopted to date; comparative progress made; and possible lessons that can be learned from the experiences of its neighbours. This is briefly conducted with reference to Tables 9.3–9.5. Table 9.3 provides details of the substantial sums that have already been spent, or committed, by governments of the crisis afflicted economies in the region, in terms of providing liquidity support to their banks and then in recapitalising their banking systems (see World Bank 2001). The governments of Korea and Indonesia have had to provide the most support. Indonesia's government debt, consequently, now approaches 100 per cent of GDP from a pre crisis level of 23 per cent, with the gross costs of bank restructuring estimated at 55 per cent of 2000 GDP as alluded to previously.

Asset management companies have been the primary vehicle utilised throughout the East Asian region to acquire significant NPLs from domestic banks, thereby reducing the NPL ratios on the banks' balance sheets (see Table 9.4). The reduction in NPLs, recapitalisation by governments, and infusion of new equity by existing and new owners, has improved banks' capital throughout the region. Average CARs now exceed the 8 per cent Basle minimum standard in Korea, Malaysia and Thailand. Even in Indonesia, recapitalisation is reported to have raised banks' capital to about 4 per cent of risk weighted assets from −8.1 per cent at the end of 1999. Indonesia's target for end 2001 is to reach the 8 per cent BIS[11] guideline.

Through their acquisition of NPLs, AMCs in Indonesia, Korea and Malaysia have become major holders of their countries' assets, and have made varying progress in asset disposal (see Table 9.5).[12] The book value of Indonesia's IBRA amounts to some 57 per cent of GDP. It is noticeable that Indonesia's AMC lags considerably behind other regional AMCs in terms of assets disposed of. Disposal of IBRA's assets has been more problematic, however, reflecting poor asset values, politically powerful debtors and an inadequate legislative and regulatory environment as mentioned previously.

9.3.3   Corporate Debt Restructuring

As with the financial sector, Indonesia's efforts at corporate reform initially focused on creating new institutions and improving legislation. The Frankfurt Agreement of 4 June 1998 paved the way for the establishment of the Indonesian Debt Restructuring Agency (INDRA) on 2 July 1998 to assist in restructuring corporate foreign debt. This agency allows debtors and creditors to insure themselves against exchange risks, once they have reached rescheduling agreements. The Indonesia government then created the Jakarta Initiative, launched on 9 September 1998, to facilitate out-of-court corporate settlements between debtors and creditors, following the London approach to corporate workouts.[13] A Corporate Restructuring Task Force (CRTF) was set up to oversee the Jakarta Initiative process.[14] Apart from providing a one-stop service for government approvals to complete a restructuring deal, the CRTF can recommend to the public prosecutor the filing of bankruptcy proceedings against debtors in the public's interest. This gave substantial authority to the CRTF to nudge debtors toward negotiations.

In addition, legislation to improve corporate governance was introduced, including a new bankruptcy law in August 1998 and anticorruption laws. The new bankruptcy law modernised the legal infrastructure for bankruptcy and facilitated the rapid resolution of commercial disputes. Several other changes in the legal and regulatory

Table 9.3
Financial Restructuring in Indonesia and Other East Asian Economies
(end 2000)

Action	Indonesia	Korea	Malaysia	Thailand
Initial government response:				
Liquidity support	US$21.7 billion (18 per cent of GDP)	US$23.3 billion (5 per cent of GDP)	US$9.2 billion (13 per cent of GDP)	US$24.1 billion (20 per cent of GDP)
Non performing loans				
NPLs/total loans* (%)	58.8 (Nov., 2000)	17.9 (Oct., 2000)	23.2 (June, 2000)	26.5 (Dec., 2000)
NPls/total loans after transfers to AMCs (%)	23.9 (Nov., 2000)	12.3 (Oct., 2000)	15.3 (Dec., 2000)	17.7 (Dec., 2000)
Provisioning as a % of NPLs	76 (Nov., 2000)	63.1 (June, 2000)	40.7 (Dec., 2000)	39.0 (Oct., 2000)
Financial distress resolutions:				
Bank closures	70 of 237	None	None	1 of 15
Closure of other financial institutions	None	More than 200	None	59 of 91 finance companies
Mergers	9 nationalised banks and 4 state banks have been merged	9 of 26 banks absorbed by other banks	50 out of 54 banks were merged into 10 groups by the end 2000 deadline	3 banks and 12 finance companies
Banks temporarily nationalised	4	4	1	4
Bank recapitalisation strategies:				
Public funds for recapitalisation	A total of US$67.8 billion of sovereign bonds have been issued, of which US$44.8 billion were used to recapitalise 4 state banks, 4 national-ised banks, 7 private banks and 27 regional banks. The balance of the bonds were used for liquidity support.	Government injected US$50 billion into 9 commercial banks plus NBFIs; 3 major banks now 80% controlled by the state. Additional US$36 billion being made available for banks/NBFIs	Danamodal injected US$1.3 billion into 10 institutions	Government injected US$1.7 billion into private banks and about US$12 billion into public banks. US$7.8 billion funds injected as tier 1 capital

(continued)

Table 9.3 (continued)
Financial Restructuring in Indonesia and Other East Asian Economies
(end 2000)

Action	Indonesia	Korea	Malaysia	Thailand
Majority foreign ownership of banks	1 pending	1 bank sold with majority stake. 6 other major banks now significantly owned by foreign stakeholders	13 wholly owned foreign banks hold 30% of total commercial bank assets. Foreign banks' branch expansion is limited.	4 completed, 2 pending (included BMB)
Weak financial institutions still in system	Many weak commercial banks	Many weak NBFIs. Reform of the deposit insurance coverage has had major impact.	Difficult to assess	Some weak public and private banks

Notes: * Includes non banks and loans transferred to asset management corporations (AMCs). For Malaysia figures include commercial banks, finance companies, merchant banks and Danaharta.
Source: World Bank (2001)

framework to speed up corporate restructuring were also completed in 1998. On 30 October 1998 the government signed a regulation providing tax neutrality for mergers and removing key tax disincentives to restructuring. A regulation to remove obstacles to debt-to-equity conversion under the Company Law was issued. A review of legal changes needed to create an effective and predictable system of security rights was also undertaken with the assistance of the World Bank. In 1999 a law against corruption, collusion and nepotism was passed.

Despite the comprehensive nature of the legal and institutional framework developed, progress toward corporate restructuring was slow and disappointing. For example, one year after its establishment INDRA had registered little debt, only 80 bankruptcy cases had been registered, although almost half of Indonesian corporations were insolvent and experiencing increasing difficulties in meeting debt service obligations. One of the biggest constraints on the speed of corporate debt restructuring during this period was an associated lack of financial sector reform as discussed previously. Weak and undercapitalised banks lacked the resources or technical skills to resolve corporate debts within the framework of the Jakarta Initiative. Another constraint was the sheer enormity of Indonesia's foreign debt. Without debt relief from foreign creditors, including Japan, Indonesia appeared unable to service its debt, and in particular that of the US$36 billion owed to foreign banks (ADB 2000).

Table 9.4
NPLs of Crisis-affected Countries (% of total loans)

	1997 Dec.	1998 Dec.	1999 Dec.	2000 March	2000 June	2000 Sept.	2000 Latest
Indonesia[a]	–	–	64.0	62.4	63.5	61.7	58.8 (Nov.)
Excl. IBRA	7.2	48.6	32.9	32.1	30.0	26.9	23.9 (Nov.)
Korea[b]	8.0	1 6.1	1 5.8	1 7.9	1 8.9	1 7.9	
Excl. KAMCO/KDIC	5.9	10.4	10.9	10.9	13.6	12.3	
Malaysia[c]	6.0	22.6	23.6	23.3	23.2		
Excl. Danaharta	–	18.9	16.7	16.7	16.2	16.1	15.3 (Dec.)
Philippines[d]	4.7	10.4	12.5	14.4	14.6	15.3	15.1 (Dec.)
Thailand[e]		45.0	41.5	39.8	34.8	30.6	26.5 (Dec.)
Excl. AMCs		45.0	38.9	37.2	32.0	22.6	17.7 (Dec.)

Notes:
a   The first line uses the 'stringent' definition of an NPL; the second line excludes transfers to IBRA.
b   NPL figures use the BLC.
c   Figures include commercial banks, finance companies, merchant banks, and Danaharta.
d   Figures are for commercial banks.
e   Commercial banks. First line includes commercial banks, finance companies, and the estimated amount of NPLs transferred to wholly owned private AMCs.
Source: World Bank (2001).

Available evidence suggests that the pace at which IBRA and private creditors were finalising restructuring deals with corporate debtors gathered some momentum throughout 2000 (see Table 9.6), although this appeared to have dissipated by early 2001. By December 2000, IBRA's AMC had provisionally resolved 88 per cent of its Rp 88 trillion in loans to its top 21 obligors. For the top 200 obligors the percentage in late stage rose from 9 per cent to 57 per cent over the same period. Despite this progress there were concerns over the quality of many of the restructuring deals, and the recent deterioration in the investment environment was likely to slow progress further. Progress in this area has become crucial and needs to be accelerated. However, such progress will depend upon exchange rate and interest rate stability and the credibility of the commercial court to arbitrate disputes effectively. However, Indonesia's relatively limited high-quality human resources in the finance sector still present it with a particularly difficult challenge in addressing the massive corporate debt overhang. However, until this debt overhang is tackled successfully, the economy has only a very limited prospect for sustainable growth.

By early 2001 Indonesia's corporate sector remained weak on a number of fronts, and the deteriorating economic environment was contributing to even greater fragility.

Table 9.5
Asset Resolution Strategies in Indonesia and in East Asia

Strategy	Indonesia	Korea	Malaysia	Thailand
Establishment of Centralised Asset Management Corporation				
Set up centralised management corporation to which the banking system's non-performing loans are transferred	Yes. IBRA has accumulated about US$57.8 billion in assets, NPLs, investment in re-capitalised banks, pledged assets from shareholder settlements.	Yes. KAMCO has accumulated assets at Dec. 2000: US$84 billion (face value); US$32 billion purchase price. Recently KDIC has received NPLs from ailing and bank-rupt institutions (US$4.2 billions) face value.	Yes. Danabarta has accumulated US$10.3 billion in assets.	Established Financial Re-structuring Agency (FRA) to liquidate failed finance companies. NPL workout for private institutions is decentralised. BOT has approved the establishment of 8 AMC subsidiaries by 7 banks and 1 finance company and is reviewing applications to set up 4 more.
Nature of Asset Management Corporation				
Purchase of assets at subsidised prices	Yes	Assets were initially purchased above market clearing prices with recourse. Since Feb. 1998 purchases have been attempted at market prices.	Purchased assets are valued by independent outside auditors and transferred at close to market values.	Not applicable for private institutions
Restructuring or disposition	IBRA created to resolve problem banks; manage and dispose of frozen bank assets; and resolve NPLs transferred from recapitalised banks.	Mostly engaged in disposing of assets but recently CRVs have been established to restructure companies.	Restructuring and disposition	Not applicable for private institutions. For state banks, selection of third party managers to manage SAM has been suspended pending a proposed National AMC.

(continued)

Table 9.5 (continued)
Asset Resolution Strategies in Indonesia and in East Asia

Strategy	Indonesia	Korea	Malaysia	Thailand
Asset Transfer and Disposal				
Type of assets transferred	Assets of frozen banks and worst assets	Limited to ailing financial institutions	Loans larger than RM 5 million and mostly loans secured by property or shares	Not applicable to private institutions. All assets of failed finance companies transferred to FRA.
Assets transferred	IBRA's total assets amount to 57% of GDP; transferred NPLs amount to 30% of GDP	49% of NPLs, equal to 11% of GDP	36.2% of NPLs, equal to 12.3% of GDP	Only assets from failed finance companies sold by the FRA (Bt600 billion of core assets; 13% of GDP).
Assets disposed of as a share of total assets transferred	7%	48%	61%	70% of closed finance company assets.

Source: World Bank (2001)

Table 9.6
Status of IBRA AMC's Efforts to Resolve Credits, December 2000
(rupiah trillion)

Group of obligor	Early stage	Middle stage	Late stage	Total
Top 21	6.1 (7%)	4.4 (5%)	77.0 (88%)	87.5
Top 22–200	21.3 (21%)	57.0 (58%)	20.9 (21%)	99.2
Others	48.6 (63%)	22.8 (29%)	6.3 (8%)	77.7
Total	76.0 (29%)	84.2 (32%)	104.2 (39%)	264.5

Source: IBRA

Firstly, Indonesian corporations remained very vulnerable to further devaluations of the rupiah. According to a recent quarterly survey of corporate indebtedness conducted by the Jakarta Initiative Task Force (JITF), total corporate debt in Indonesia amounted to US$119 billion as of December 2000. Of this around 48 per cent (US$57 billion) was owed to offshore creditors and the other 52 per cent (US$62 billion) to onshore creditors. Almost half of the latter (US$29.4 billion) was denominated in foreign exchange. Rising domestic interest rates also exacerbated the repayment of domestic currency denominated debt.

Indonesian corporations have continued to accumulate arrears on debt service payments. Around 62 per cent (US$37.3 billion) of the onshore portion of the corporate debt is classified as non-performing. The percentage of offshore loans that are non-performing is not yet known, but if the same ratio were applied to that of the onshore loans, after deducting Japanese loans which are largely performing, then around US$22.6 billion of the offshore loans would also be non-performing. At the end of 1997 around 95 per cent of total loans in the domestic banking system were categorised as performing. By the end of 1999 this had fallen to around 36 per cent and in June 2000 remained at around 36 per cent. By December 2000 it had fallen to 30 per cent, indicating a deterioration in the domestic banks' portfolios during the second half of the year. Among the offshore creditors Japanese banks are the largest group, accounting for 31.2 per cent of offshore loans. The second largest group is the US banks (13.6 per cent) followed by the Netherlands (10.7 per cent) and Germany (6.4 per cent). The three largest creditor countries therefore accounted for more than 55.5 per cent of Indonesia's offshore corporate loans.

IBRA holds 80 per cent (US$29.9 billion) of the onshore distressed loans. Large private corporations (debts of more than Rp 50 billion) account for 80 per cent of this amount. Of the US$24.7 billion offshore performing loans (loans of less than Rp 50 billion) small and medium enterprises account for 60 per cent, state owned enterprises for 5 per cent and the remaining 35 per cent is accounted for by large private corporations.

Indonesian corporations are still undergoing little fundamental restructuring and could emerge from the crisis largely intact and still very vulnerable. In the restructuring deals to date, term extensions and grace periods have been predominant. Sales of non core businesses or assets to foreign or domestic investors, mergers or spin offs, additional equity financing, management changes, or court supervised reorganisations or liquidations have not played as great a role in Indonesia as in other East Asian countries. Corporations and financial institutions can only regain their health through deeper restructuring through sale of assets, new equity injections and debt equity conversions.

As of early 2001, JITF was handling 111 cases of voluntary debt settlement valued at US$19 billion. This represented important progress when compared with the 67 cases valued at US$13.3 billion in August 2000. By the end of 2000 JITF had rescheduled about US$9.4 billion in corporate debt, nearly twice that restructured as of August 2000. Under its programme with the IMF it needed to restructure US$12 billion in debt by April 2001. JITF was ahead of its quantitative targets. Particularly useful in achieving this have been JITF's time bound mediation procedures and the improvements in regulatory incentives, particularly tax breaks, for corporate restructuring. As with IBRA, however, there remain questions about the quality of the restructuring deals concluded.

Although the quantitative results from the enhanced corporate restructuring framework are encouraging, there is a continuing need for Indonesia's legal system to provide more reliable protection for creditors. Reform of Indonesia's legal system will take time and ongoing efforts to promote corporate restructuring cannot assume the availability of a robust bankruptcy option. The relevant parties – including Bank Indonesia, BAPEPAM, Jakarta Stock Exchange, and the tax authorities – should continue efforts to remove unwarranted impediments to corporate restructuring transactions. The current requirement for financial institutions to sell converted equity within 2–5 years is of particular concern, since debt/equity conversions are likely to feature prominently in Indonesian corporate restructuring transactions (World Bank 2001).

Improved access to financing for working capital and capital investment is likely to be the greatest incentive for corporations to undergo necessary corporate restructuring. Financial institutions are likely to be more willing to provide additional loans or equity investments in companies whose management teams have demonstrated readiness to focus on core competencies, sell non core assets, exit from non competitive businesses, eliminate cross guarantees and otherwise adopt more straightforward capital structures, seek strategic investors, provide or raise additional equity financing, pay down debt, improve financial disclosure, and strengthen corporate governance (World Bank 2001).

9.3.4 Governance

In Indonesia, decades of unaccountable and centralised administration degraded the quality and efficiency of several public administrations. Strong growth and rising prosperity for years before the crisis gave rise to complacency, resulting in a delay in implementing necessary governance reforms. Poor governance was also responsible, in large part, for the magnitude of the financial, economic and social collapse that occurred in 1997–98. The government recognised that unless governance reform was accelerated and fundamental change brought about, sustained future growth and development would be further jeopardised. Major priorities, as a matter of urgency, in improving governance include: combating corruption; improving decision-making and administrative structures; and strengthening public institutions (ADB 2000).

The government took important steps in 1999 to combat corruption in a country widely perceived as being the most corrupt in the region (see Table 9.7), when it passed several new laws. The Clean Government Law required public officials to declare their assets before assuming their posts, and to agree to open their assets to official audit during and after their term of office. The Eradication of Criminal Acts

Table 9.7
Perceptions of Regional Corruption, Transparency and Potential
for Social Unrest, 1999

Country	Corruption	Transparency	Potential for social unrest
Indonesia	9.91	8.00	9.64
Malaysia	7.50	6.50	4.88
Philippines	6.71	6.29	4.43
Singapore	1.55	4.55	1.18
Thailand	7.57	7.29	3.86
Vietnam	8.50	9.50	5.00
Japan	4.25	7.13	0.88

Notes: Scores based on response by 600 regional businessmen, where 0=best and 10=worst.
Source: Political and Economic Risk Consultancy, Singapore.

of Corruption Law defines corrupt practices as those that are harmful to the finances of the economy of the state, and establishes the basis for legal prosecution and criminal charges. It also provides for public participation in legal surveillance and the establishment of an independent anticorruption commission for legal enforcement.

New regulations to reform public procurement and project implementation, including the provision of infrastructure services practices, were introduced. A ministerial decree elaborated upon the criteria and institutional arrangements for project screening, selection, and review, including transparent competitive bidding procedures, providing a framework for consistent sector-specific norms. While these steps are important, much more remains to be done to: promote competition and efficient, transparent and accountable administration; encourage citizen participation; and strengthen legal reforms and the role of official oversight agencies. However, progressive institutional change across many sectors have met with significant resistance from vested interests (ADB 2000).

Parliament's approval of the Law on Regional Autonomy and the Law on Fiscal Balances in 1999 gave districts and provinces impetus to decentralise. This is intended to improve accountability of the government's decision making process, strengthen participation of beneficiaries, and increase transparency. Implementing the government's wide ranging decentralisation agenda, which includes introducing new systems, structures, and procedures to transfer developmental and administrative functions and fiscal responsibilities to local levels, will, however, pose difficult challenges. Among other things, this implies that many central government agencies will need to make their respective mandates consistent with a decentralised framework. It also implies substantial strengthening of capacity of the public institutions, especially at lower tiers of public administration (ADB 2000).

Elsewhere, with assistance from the World Bank, the government has addressed governance concerns in the banking sector and capital market institutions under the Financial Governance Reform Sector Development Programme. The Programme focuses on best governance practices, disclosure and transparency, and the regulatory framework of the banking sector and the capital market. An antimonopoly law was passed by Parliament in February 1999.

The government has also undertake a comprehensive review of all public services to assess their financial and economic viability, and to identify those services that could be more efficiently delivered by the private sector. The government agreed to release to the public detailed financial information on BULOG, Pertamina, PLN, and the reforestation fund.[15] International standard audits were completed for PLN. Auditors were appointed for the other two institutions and the reforestation fund, and their audits were completed by the end of June 1999. Such audits were extended to other key SOEs with substantial market or debt exposure, with the intention of reducing KKN.

The crisis has exposed deep-seated governance problems in Indonesia. KKN was a major factor in the collapse of the finance sector. Apart from raising the transaction costs of business, and encouraging misallocation of resources, the rent-seeking behaviour associated with KKN has imposed high economic costs on Indonesia (ADB 2000). While the government is moving in the right direction to improve governance, the agenda for reform needs to be broadened and deepened substantially. The Government's commitment needs to be sustained over a long period to root out KKN. However the legal reforms implemented so far are aimed at strengthening the institutional basis for promoting good governance across all sectors of the economy.

9.3.5   Privatisation

Most state owned enterprises (SOEs) in Indonesia are in poor economic and financial health, and represent a drain on scarce public resources. The onset of the crisis further constrained scarce fiscal resources. With this backdrop, the government prepared a privatisation and restructuring masterplan for SOEs in September 1998.[16] The masterplan envisaged the divestiture of 150 SOEs over the next decade, leaving only a few enterprises under State ownership. The masterplan envisaged that privatisation of the first batch of 12 SOEs that could not be completed in FY1999 would be completed in FY2000, with a second batch of 25 SOEs in FY2000, and another 35 SOEs in FY2001. This schedule took into consideration the capacity constraints of the Ministry of SOEs and the Agency for SOEs. The major focus of the privatisation programme for FY2000 was on hotels, trading, construction, mining, civil engineering companies, and fertiliser firms. PLN and Garuda, the national airline, were included among the SOEs to be restructured in preparation for privatisation (ADB 2000).

The government has expressed commitment to follow international best practice and transparency in contract design and bidding procedures in the privatisation process. There have been, however, significant concerns, particularly in view of the events related to the privatisation of the Krakatau Steel Company and the Semen (cement) Gresik Company. There was also concern regarding attaining the privatisation targets scheduled. The process needs to be accelerated and future targets made to avoid major shortfalls in fiscal revenues.

9.3.6   Poverty

Even before the crisis, poverty was a major concern in Indonesia. The crisis further exacerbated the poverty problem, reversing in the span of less than one year the impressive gains in living standards and poverty reduction attained over nearly three decades (ADB 2000). As indicated in Table 9.8 the impact of the crisis on poverty in Indonesia has been severe, with the number of poor, those earning less than US$1 a day, increasing from 15.4 million in 1996, before the crisis, to 24.7 million in 1999 after the worst of the crisis. The crisis, consequently, brought poverty reduction to the top of the policy agenda again. Projections by the World Bank (World Bank 2001) suggest that while the extent of poverty reduction in Indonesia is recovering, it will not be until 2002, at best, before Indonesia returns to the levels of poverty achieved before the crisis in 1996. However, social vulnerability remains high. In 1999 two-thirds of the population lived on less than US$2 a day and this figure was projected to fall to 58 per cent of the population by 2002. The extent of the fall in poverty in the medium term will crucially depend upon the success of structural adjustments in the economy which are not yet complete, and in some cases have some considerable way to go. Hence the necessity of accelerating these as rapidly as possible.

In response to the increased poverty, the government strengthened the social safety net for poor and vulnerable groups. To address food security concerns in the wake of rapidly rising prices, a seven-point strategy for rice was put in place from mid-1998. During the low season, rice price stability was maintained through larger releases from public stocks. The subsidised programme to supply rice to the poorest was expanded to 17 million families in late 1998. The monthly allocation of rice per family was doubled to 20 kg for the poorest 5 million. To supplement government efforts, the World Food Programme also undertook food aid programmes and expanded the food-for-work programme. The government also launched labour-intensive projects in 4600 rural and urban areas throughout the country to enhance wage employment opportunities (ADB 2000).

The large expenditures on social safety nets and employment generation programmes required careful assessment and continuous monitoring by the government. The administrative machinery of the government and related agencies were seriously tested by these safety net programmes. To strengthen management and ensure transparency and accountability of these programmes it was essential to ensure greater involvement of non-government organisations and local civic and community representatives. Preliminary findings of poverty studies undertaken suggested a need to allocate adequate resources to combat urban poverty and poverty of women (World Bank 2001). The results also suggested that poverty reduction

Table 9.8
Mean Consumption, Inequality and Poverty in Indonesia

	Mean consumption (1993,PPPUS$ /person/day)	Gini (%)	Headcount index (%) US$1 a day[a]	No. of poor ('000) poverty line	Headcount index (%) US$2 a day[b]	No. of poor ('000) poverty line
1984	1.64	30.3	36.7	58 730	80.0	128 119
1987	1.83	30.8	25.7	43 363	74.2	125 391
1990	2.02	28.9	20.6	36 690	71.1	126 691
1993	2.25	31.7	14.8	27 818	61.6	115 534
1996	2.85	36.5	7.8	15 398	50.5	99 583
1999	2.20	31.0	12.0	24 726	65.1	134 038
2000	2.24	30.7	10.5	21 931	63.3	132 299
2001[c]	2.32	30.9	8.9	18 827	60.5	128 055
2002[c]	2.40	31.0	7.5	16 010	57.8	124 090

Notes:
a   More precisely this is a poverty line of US$32.74 per person per month (or US$1.08 per person per day) at 1993 PPP US dollars, widely used for international comparisons of poverty (World Bank 1990, 2000a, 2000b).
b   More precisely this is US$2.15 per person per day (at 1993 PPP US$s).
c   Projections based on World Bank Unified Survey growth forecasts for 2001–2003.
Source: World Bank (2001)

programmes should be targeted increasingly at areas with depressed labour demand. That is in areas that suffered the largest decline in real wages and not necessarily in areas with the highest open unemployment rates. The government's fiscal revenues are, however, constrained. These programmes in their present scale can therefore only be undertaken for a limited period. Beyond that, sustainable poverty reduction must rely on reviving strong growth of the economy (ADB 2000). It is worth mentioning that the fiscal constraints imposed on the government from the crisis have resulted in reduced expenditure on health and, of particular concern, education (World Bank 2001).

9.3.7   Political Developments

The resignation of President Suharto in May 1998 following three decades of rule was a major landmark event, which resulted in major political instability thereafter. When Suharto's deputy B.J. Habibie took over as President the desire for change and reform amongst the population was so great that he had little option but to accede to this. Indonesia's first free elections in almost four decades were promised for June 1999. Ethnic and separatist violence began to plague the country and even began to break out in a number of the country's far flung provinces, triggered by the new President's decision to allow East Timor to vote on independence in August 1999. The Parliamentary elections of June 1999 were relatively clean but failed to produce a clear outcome, leaving the country more divided than ever. This did not bode well in terms of the country making difficult decisions essential for its recovery from the economic and social crisis. The Indonesian Democratic Party of Struggle, led by Megawati Sukarnoputri, the daughter of Indonesia's first President, won the most votes, but lacked an overall majority as did the Golkar Party. In a surprise decision Adurrahman Wahid was elected as president in October 1999 and Megawati Sukarnoputri, who was expected to be elected as president, failed to build a coalition prepared to back her, and instead became vice-president. Since becoming president Mr Wahid has, like his country, appeared fragile, with many forecasting that he would be unable to hold together his 'national unity cabinet' composed of members of all the main political parties and the military. At the beginning of 2001 he had himself become tainted by scandal and corruption allegations, which have undermined his authority and diverted attention away from the necessary tasks involved in bringing about a recovery of the economy. Many political pundits were forecasting that his presidency would come to an end in 2001, and would be hastened by sustained acts of sectarian strife in a country traditionally lauded for its tolerance. Peaceful transition after over 30 years of authoritarian rule characterised by corruption, collusion, and nepotism (KKN) to a stable democratic order is a key ingredient to greatly improve investor confidence and Indonesia's economic outlook.

9.4   OUTSTANDING ISSUES TOWARDS SUSTAINABLE RECOVERY – A SHORT- AND LONG-TERM AGENDA

While Indonesia has made progress towards attaining macroeconomic stability and in reforming its financial and corporate sectors, much more remains to be done to ensure the country's sustainable recovery from its economic crisis. It will depend in particular how expeditiously, yet prudently, the following short- and long-term tasks are tackled.

9.4.1   Short-term Tasks

Agreeing on a programme with the IMF
Investor sentiment towards Indonesia continues to be negative, especially when compared to other crisis countries in the region. A critical ingredient to improving foreign investor confidence in the near term will be a resumption in the reform programme supported by the IMF which has been stalled since December 2000. This

will also trigger the second consolidation phase of the Paris Club debt rescheduling agreement and will allow it to proceed forward smoothly. Together with actions on poverty and governance this will facilitate access to higher levels of lending from the World Bank. A high level advisory group to the President, re-emphasised the necessity for the government to consider carefully the serious risks of further delays in implementing the programme agreed with the IMF.

Adopting measures to improve investor confidence
Related to the previous issue is the need to increase investor confidence in general in Indonesia, essential for supporting macroeconomic stability (through a less volatile exchange rate, stronger stock market index, and lower risk premiums) and in attracting non debt private capital flows (including foreign direct investment). With growth in external markets slowing for many export products, continued political uncertainty in the country, and delays in implementing the reform programme supported by the IMF, investor confidence in Indonesia has once again waned. Generating positive investor sentiment is a multi faceted endeavour and will require from the government: clarification of the 'rules of the game' for investors; increased predictability of government actions; and that laws are implemented even-handedly and credibly. To this end, a number of outstanding issues need to be addressed. Firstly, there is a lack of transparency in IBRA's corporate debt restructuring principles. In the absence of such principles, there are fears that large debtors will be able to strike deals that will not serve the best interests of the State. There are also concerns as to whether the government will take action against non cooperative debtors and whether IBRA will continue with its successes in its bankruptcy and foreclosure actions. Progress in corporate restructuring has been largely voluntary and it remains to be seen whether major non-cooperative debtors can be successfully pressured into reaching agreements. Some of the bankruptcy cases won by IBRA were still subject to possible reversal by the Supreme Court. Until there is an assurance of more reliable court decisions, referrals may serve only to re-emphasise the relative weakness of creditors and deter foreign investors.

Secondly there is a need to enhance the credibility in the legal system. In recent high profile cases phantom creditors have emerged to offset bona fide creditor claims, gaining court approval of debtor friendly composition plans. It remains to be seen whether these court decisions will be successfully appealed or whether more similar cases will emerge and further erode the already very low confidence in the judicial system. Other unscrupulous practices have included non disclosure and exclusion of debtor assets and asset sale proceeds from debt restructuring negotiations, creation of phantom shareholders to block foreign equity investment, and use of nominee shell companies by Indonesian conglomerates to buy back assets from creditors at a percentage of the amounts owed creditors.

Thirdly, recent agreements between debtors and creditors need to be implemented. While recent progress by IBRA's AMC in reaching debt restructuring agreements with its top 200 obligors is encouraging, some bankers continue to question whether debtors have the cash flows and the will to implement these deals. IBRA will need to monitor implementation of these agreements and respond to lags or shortfalls in implementation.

Finally, progress by IBRA's AMC in resolving the corporate debts of its smaller obligors bears watching along with the manner in which it disposes of the restructured corporate loans that fall under its purview. In all cases, these credits should be priced through a competitive auction process. Appropriate pricing and provisioning of loans is essential for acquiring banks to push for additional corporate restructuring measures, that is sales of non core assets and exits from unprofitable businesses, that may require banks to recognise losses along with their corporate clients (World Bank 2001).

Disposal of assets acquired by IBRA

Prior to October 2000 the focus of Indonesia's restructuring effort was primarily upon resolving NPLs and recapitalising weak financial institutions. With this now complete the short-term agenda must now focus upon disposing of the assets accumulated by IBRA's AMC. By the year 2000 about 66 per cent of NPLs in Indonesia had been transferred to IBRA, equivalent to about 30 per cent of GDP (see Table 9.5).[17] However, the proportion of NPLs actually resolved or disposed of as a share of the total assets transferred was very low, only 7 per cent, both in absolute terms and relative to progress made in other crisis afflicted economies (see Table 9.5). Further improvement in the regulatory framework to speed up the resolution of IBRA's portfolio of assets is therefore a priority. The purchase, transfer, management and sale of such assets needs to be made easier. The sale of such assets will provide much-needed revenue for the government and consequently will reduce pressure on fiscal sustainability.

Improved governance

Poor governance was a major weakness in Indonesia's financial and corporate sectors, exacerbating the extent of the financial and economic crisis. Symptoms included intricate formal and informal relationships between government, financial institutions, and corporations; inadequate disclosure requirements; and widespread corruption and favouritism (ADB 2000). A focus of ongoing reforms must be upon further strengthening of governance in both the public and private sectors by: improving market discipline; improving corporate governance; privatisation of SOEs; introducing competition policies; and the introduction of anticorruption policies. The impact of these reforms, however, will take time as they will require an entirely new corporate framework and culture.

Despite the progress made in Indonesia more effort will be needed to establish a modern legal and regulatory framework, reduce the risk of bureaucratic and corruption-prone administrative procedures, reform the ownership structure of large business groups, adopt modern financial management techniques, and reduce corruption. Corruption remains a serious systemic problem in Indonesia, and, as indicated in Table 9.7, is widely perceived by business people within the region to be so. In the public sector this can involve either monopolistic firms or rent seeking bureaucracies that extract rents in return for licensing privileges. Such monopolistic firms are best addressed through well designed privatisation programmes. Eradication of rent-seeking corruption is more entrenched and difficult, and badly devised efforts to do so could increase inefficiency.

9.4.2   Longer-term Tasks

Maintaining fiscal sustainability

Before the onset of the financial crisis Indonesia enjoyed a strong fiscal position with budget surpluses and a negligible public sector debt. When the crisis hit the country fiscal policy was initially kept tight, but was later relaxed in the wake of rapidly deteriorating economic and social conditions. Fiscal resources were increasingly devoted to: financial restructuring, including the buying of NPLs; recapitalising insolvent banks; protecting depositors and creditors; providing subsidies on food and fuel to reduce as much as possible the impact of the crisis upon the poor; and stimulating economic recovery and providing social safety nets for the poor and vulnerable. Consequently fiscal deficits have risen substantially and public debt has rapidly accumulated (see Table 9.1). With the recent depreciation of the rupiah and the rise in domestic interest rates the fiscal position has deteriorated further. The currency depreciation is pushing up spending on fuel and electricity subsidies as well.[18] Revenues go up as well when the rupiah depreciates, but under the new decentralised system of government these increases are shared with the regions. The rising domestic interest rates are increasing the burden of servicing the outstanding bank recapitalisation bonds, and at the same time are increasing the risk of a deterioration of the banks' balance sheets.

Also related to the issue of fiscal stability is the government's recent decision to move towards greater fiscal decentralisation and with it the need to ensure appropriate safeguards and public service delivery standards. The government has issued a decree forbidding local governments from domestic borrowing in 2001, except through the central government. For 2002 and beyond, the government will need to rapidly put in place proper principles and safeguards for sub-national borrowing in the implementation of fiscal decentralisation. The issue, if left unattended, may put Indonesia's fiscal sustainability at risk. There remains considerable confusion about the division of regulatory powers between the centre and districts, especially in areas that affect private sector activity. To facilitate private sector activity, the government needs to clarify responsibilities for tax, investment approval, and private sector regulation; and to ensure that administrative courts are better able to enforce the rights of citizens against arbitrary actions by local governments (under Administrative Law 5/1986).

The prospects for greater fiscal imbalance therefore require remedial action over the medium to longer term, otherwise economic recovery may be slowed as private investment is crowded out and debt servicing requirements impede the public sector's infrastructure development. Hence the country will be required to give higher priority to reducing fiscal imbalances as soon as possible. Additional revenue can be generated from privatisation of nationalised banks and SOEs, and by selling accumulated assets acquired by IBRA. Attracting more domestic and foreign private investment into the ailing financial and corporate sectors would also alleviate the fiscal burden. So too will more consistent efforts to recover defaulted bank loans through systemic investigations into corporations' uses of such loans.

Developing financial markets and a comprehensive financial sector strategy

It is generally accepted that one of the major causes of the region's financial crisis was excessive reliance on short-term bank loans from abroad, either through the domestic banking system or, as was the case primarily in Indonesia, directly by the corporate sector in order to finance long-term investments at home or abroad. Asian finance has traditionally been overwhelmingly bank based, which will require a fundamental change. An important lesson from the crisis is the urgency required to develop financial markets that can efficiently allocate domestic savings to long-term projects. Therefore the crisis afflicted countries, including Indonesia, need to modernise and develop their capital markets, particularly bond markets, and maximise the efficiency with which long-term savings are channelled into profitable industrial and infrastructure projects.

The government therefore needs to articulate a comprehensive financial sector strategy as a useful way to prepare for such a fundamental change that is accepted by all stakeholders within and outside the government. This would serve as a basis for financial sector reforms over the medium term and towards the implementation of an agreed action plan with the necessary 'buy in' among all stakeholders. Further delays in determining the government's approach to the shape of the future financial landscape may hamper coordination of various financial sector reform efforts at a crucial point in Indonesia's recovery process.

The strategy should aim to ensure greater diversification and market orientation in the financial sector by increasing operational efficiency, developing human resources, maximising synergy between various subsectors, and facilitating resource mobilisation. It should cover the banking sector, non-bank credit institutions, insurance sector, capital markets, and newer financial institutions such as venture capital entities.

All types of long-term financial markets, equity, bonds, and insurance, need to be fostered. However, bond markets deserve particular attention because they have been long neglected, while efforts at developing equity markets began long before the crisis. Bond markets were underdeveloped because government surpluses meant that the government had little, if any, outstanding government debt. Therefore, there was no benchmark yield curve of returns on safe government debt, making it difficult to price other bonds. The investor base for bonds was also limited; the market infrastructure was inadequate. Moreover, weak corporate governance and underdeveloped regulatory and supervisory arrangements reduced the attractiveness of corporate bonds. Given the rudimentary nature of domestic bond markets, a gradual approach is desirable. First, the market for primary government securities issues must be developed. Then a secondary market for these issues should follow, and corporate bond markets should then develop.

9.5   SUMMARY AND CONCLUSIONS

Indonesia's economic fundamentals before the onset of the currency contagion in East Asia, during the summer of 1997, appeared to place it in a good position to weather the storm. Indeed, the government was praised for acting responsibly by requesting assistance from the IMF early on in its crisis in October 1997. By April 1998, however, the country was in the weakest position of all the countries affected by the crisis. Consequently, the extent and speed of reform required has been more pressing for Indonesia than for many of its regional neighbours. As with many of the other crisis afflicted economies the country's weakest link was the financial sector, however this was compounded by an equally weak corporate sector. Sustainability of the country's recovery, therefore, fundamentally depends upon restructuring and reforming its financial and corporate sectors. This initially entailed cleaning up the financial sector by recapitalising the banking system through purchase of non performing loans by IBRA. With this now effectively complete, the next stage, involving asset disposal, has become the focus of policy. The success of this will also go considerably towards attaining longer term fiscal sustainability. Corporate sector restructuring and reform has been slow, has lacked transparency, and does not appear to have gained the confidence of foreign investors. The latter, in fact, will be crucial for the sustained recovery of the economy. Hence a further key policy priority is acceleration of corporate sector restructuring.

The tasks facing the country are therefore enormous, and only if there is a determined, credible, and transparent government policy response to tackle and overcome these will investor confidence and sustained growth be possible. Ongoing political instability, regional and ethnic tensions and general social unrest are adding to the enormity of the task, a dimension to the recovery process not apparent, to anywhere near the same degree, in other crisis afflicted economies in the region.

NOTES

1   The outcome of these upheavals was the replacement of President Suharto with his right-hand man President Habibie.
2   The first truly democratic elections in nearly four decades.
3   Oil remains a key export commodity for the economy.
4   Law on Regional Autonomy and the Law on Fiscal Balances 1999.
5   To support bank restructuring, as of October 2000, the government had issued

bonds valued at Rp 650 trillion.

6   IBRA and its Asset Management Unit (AMU) are under the close supervision of Bank Indonesia.

7   Banks that did not achieve the minimum CAR level of –25 per cent were restructured through mergers or closed.

8   The business plans were reviewed by committees comprising representatives of BI, the Ministry of Finance, IBRA, and independent observers from the World Bank, IMF, and the Bank.

9   Before the crisis Indonesia had 160 private banks.

10   However, the actual cost has turned out to be much higher than this.

11   Bank for International Settlements.

12   Consequently the AMCs, and therefore the governments in these countries, will have enormous influence in shaping the future development of their respective private sectors, both financial and corporate.

13   The London approach evolved in the United Kingdom when numerous firm bankruptcies occurred in the recession of the early 1990s. During this period more than 160 British companies used this approach, which involved creditor financial institutions and indebted firms working under the close coordination of a government institution (in this case the Bank of England) but outside the formal judiciary process. To be successful this approach required confidence in the official mediating institution. Superficially, at least, the corporate debt workouts under government coordination in Indonesia, Korea and Thailand resemble the London approach.

14   More generally referred to as the Jakarta Initiative Task Force (JITF).

15   Pertamina is the SOE for petroleum, while PLN is the State-owned electricity corporation. Bulog is the State logistics agency.

16   Government of the Republic of Indonesia (1998), Masterplan for the Reform of State-Owned Enterprises. State Ministry for State-Owned Enterprises/Agency for State-Owned Enterprises, Jakarta.

17   Latest figures from the Asian Development Bank (April 2001) suggested that by December 2000, IBRA had acquired 82.6 per cent of banking sector NPLs as alluded to in an earlier section of this chapter.

18   The increased spending on the development budget is largely foreign financed, and thus does not significantly impact the fiscal deficit. However, availability of these funds is mostly contingent on continued progress on implementation of the ongoing reform programme.

REFERENCES

Asian Development Bank (ADB) (2000), *Asian Development Outlook 2000*, Manila, Philippines: Asian Development Bank.

Asian Development Bank (ADB) (2001), *Asian Development Outlook 2001*, Manila, Philippines: Asian Development Bank.

Bank of America (1999), 'Banking reform in Asia: comparative rankings of progress made', *Asian Financial Outlook*, **25** (August).

Deutsche Bank (1999), 'Is Asia's recovery sustainable', *Global Emerging Markets*, **2** (3), May.

Harvie, C. (2000a), 'The financial crisis in Indonesia: the role of good governance', in Tran Van Hoa and C. Harvie (eds), *The Causes and Impact of the Asian Financial Crisis*, Basingstoke, UK: Macmillan, pp. 95–130.

Harvie, C. (2000b), 'Indonesia: the road from economic and social collapse', in Tran Van Hoa (ed.), *The Asia Crisis: the cures, their effectiveness and the prospects after*, Basingstoke, UK: Macmillan, pp. 110–139.

JP Morgan (1999), 'The budgetary legacy of the Asian crisis', *Asian Financial Markets* (fourth quarter), Singapore.

World Bank (1990), *Poverty, World Development Report 1990*, Oxford: Oxford University Press.

World Bank (1999), Global economic prospects and the developing countries, Washington, DC: World Bank [available at <www.worldbank.org>].

World Bank (2000a), *Attacking poverty*, World Development Report 2000/1, Oxford: Oxford University Press.

World Bank (2000b), Global economic prospects and the developing countries 2001, Washington, DC: World Bank [available at <www.worldbank.org>].

World Bank (2001), *East Asia Update – Indonesia*, Washington, DC: World Bank, March.

10 Singapore: Economic Management During and After the Asia Crisis

Tran Van Hoa

10.1 INTRODUCTION

Tumasik, currently known as the Republic of Singapore, is small in area (646.1 sq km) and in population (3.164 million in 1998), less endowed with natural resources as are its neighbouring countries (for example, Indonesia, Malaysia and Thailand), but fairly influential in world economic and political affairs. It has had a long and chequered history, especially during the last 200 years or so. Singapore (with an annual income of US$30 550 per capita in 1996) has a essentially market economy based largely on international trade and finance. It has no mining projects other than granite quarrying but more than 100 commercial banks. Singapore's manufacturing industries (producing transport equipment and electronics products and using electricity that is generated entirely from imported fuels) account for more than a quarter of its gross domestic product and employ more than 25 per cent of the workforce. Singapore has become one of the few economies in Asia to join the rank of the developed nations of the Western world, even though some of its administrations still are, to some critics, far from being fully developed in the true Western framework, culture and *opus operandi*.

Starting out as an island inhabited by fishermen and pirates and an outpost of the Sumatran empire of Srivijaya until the 14th century, Tumasik became part of the Malacca empire in the 15th century, and part of the Portuguese hegemony over the area in the 16th century, and then the Dutch in the 17th century. After the treaty with the sultan of Johore in 1819, Sir Stamford Raffles established the island as the port settlement of Singapore which became the centre of British colonial activity in Southeast Asia. Straits Settlement was founded in 1832 and Singapore became its administrative seat. At the time of its early development, the growth of the port was steady but slow due to a number of other development activities in the neighbouring region at the same time by either the British (the acquisition of Hong Kong) or French (Saigon, now Ho Chi Minh City) or Dutch (Dutch East Indies, now Indonesia) administrations. However, as Singapore is located strategically and importantly on the main sea routes in Southeast Asia through which trade between the West, Middle East and Far East could be more economically and commercially conducted, its growth prospered especially after the opening of the Suez Canal in Egypt in 1869 and the advent of steamships. This growth was initially linked to the demand for tin and rubber of the Malay Peninsula. After a brief occupation by the Japanese forces (1942–45) and after World War Two, the Straits Settlement was dissolved and Singapore became a separate crown colony in 1946, achieved full internal self-government in 1959, part of Malaysia in 1963, and became independent in 1965. From this date, Singapore's economy grew rapidly and achieved by the end of the 20th century the well coveted status of a developed nation in Southeast Asia (Britannica 2001).

This chapter first surveys the path of Singapore's growth over the last four decades (or whenever data are available), and focuses mainly on the principal determinants or inherent infrastructure responsible for or conducive to this remarkable growth. The chapter then discusses economic management policies in the economy especially during the last few years of the economic crisis in Asia that has had lingering worldwide repercussions. It then investigates Singapore's outlook and prospects in the face of a slow-down in the globalised world economy in the medium and long terms.

10.2   STRUCTURE OF SINGAPORE'S DEVELOPMENT AND GROWTH SINCE 1965

As noted above, Singapore's growth in its initial economic development was based principally on the supply of tin and rubber to meet their demand in the Malay Peninsula. This kind of trade was then a significant growth determinant but, in the last few decades, it had been replaced by exports of goods and services that represent more current demand and supply and other activities of international trade. From the data of 2000 CHELEM-CEPII international trade databank, we can list nine of the world's major trading blocs with Singapore. These blocs are: the US, Japan, Australia and New Zealand, Africa (OPEC), India, three major Asian newly industrialised economies (Malaysia, the Philippines and Thailand), the former USSR, Central Europe, and China). The trends of Singapore's exports to these trading partners are given in Figures 10.1 (in US$ million) and 10.2 (in percentage of total trade).

From Figures 10.1 and 10.2, we note that Singapore's important trading partners during 1967 and 1998 were Malaysia, the Philippines (the Asian newly industrialised economies – NIE), the US and Japan. In 1967, these three trading blocs took over 85 per cent of Singapore's total exports and, in 1998, they still took over 84 per cent of all exports. While Singapore's exports to these countries remained almost the same in 1967 and 1998, the dynamics of these export trends during 1967–98 had changed quite dramatically.

In 1967, the Asian NIE 3 took 61.3 per cent of Singapore's exports, while Japan

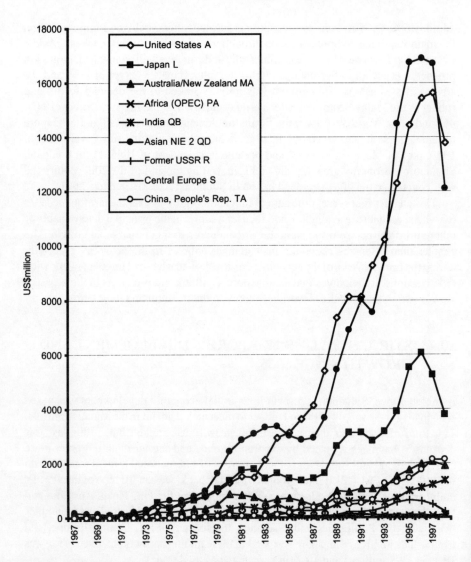

Figure 10.1   Singapore's Exports to the World's Major Trading Blocs

and the US took 17.7 and 6.7 per cent respectively. This ranking in trade importance remained until 1973, when the US took over the lead with 32.7 per cent (US$313.8 million) compared to 31.1 per cent (US$298.8 million) for the Asian NIE 3. In 1973, Japan also increased its imports from Singapore to US$195.4 million or 20.3 per cent. Also from Figures 10.1 and 10.2, the fastest growth rate of Singapore's exports seem to be equally with the US and the Asian NIE 3, and Japan only scored a moderate

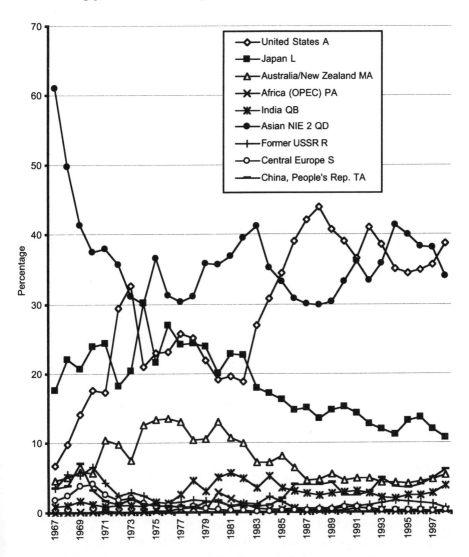

Figure 10.2   Singapore's Exports to the World's Major Trading Blocs (%)

growth rate. Singapore's exports to both the Asian NIE 3 and Japan started a decline as early as 1996 a year before the emergence of the Asia crisis, while those to the US showed a sharp fall in 1998. In terms of export shares however, the picture on the trends of Singapore's exports to these major trading blocs is more telling. Japan's imports from Singapore peaked in 1974 with 30.2 per cent (US$584.2 million) of

Singapore's exports and since then the share had been falling steadily ending at 10.7 per cent in 1998. After catching up with Japan's imports from Singapore in 1972 and the Asian NIE 3 in 1973, the US imports from Singapore fell dramatically since and only caught up again with the Asian NIE 3's imports in 1984. Remarkably, in 1998, while the share of Singapore's exports to the Asian NIE3 and Japan declined to 34.0 (from 38.2 in 1997) and 10.7 (from 12.0 in 1997) per cent respectively, that of the US increased from 35.8 in 1997 to 38.8 per cent in 1998. This change in the structure of exports from Singapore during the Asia crisis is very similar to that observed for Australia's exports at the same time.

In this chapter, Singapore's tradable commodities exported to the world according to 2000 CHELEM-CEPII classification consist of 10 broadly defined groups: construction products, basic metals, textiles, wood paper, metal products, chemicals, mining, energy, agriculture, and food products. In terms of commodity exports (see Figures 10.5 and 10.6), Singapore' exports to its major trading blocs were concentrated on three groups, namely, metal products (principally computer equipment, electronic components, telecommunications equipment, and electrical apparatus), energy (refined petroleum products and natural gas), and chemicals (basic organic chemicals, plastic articles, toiletries). These three groups accounted for 59.8 per cent of all groups in 1967 but about 92.7 and 92.8 per cent in 1997 and 1998 respectively.

In 1998, the proportion of metal products was 71.47 per cent of all exports. In this group, computer equipment accounted for 49.16 per cent, electronic components 21.01 per cent, telecommunications equipment 6.81 per cent, and electrical apparatus 5.49 per cent. Energy accounted for 13.5 per cent of all exports and, in this group, refined petroleum products shared 97.84 per cent and natural gas 1.94 per cent. Chemicals were 7.8 per cent of all exports with basic organic chemicals sharing in this group 40.37 per cent, plastic products 24.76 per cent and toiletries 11.94 per cent.

Agriculture played an important part of Singapore's exports in the late 1960s reaching 33.6 per cent of all exported commodity groups in 1970, but ending at about 0.63 and 0.62 per cent in 1997 and 1998 respectively. Food products showed a small increase in total exports in 1997 and 1998 with a share of 1.14 and 1.18 per cent respectively. Energy exports from Singapore to the world occupied the largest share during the period 1967–83 peaking at 51.0 per cent in 1983, but since then, it had fallen to 13.5 per cent in 1998. In 1986, metal products overtook energy as the largest export commodity group reaching 45.7 per cent compared to 30.9 per cent for energy. Chemical exports (5.4 per cent) overtook food product exports (5.0 per cent) in 1979 and they had remained fairly steady in the 1990s at about 7.0 per cent of all groups of export commodities.

The trends of Singapore's imports from the world's major trading blocs are given in export value in Figure 10.3 (US$ million) and in Figure 10.4 (in percentage of all imports).

From these figures, we note that Singapore's imports had increased almost exponentially during the period 1867–1998, especially from 1985. These imports came from three main trading blocs: Japan, the Asian NIE 3, and the US. In 1967,

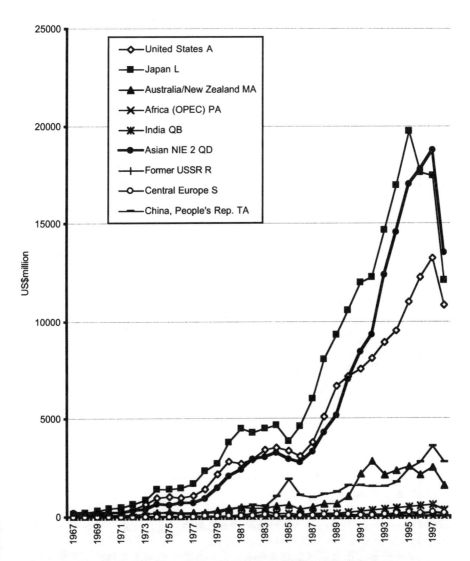

Figure 10.3   Singapore's Imports from the World's Major Trading Blocs

these three blocs accounted for 76.0 per cent of all imports by Singapore (the Asian NIE 3 31.0, 27.9, and 17.1 per cent respectively). In 1998, they accounted for 88.0 per cent (the Asian NIE 3 32.6, Japan 29.2, and the US 26.2 per cent respectively). Japan had played an important part in its exports to Singapore from 1968 to 1996, peaking at 44.7 per cent (US$2343.9 million) of Singapore's total imports in 1978. This trend had however declined since 1996, ending at about US$12 128.1 million in

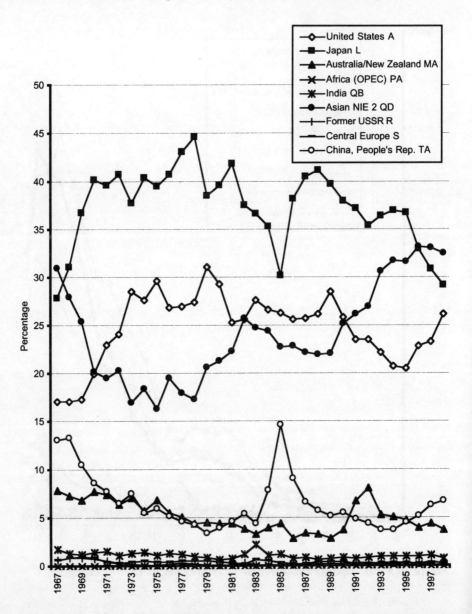

Figure 10.4   Singapore's Imports from the World's Major Trading Blocs (%)

1998. In 1996, the Asian NIE 3 overtook Japan's leading role in imports to Singapore with a share of 32.6 per cent (or US$13 512.9 million). The share of imports from the Asian NIE 3 and Japan to Singapore had fallen since 1996, but that for the US had

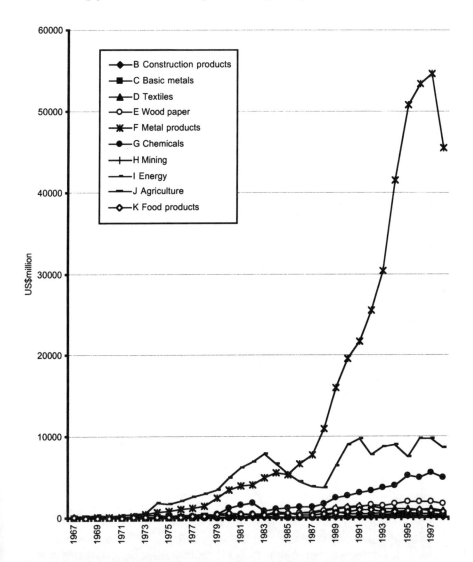

Figure 10.5   Singapore's Main Exports to the World

increased instead since 1995 (20.5 per cent) to 22.9 per cent (in 1996), 23.4 per cent (in 1997).

China was ranked fourth (13.1 per cent or US$86.8 million) in Singapore's imports from the world in 1967 and remained so for much of the period 1967–98 (except for a brief duration early in the 1990s). Its share of these imports peaked in 1985 at 14.7 per cent (or US$1891.5 million). After a decline in the early 1990s due chiefly to the

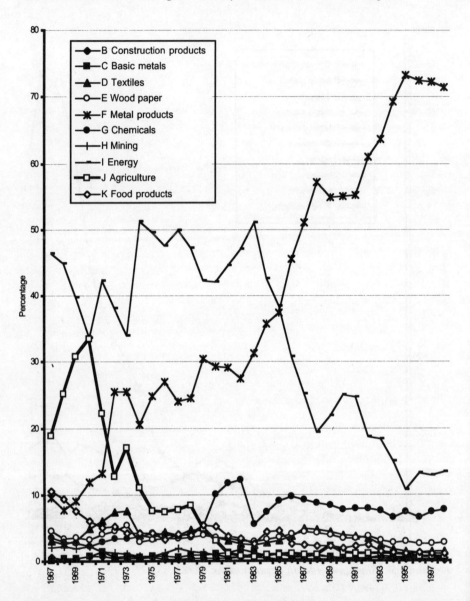

Figure 10.6   Singapore's Main Exports to the World (%)

internal turmoil in China when the import share from Australia and New Zealand overtook its share, China had come back as a major exporting country to Singapore.

Singapore's imports, which have been broken down into ten tradable commodity groups from the world's nine major trading blocs are given in Figures 10.7 (in US$

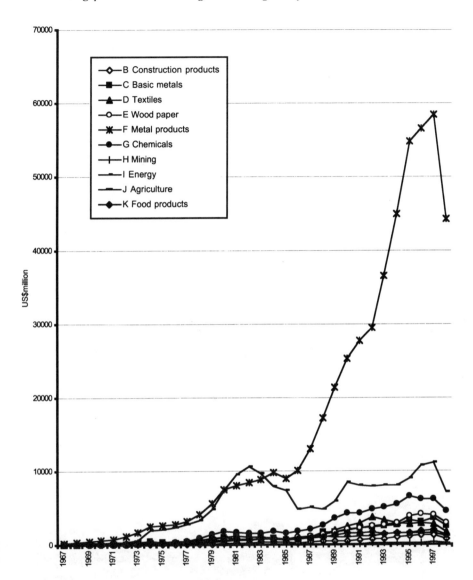

Figure 10.7   World's Main Exports to Singapore

million) and 10.8 (percentage). From these figures, we note that the country's largest imports were metal products, followed far behind by energy and chemicals. In the initial development stage, in 1967, these accounted for 58.3 per cent (or US$700.9 million) of all imports (US$1201.3 million) into Singapore with 27.4 per cent (US$329.0 million) for metal products, 25.0 per cent (US$300.7 million) for energy,

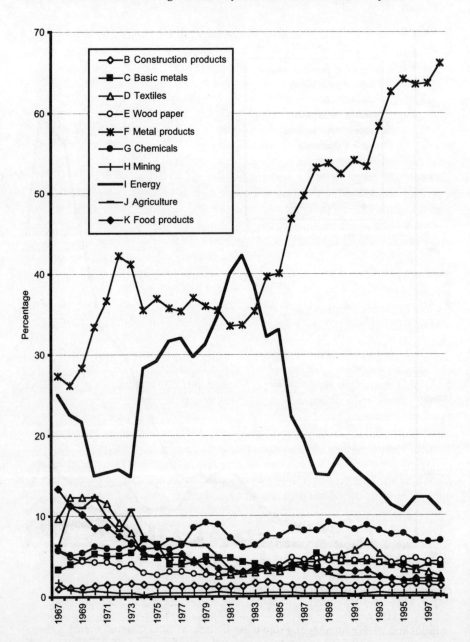

Figure 10.8   World's Main Exports to Singapore (%)

and 5.9 per cent (US$71.2 million) for chemicals. At the end of our sample data in 1998 however, the share of the three largest import groups rose to 83.7 per cent (US$58 583.2 million) with 66.2 per cent (US$44 352.9 million) for metal products, 10.6 per cent (US$7135.2 million) for energy, and 6.9 per cent (US$4634.3 million) for chemicals. In the metal products group, the share of electronic components was 27.0 per cent, computer equipment 18.6 per cent, electric components 10.5 per cent and telecommunications equipment 6.0 per cent. In the energy group, crude oil accounted for 68.8 per cent and refined petroleum products 30.7 per cent. In the chemicals group, basic organic chemicals accounted for 20.4 per cent, plastic articles 27.3 per cent, paints 18.36 per cent and toiletries 13.0 per cent.

The dynamics of the world's commodity exports to Singapore during the three decades of the island's economic development is interesting. While metal products had remained a dominant group of imports for much of the period, they came second in importance during the second world oil crisis of 1981 and remained so for a few years until 1984. In fact, during this crisis period, energy share of Singapore's imports reached a peak of 42.3 per cent (33.7 per cent for metal products) in 1982. Chemicals had remained fairly steady in their movements especially since the late 1970s.

The above historical data and their analysis show that during its different stages of economic development in the past 32 years since 1967, Singapore had relied mainly on what it set out to do in the first place in its economic management of the state, namely, to develop its economy through trade (exports and imports) and investment. Our analysis also shows that Singapore had realigned its economic activities to meet the world's demand for its goods and services at the different stages of development. The alignment or flexibility is a necessity as historical evidence seems to indicate that world demand is an unpredictable phenomenon in economics, trade and investment, business and commerce, and it is regularly subject to many fluctuations, political turmoil, policy change, and crises. In this context, Singapore's economy, like many other economies that depend crucially on trade and investment for their growth, is a fragile economy. It has to face many risks not only in formulating and implementing its own domestic economic management but also the risks associated with external factors that originated in the countries it was trading with. Some of these external risks that had had great impact on Singapore's economy, as seen through the movements of trade and tradable commodities over time in our discussions above, are beyond its control.

The following sections will look critically at Singapore's economic issues and management in the recent period as compiled and assessed by authors from national and international organisations and agencies. The period covers the years after the Asia crisis of 1997 and the data used for analysis supplement the 2000 CHELEM-CEPII international trade data for Singapore that end in 1998. The sections will also present discussions on Singapore's economic management and its implementation and impact from a long-term perspective.

10.3 SINGAPORE'S ECONOMIC GROWTH AND MANAGEMENT THROUGH THE ASIA CRISIS AND PROSPECTS

10.3.1 Recent Trends and Outlook

During its development and growth since 1964, Singapore has achieved a remarkably high rate of income per head and attained the status of being a high-income country of the world. Singapore's income per head during the period 1964–98 is given in Figure 10.9, where it is plotted against income per head of two other Asian high-income countries (Japan and Korea) and the US. Income is defined here as gross national product at current prices and in US dollars. The data are obtained from the 2000 World Bank World Tables databases. From this figure, we note that Singapore's income per head was about US$540 in 1964, but it reached US$30 170 in 1998. After trailing the US for most of the sample period, Singapore with an income per head of US$30 700 overtook the US with US$27 520 in 1996. In contrast, Japan that had an income per head of US$810 in 1964, overtook the US in 1988 with US$23 620 per head as compared to US$21 810 per head for the US. An important observation from Figure 10.9 is that, in spite of their high income levels and the advanced stages of their development, all four countries in our figure show the damaging impact of the Asia crisis of 1997 on their economies. Japan which had had the highest income level since 1988 among the four countries in our comparison suffered the biggest decline even in 1997 (from US$41 280 in 1996 to US$38 260 in 1997) and more in 1998 (US$32 350). Korea, while seemingly escaping the immediate effect of the Asia crisis in 1997 (with an income of US$11 390 in 1997 as compared to US$11 380 in 1996), posted a dramatic fall to US$8600 in 1998. The US also had a fall in income from 1997 (US$29 440) to 1998 (US$29 240), even though the fall was slightest of the four economies.

A few years after the 1997 economic crisis in Asia, Singapore seems to have managed its economy fairly and achieved some of its previous levels of international trade and finance. In 2000 for example, Singapore's external trade posted a sturdy performance with total trade growth up by 22.9 per cent from 1999, substantially higher than the 8.1 per cent growth in 1999 from 1998, bringing a record value of S$470 billion in total trade. This growth was achieved through a robust growth of global demand for semiconductors as well as rising demand from major Asian countries. Non-oil domestic exports grew by 11.7 per cent in 2000 as compared to 9.5 per cent in 1999, but these had weakened as a result of a decline in electronics exports in the fourth quarter of 2000. Non-oil re-exports expanded by 30.8 per cent in 2000, sharply higher than the 0.1 per cent increase in 1999. As in the case of non-oil domestic exports, the expansion was broad-based across all products and markets, supported by the strong global demand for electronics as well as rising demand from the developed as well as major Asian countries (Trade Development Board 2001).

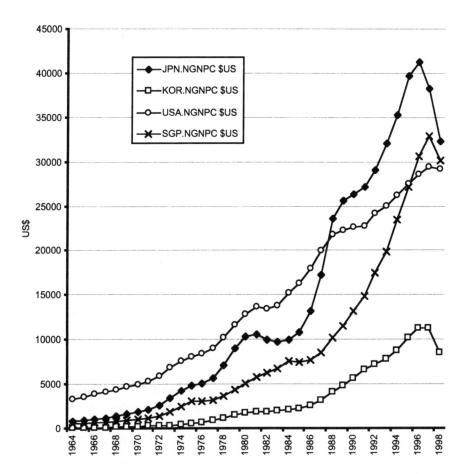

Figure 10.9   Income per Head of Singapore, Japan, Korea and the US (1964–
*   1998)*

Singapore's position in the International Monetary Fund was also healthy as of 31 December 2000 (see Table 10.1). In the general resources account, it fulfilled all its quota requirements (that is, 100 per cent of quota) at SDR862.5 million, had a fund holding of currency of SDR624.8 million or 72.4 per cent, and a reserve tranche position of SDR237.7 million or 27.6 per cent. In the SDR department, Singapore had a net cumulative allocation of SDR16.5 million or 100 per cent of allocation and SDR105.3 million in holdings or 639.3 per cent. It had nil outstanding purchases and loans, nil financial arrangements, and nil projected obligation to the Fund.

As an important economy whose growth in output depends principally on international trade and finance, Singapore's outlook and prospects in 2001 and beyond will depend crucially on international development and demand for its exports. It has

Table 10.1
Singapore's Position in the IMF
as of 31 December 2000

Membership status	Joined 3 March 1966	Article VIII
General resources account	SDR Million	% Quota
Quota	862.50	100.0
Fund holdings of currency	614.81	72.4
Holdings exchange rate		
SDR Department	SDR Million	% Allocation
Net cumulative allocation	16.48	100.0
Holdings	105.32	939.3
Outstanding purchases and loans	None	
Latest financial arrangements	None	
Projected obligations to fund	None	

Source: IMF, *Internet*, 29 January 2001

been predicted that, in 2001, Singapore's total trade will be expanded at a moderate rate of 7 to 9 per cent, compared to 22.9 per cent in 2000. This forecast is based on a number of factors. This includes: a softening of global demand for electronics products due to their high growth in the past and current saturation of the markets, a slow-down in the US economy, weaker growth and lingering turmoil in many Asian economies with which Singapore trades, a decline in oil trade (due principally to higher prices and lower production of crude oil), and a moderate growth of non-oil retained imports (a short-term indicator for manufacturing activities in Singapore's economy) (see Trade Development Board 2001).

Early in 2001, there were signs that the US economy was in trouble after many years of strong growth. The problem persisted even after help in the form of several interest rate cuts from the Federal Reserve Board. The greatest risk for 2001 is, however, the prospect of the US going into a real recession and with it the slowing down of the global economy. Under this scenario, global demand for Singapore's exports will be substantially curtailed and Singapore's trade and growth will be severely affected.

10.3.2 Issues in Economic Management

The assessment from the Asian Development Bank late in 2000 and other authors working on the area seems to indicate that the Singaporean economy had initially survived well the impact of the Asia crisis starting in July 1997 in Thailand. The main reasons for this survival were the economy's institutional strengths and flexible and pragmatic economic management policies that had been strictly adopted by the government. The economy had rebounded strongly in 1999 and 2000 from economic stagnation in 1998. These policies were helped not in a small way by strong global demand growth for IT (information technology) products and services in these years. However, this assessment is tampered by the fact that, despite the strong rebound in economic activity and increased investment commitments in 1999, overall growth in fixed investment by both the private and public sectors remained below its historical rate in the pre-crisis period. This was due to insufficient credit expansion and industrial overcapacity. In addition, fiscal policy (with a planned deficit of S$5.1 billion or 3.4 per cent of GDP in 1999) provided less of a stimulus to the economy than was originally expected (that is, with a budget surplus instead).

The realities of the post-crisis and new international economic and financial developments in 2001 and beyond will be more challenging for Singapore. To remain competitive in a global economy, Singapore needs not just temporary measures (such as those adopted in the late 1990s to reduce business and labour unit costs in the face of the sharp depreciation of the region's currencies) to make more meaningful adjustments to its economic management policies and changes in its institutional, financial and production structures (Asian Development Bank 2001).

An important aspect of economic management is monetary policy. Singapore which is the headquarters for the Asian Dollar Market and channels foreign investments into primarily Asian ventures, had been cautious toward the internationalisation of the Singapore dollar, although restrictions on the use of the Singapore dollar by non-residents were considerably eased. An example is this: despite the removal of the ceiling on foreign ownership of local banks, these banks must however retain at least 50 per cent of residents' deposits so that the Monetary Authority of Singapore (effectively Singapore's Central Bank) can control Singapore dollar transactions. The restrictions, it has claimed, were based on concern that a large off-shore market in Singapore dollars could destabilise domestic exchange and interest rates. The policy is however at odds with the fast growing trend in globalisation of economic and financial transactions around the world. Singapore which wants to become an important international financial centre is likely to have to contend with the internationalisation of its dollar (Asian Development Bank 2001).

Singapore, in spite of its developed status in economic development, does not have an antitrust law and competition policy agency. It has however a Committee on Singapore's Competitiveness which deals essentially with competitiveness on the international level. This Committee had called for a knowledge-based economy to help long-term competitiveness, and the government had been developing an institutional structure to support it. In addition, the Ministry of Communications and Information was created, and the existing National Computer Board of Singapore were merged into the Info-Communications Development Authority. This Authority was given the task of preparing a master plan to develop the information and communications industry. The government had also initiated measures to provide incentives for entrepreneurs entering high-tech industries, and to train people in skills related to information technology. However, there is no certainty that retraining will enable workers with limited skills and education to qualify for jobs being created in the semiconductor and chemical industries (Asian Development Bank 2001).

In the banking and financial sector, many other challenges remain to be dealt with. As in most other Asian economies where the government has always played a more important role in managing the economy, Singapore has a domestic banking sector that is overregulated and characterised by high cost and low liquidity. This sector needs improvements. It was a good sign that in 1998 and 1999, in a move to develop the island state as an international financial centre, the Singapore Monetary Authority introduced a series of measures to liberalise the financial market. These included the merger of the Stock Exchange of Singapore and the Singapore International Monetary Exchange into the Singapore Exchange in December 1999, the first fully integrated financial market in Asia. The government also liberalised entry into the Singapore Exchange by gradually lifting the restrictions on the number of foreign brokers who can participate and on the value of their trades. Beginning in 2001, freely negotiated broker commissions were replaced by a system of fixed commissions which the authorities expect will lower transaction costs. Bank disclosure rules were also strengthened by measures recommended by the Committee on Banking Disclosure in May 1998.

The various liberalisation measures adopted by Singapore have led to a fundamental change in emphasis from regulation to risk-focused supervision and increased disclosure. The authorities expect this policy will help reduce risks of contagion (if further economic crises in the region ever occur again), broaden and deepen the capital market, decrease costs, and improve efficiency. Now that the desire of Thailand to be the region's financial centre has been squashed due to its economic crisis in 1997 and Hong Kong's return to China has diminished its importance as a major financial centre, Singapore hopes that the changes and adjustments to its economic management will increase its chance of being the region's major financial centre. This policy also will improve its international competitiveness in relation to Hong Kong or, more appropriately, China.

10.4   CONCLUSIONS

Singapore is a city-state with very limited national and human resources and short on history and modern politics. Its initial stage of development started with its independence from Britain in the mid-1960s, and, like many of its neighbouring countries in the region over a similar timeframe, its economic development and growth has successfully grown through trade and foreign investment. In spite of its shortcomings, Singapore now is a major developed economy in Asia and ranked high in the high-income countries in the world.

In its four decades or so of development, Singapore has seen international turmoil and regional unrest in various shapes and forms of the economic, financial, political or social kind. At the same time, it has always achieved or maintained political stability, steady growth, increasing living standard, and international standing in economic, financial and political affairs. Being a country dependent principally on international trade, investment and finance from its earliest stage of development, Singapore has had to manage its economy in the context of the volatility of external factors, regional and international. Singapore's economic management has had a flexible or pragmatic style in times of great fluctuations of regional and international activities. It has also been identified as having a market economic style of an Asian kind in which it has all the marks of a free market economy but is deeply affected by pragmatic interventionist considerations and policies. This type of economic crisis management, while successful in the case of Singapore or Taiwan in recent years, may not be able to accommodate the inevitable appeoaching globalisation and all of its implications for borderless trade, investment and finance, and government and corporate governance according to the requirements of regional or international economic integrations such as the Asia and Pacific Economic Cooperation or, more importantly, the World Trade Organization.

The issues and problems above can be seen as the challenges and possible changes and adjustments for Singapore to consider and to come to grips with in the years to come. With its pragmatic but successful economic management policies over its entire stages of development since 1965, however, it is our prediction that Singapore will be able to adapt or even adopt full implementations of a free-market mechanism for its own long-term benefits in a globalised economy. In this context, the long-term prospects for the Singapore economy remain bright.

REFERENCES

Asian Development Bank (2001), Asian development outlook data for 2000 – Singapore, March, available at <www.adb.org>.

CHELEM-CEPII (2000), *International Trade Databases*, Paris: CEPII.

Encyclopaedia Britannica, 'Singapore', March, available at <www.britannica.com>.

International Monetary Fund, 'Singapore', January, available at <www.imf.org>.

Singapore Trade Development Board, 'Review of Year 2000 Trade Performance and Outlook for Year 2001', January, available at <www.tdb.gov.sg>.

Singapore Trade Development Board, 'Singapore's External Trade – January 2001', February, available at <www.tdb.gov.sg>.

11 Management of Economic and Financial Crises: Synthesis and the Road Ahead

Tran Van Hoa

11.1 SYNTHESIS OF ISSUES AND FINDINGS

In the preceding chapters, we have dealt in detail with recent economic and financial crises and crisis management in a number of major newly industrialised economies and developing and transition countries alike in the Asian region. We have presented assessments by well-known experts, knowledgeable in the countries under study, on the outcomes of this management as implemented by governments and monetary authorities in the crisis economies. A general evaluation of these outcomes indicates that economic and financial management policies, strongly recommended by international organisations and agencies and adopted voluntarily or involuntarily by crisis countries, have not been effective in crisis resolution. The obvious evidence is that, almost five years on since the emergence of the so-called Asia meltdown, its impact is still causing havoc at all levels of activity of the country, economic, financial, political and social. We have also discussed plausible and more effective alternative policies for similar crisis issues, and analysed aspects of crisis management that would achieve better short-term and long-term resolutions in similar future economic turmoil. The relevance of our discussion and analysis to economic and financial crises in other regions (such as Latin America) in the early 1990s is straightforward.

11.2 ALTERNATIVE ECONOMIC CRISIS MANAGEMENT POLICIES

Our general assessment of the outcomes of economic crisis management in these Asian economies in recent years is that the simple one-instrument policy of the Keynesian (demand management or fiscal expansion and contraction) or monetarist

238

(money supply or interest rate manipulation) kind has been inappropriate in dealing with what emerged as immense issues of diverse economic, regional, political, cultural and social complexity.

Among the alternative and (in our view) more appropriate multi-instrument policies was the macroeconomic mix theory proposed in the mid-1980s by Perkins and Tran Van Hoa (2000) and, more importantly, its adoption in conjunction with deep understanding or knowledge about the long-term and fundamental construct of the troubled economies under consideration. An example of the importance of the local social construct is the underestimation by international organisations of the effect of price subsidies removal (resulting from a budget deficit reduction policy) from energy commodities in Indonesia during the peak of its economic crisis. The ensuing hardship and unrest caused a delay in the country's major economic and administrative reform. Another example is the misdirected focus (or blame) on the public sector in Thailand for having started the initial Asia turmoil (resulting in severe budget cuts and massive unemployment). Later analysis shows that the real cause of the crisis was the uncontrolled explosion of easy money and borrowings in the private sector itself a year or so before 1997.

It is unfortunate that the issue of proper economic crisis management for countries in trouble in Asia has been regarded as 'passé' by a number of influential countries in the world and, as a result, less attention and fewer resources have been allocated to finding proper prescriptions. There are three good reasons for this neglect. First, official reports and assessments by international organisations and agencies seem to indicate that the contagion and impact of the Asia meltdown on the non-Asian economies have been benign. Second, the complexity of crisis management in the once-miracle economies in the Asian region has been so immense that it has rendered external remedial contributions less effective and immediate. Third, the underlying orthodoxy of crisis management policies prescribed for crisis economies has been inappropriate both in the short term and also in the long term (see, for example, Desai 2000).

Early in 2001, reports by international organisations and some research institutes still maintained the erroneous view that the lingering impact of the Asia crisis on major Asian economies was only benign and the recovery was in sight (see however Tran Van Hoa, 2001). Many economic and financial forecasts that were based on this view would regard the estimated trends and prospects for these economies as being promising with rising growth prospects in 2000 and probably 2001 and later (see Figure 11.1 for growth trends of Japan and four Asian NIEs and Figure 11.2 for six major Asian developing and transition economies).

Figure 11.1 shows that, among the depicted trends of Japan and four NIEs in Asia, Korea was the only country that would still suffer the effect of the Asia crisis in 2000 (with a growth rate of 10.66 per cent in 1999 and an estimated 9.60 per cent in 2000). Hong Kong and Singapore, after their economic setbacks in 1998 (at –5.14 per cent and 0.40 per cent respectively) would recover and regain high growth rates of 10 per cent (2.91 per cent in 1999) for Hong Kong and also 10 per cent (5.35 per cent in 1999) in 2000 for Singapore.

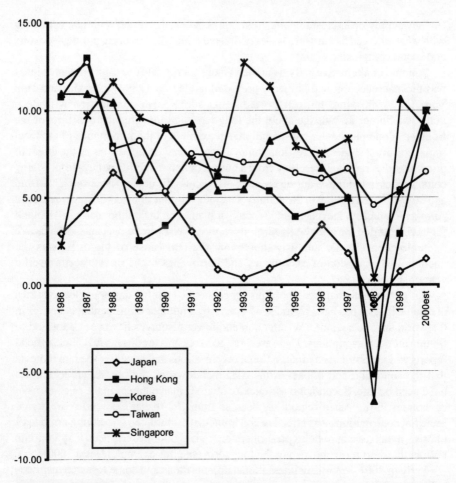

Source: ICSEAD (2001)

Figure 11.1   Growth (in Local Currency) of Japan and Major Asian NIEs (1986–2000)

Figure 11.2 shows that Indonesia's recovery was strongest in 2000 with an estimated growth rate of 4.80 per cent, compared to 0.31 per cent in 1999 and −13.01 per cent in 1998. A strong recovery was also obtained for Malaysia and Thailand which were estimated to have a growth rate of 8.80 per cent and 4 per cent respectively in 2000.

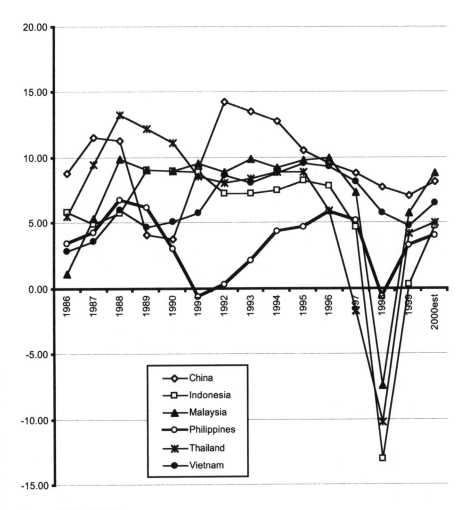

Source: ICSEAD (2001)

Figure 11.2   Growth (in Local Currency) in Major Asian Developing Economies (1986–2000)

11.3   THE ROAD AHEAD

As discussed in Chapter 2, the prospects for these Asian economies (including Japan) were rather more dismal and demand a serious reconsideration of policy options. The assessment was based on these economies' historical economic and international trade trends and projections and also on new developments in the region and the US early in 2001. The strong lingering effect of the Asia turmoil was found in deeper analysis in the preceding chapters to depend crucially on the fundamental construct of crisis economies. This construct includes economic, political, social, religious, historical and regional and international relation aspects that have both short-term and long-term implications.

The prospects for proper economic crisis management are slim unless crisis economies in Asia (or even elsewhere) and international organisations take note of the inadequacy or unsuitability of the orthodox policies (which may have been very useful during the Great Depression of the 1930s but which may be second best in late 2000 or early 2001). The prospects will also be slim unless other dimensions of the management are taken into account in designing and implementing economic crisis management.

The slowdown in two of the world's largest economies, namely the US and Japan, as observed in early 2001 demands that crisis management in economies in trouble needs effective, resilient and long-term resolutions. It also should have plausibility and minimal conditionality. Due to the great effect a crisis can have on the poor (poverty increase) and disadvantaged and vulnerable (social and welfare deterioration) of the population especially in developing and transition economies in the Asian region (where safety net and social security are not yet well developed or even seriously considered), a proper crisis management policy should also be an urgent consideration for all national governments and international organisations responsible for highly effective crisis resolution.

REFERENCES

Desai, Meghnad (2000), Discussions at the *Conference on Financial Crises and Global Governance*, London School of Economics, 13–14 October.

ICSEAD (2001), 'Recent Trends and Prospects for Major Asian Economies', *East Asian Economic Perspectives*, International Centre for the Study of East Asian Development, Special Issue, February.

Perkins, J.O.N. and Tran Van Hoa (2000), 'Towards the Formulation and Testing of a More General Theory of Macroeconomic Policy' [originally published 1987], in J.O.N. Perkins (ed.), *The Reform of Macroeconomic Policy: From Stagflation to Low or Zero Inflation*, London: Macmillan.

Tran Van Hoa (2001), *The Asia Recovery*, Cheltenham, UK and Northampton, MA: Edward Elgar.

Index